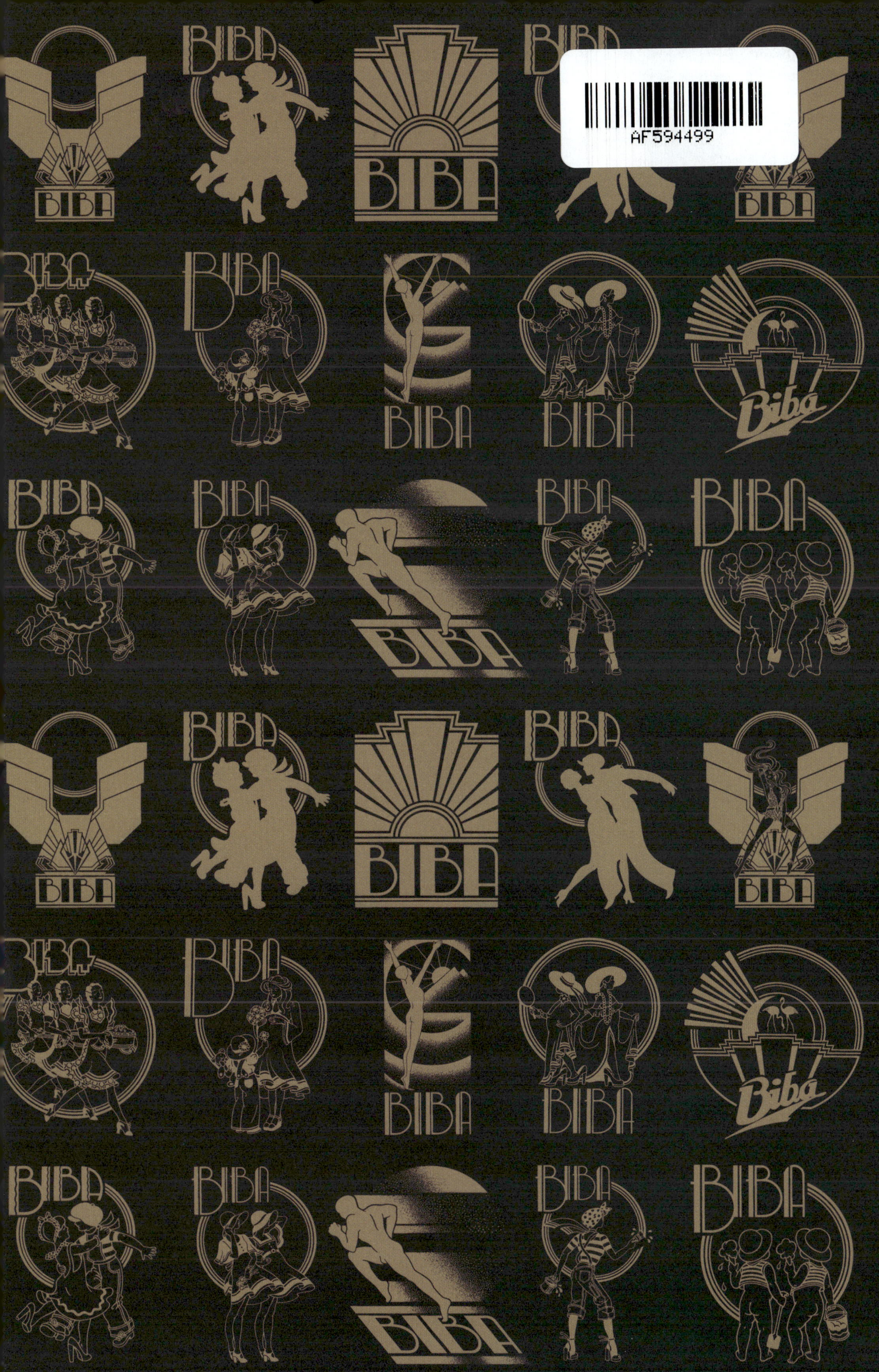
BIBA
BIBA
BIBA
BIBA
BIBA
BIBA
BIBA
BIBA
Biba
BIBA
BIBA
BIBA
BIBA
BIBA
BIBA
BIBA
BIBA
BIBA
BIBA
BIBA
BIBA
BIBA
BIBA
Biba
BIBA
BIBA
BIBA
BIBA
BIBA

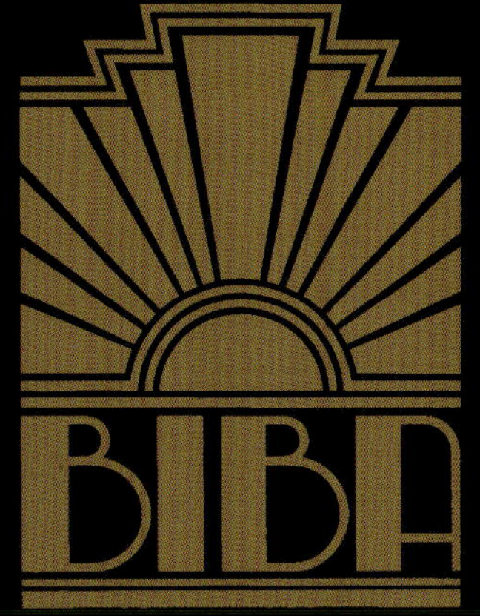

BIBA LIMITED 103-105 KENSINGTON HIGH STREET LONDON W8 5SB ENGLAND
TELEPHONE 01-937 6287 OFFICES 01-937 8060 TELEX 916123
REGISTERED IN ENGLAND REGISTER NUMBER 404312

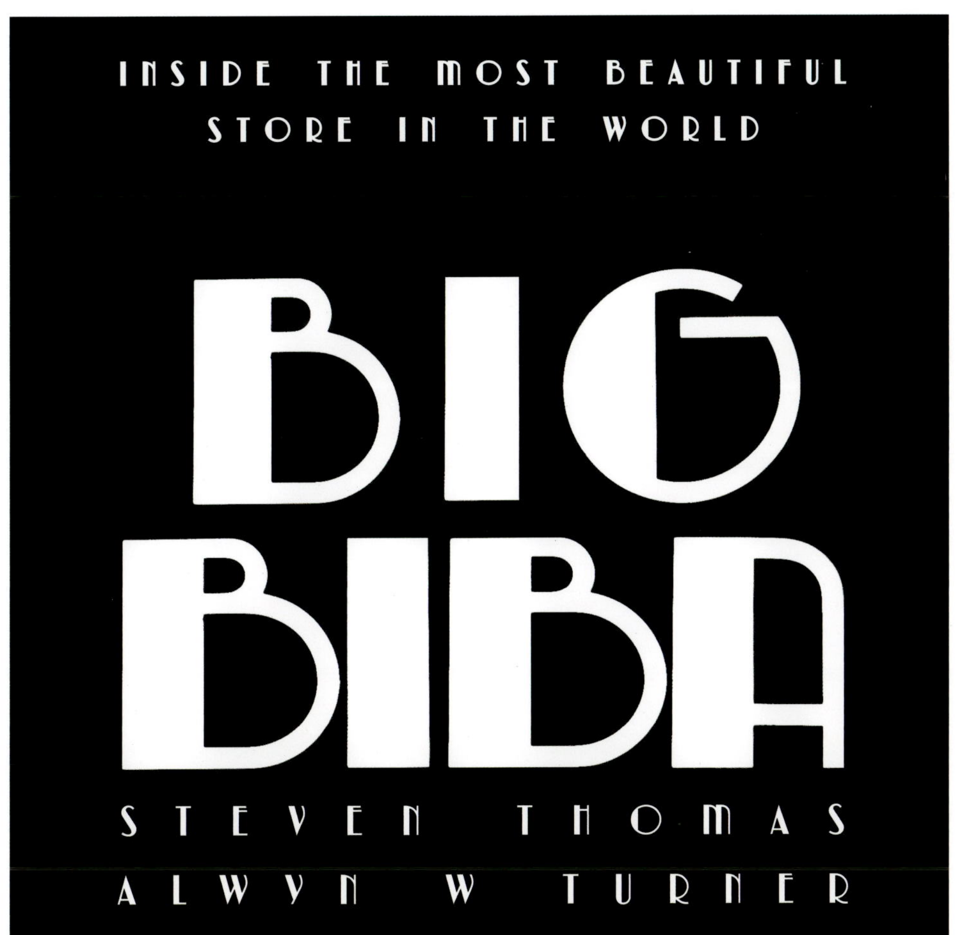

INSIDE THE MOST BEAUTIFUL STORE IN THE WORLD

BIG BIBA

STEVEN THOMAS

ALWYN W TURNER

ACC ART BOOKS

This book is dedicated to Jamie Thomas
and to Mark Eastment, an inspiration to us all

Credits and Acknowledgements

Acknowledgements: Thanks to all at ACC: Tom Conway, Matthew Freedman, Alison Hart, Susannah Hecht, Juliet Henney, Craig Holden, Stephen MacKinlay, Jennifer Monk, Anna Pearce, James Smith, Sarah Smye, Simon Walsh, Richard Weale and Corban Wilkin

Photography credits: Colour photographs of Big Biba in this book were taken by Tim White and Tim Street-Porter.

Other picture credits: p.4 Courtesy of Barbara Hulanicki; pp.8-9 Courtesy of Steve Thomas; pp.44-51 Photographer: John Bishop

The letterheads used on pages 3, 5 and 80 are the headed paper designed for the relevant departments of Big Biba

Front cover: *Mistress Room swing-ticket.* **Back cover:** *model in Rainbow Room (© John Bishop); Rainbow Room light coves*

Front endpapers: *Big Biba logos all designed by Whitmore-Thomas; Men's Floor; Kids' Rainbow Room; Ground Floor; Rainbow Room; Mistress Room; Food Hall; Pregnant Mums; Health Cosmetics Range; Children's Store; Roof Garden; Kids' Rainbow Room; Lolita Store; Men's Health Cosmetics Range; Household Floor; Babies' Department*

Back endpapers: *Big Biba typefaces all designed by Whitmore-Thomas to suit each floor and department, mainly used for packaging; 'Fitz Face' used for newspaper staff recruitment ads*

Title Page *(p.1) graphics: ground floor letterhead; Credits Page (p.3) graphics: food hall letterhead; Foreword Page (p.5): men's floor letterhead with Mistress Room Valkerie ride pattern*

First published 2006 by the Antique Collectors' Club
Reprinted 2016 by ACC Editions, an imprint of ACC Art Books Ltd.
This Golden Edition published in 2023 by ACC Art Books
ISBN: 978 1 78884 261 7

British Library Cataloguing-in-Publication Data
A catalogue record for this book is available from the British Library

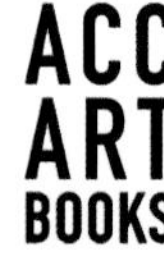

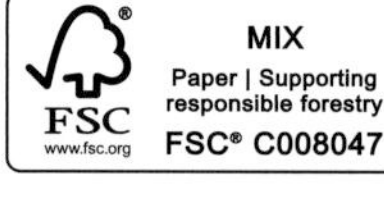

Printed in China
for ACC Art Books Ltd.,
Woodbridge, Suffolk, UK

Steven Thomas, as half of the Whitmore-Thomas Partnership, worked with Biba from 1968 and was thus responsible for transforming the Derry & Toms store into Big Biba. His clients have ranged from Paul McCartney and The Rolling Stones to the Blue Chips: Kodak, Pepsi, Levi's and BAT amongst many others. From restaurants and bars, Formula One teams to the Queen's Jubilee Silver buses, he has worked on an extraordinary array of design projects. One major omission and regret, however: he has yet to design an hotel...
www.steventhomasdesigns.com

Alwyn W Turner is the author of *The Biba Experience*, co-author of *Cult Rock Posters 1972-82* and general editor of *Portmeirion*. He is the founder of the website Trash Fiction, and a contributor to both *The Rough Guide to Rock* and to the BBC website. With his father, Gordon Turner, he is also the co-author of four volumes on British military bands. He was once described by the *Melody Maker* as 'a demented Sunday School teacher'.

BIBA LIMITED 103-105 KENSINGTON HIGH STREET LONDON W8 5SB ENGLAND
TELEPHONE 01-937 6287 OFFICES 01-937 8060 TELEX 916123
REGISTERED IN ENGLAND REGISTER NUMBER 404312

THE BIG BIBA PROJECT

CREATORS

Barbara Hulanicki

Stephen Fitz-Simon

INTERIOR & GRAPHIC DESIGN

Tim Whitmore & Steven Thomas

Whitmore-Thomas Design Associates

WTDA DESIGN TEAM

Chris Angell - Brian Temple - Brian Bousfield - Kasia Charko - Mick Partlett
Bernard Spencer - Dave Farey - David Smith

ART DIRECTORS

John Graysmark - Les Tompkins - Alan Tompkins - Bob Cartwright - John Fenner
Bill Hutchinson - Brian Ackland-Snow

BIBA TEAM

Eleanor Powell - Anne Behr - Del Howard - Eva Molnar
Daphne Black - Janice Newman - Lily Anderson - David Moxey
Alison Lang - Shirley J Shurville - Maria Rees - Lorraine Harper
Pam Linstead - Louise Melly - Patrick McDonaugh
Maureen Docherty - Aina Vasilevskis - Gunda Lenmanis
Eddy Hunt - Allan Gerring - Andrew Logan

PHOTOGRAPHERS

Tim White - Tim Street-Porter

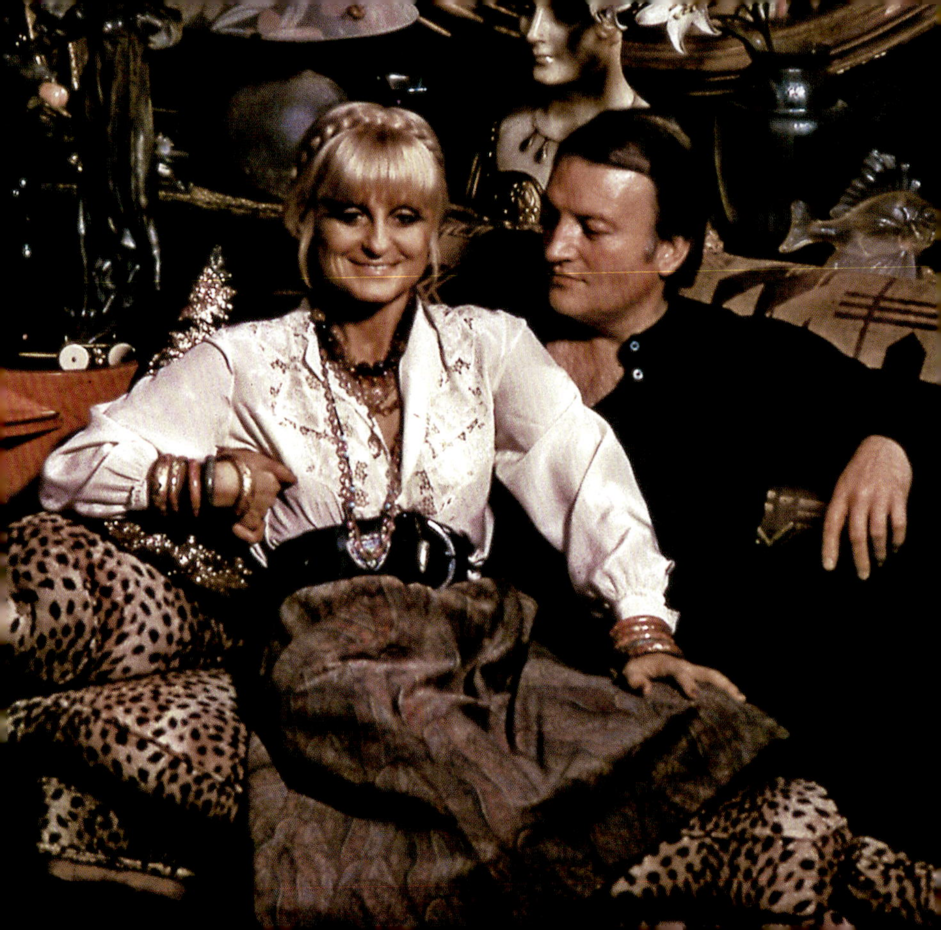

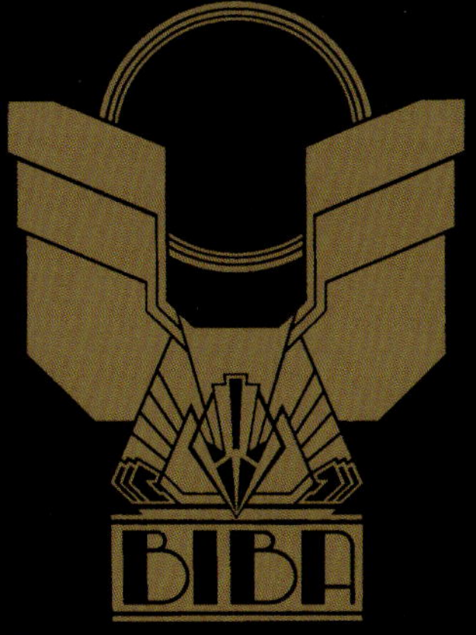

BIBA LIMITED 103-105 KENSINGTON HIGH STREET LONDON W8 5SB ENGLAND
TELEPHONE 01-937 6287 OFFICES 01-937 8060 TELEX 916123
REGISTERED IN ENGLAND REGISTER NUMBER 404312

FOREWORD

From day one of the first Biba I was never quite certain which came first, the clothes or the interiors. A 1930s movie buff, I had imagined Garbo-esque figures floating in vast spaces in languid clothes and murky lighting. The design of all the previous Biba shops had always reflected the period of the building. The last Biba, in an unwanted, abandoned and abused '30s building, was going to be an Oscar-winning performance.

Fitz & I travelled the globe to absorb and see and feel atmospheres. Whatever the source of inspiration, we would go there to experience it for ourselves. We decided that the ground floor, for example, would be mirrored like the Mistinguette bedroom at the l'Hotel in Paris, so we went and stayed there to try it out. The past Biba's Art Nouveau influences had been Beardsley, Klimt and Alphonse Mucha posters. The children's floor in the Big Biba we took from the original '30s Disneyland in LA. The giant furniture in the pregnant mums' department came from Twiggy and Ken Russell's film, The Boyfriend. The Rainbow Room? Well, it spoke for itself. We faithfully reproduced the carpets and fabrics that had lain in the old store. The roof garden, with a flowing river, was replanted by a very boisterous, Pimm's-ignited, platform-shoe-wearing, tipsy gardening club. With every beautiful deco detail preserved by the brilliant Tim Whitmore and Steve Thomas, the interiors were drawn up by John Graysmark's skilled team of draftsmen, based on the existing third floor of the Biba-to-be. The units, designed by Whitmore-Thomas, were built by factories in industrially depressed areas of Wales and Scotland and were assembled in the investors' warehouses in Bracknell. There they were tweaked and corrected to await the right moment to be reassembled on site. Fitz and Mr Trotter, the construction manager, delivered on time with weeks to spare for us to set up the merchandise in the shop. The building budget came in on the nose, not a penny over the quarter-million pounds. This would be unheard-of today.

Biba never went broke, and it even made a small profit in the first year. Fitz's projection was 5 million, but it came in at 4.95 even with all the problems of the time. Biba was the number two tourist attraction after the Tower of London, followed by Buckingham Palace.

Two nights before opening day, Fitz instructed us all to have early nights. Everything was in place, waiting, our stomachs churning. On opening day we welcomed our investors. It was the first time they had set foot in Big Biba. Later that day Fitz & I heard a rumour that the building had been sold to Marks & Spencer's. We laughed it off nervously, but no matter what the fable tells you, Goliath always wins. The suits had won. And yet, in spite of that, we broke through the corporate fence. This book is a testament to creative freedom. You can do it all as long as you learn to wear a suit. Of course, your secret will be that the suit is lined in gold lamé. They'll never know until it's too late!

Barbara Hulanicki
Miami Beach 2006.

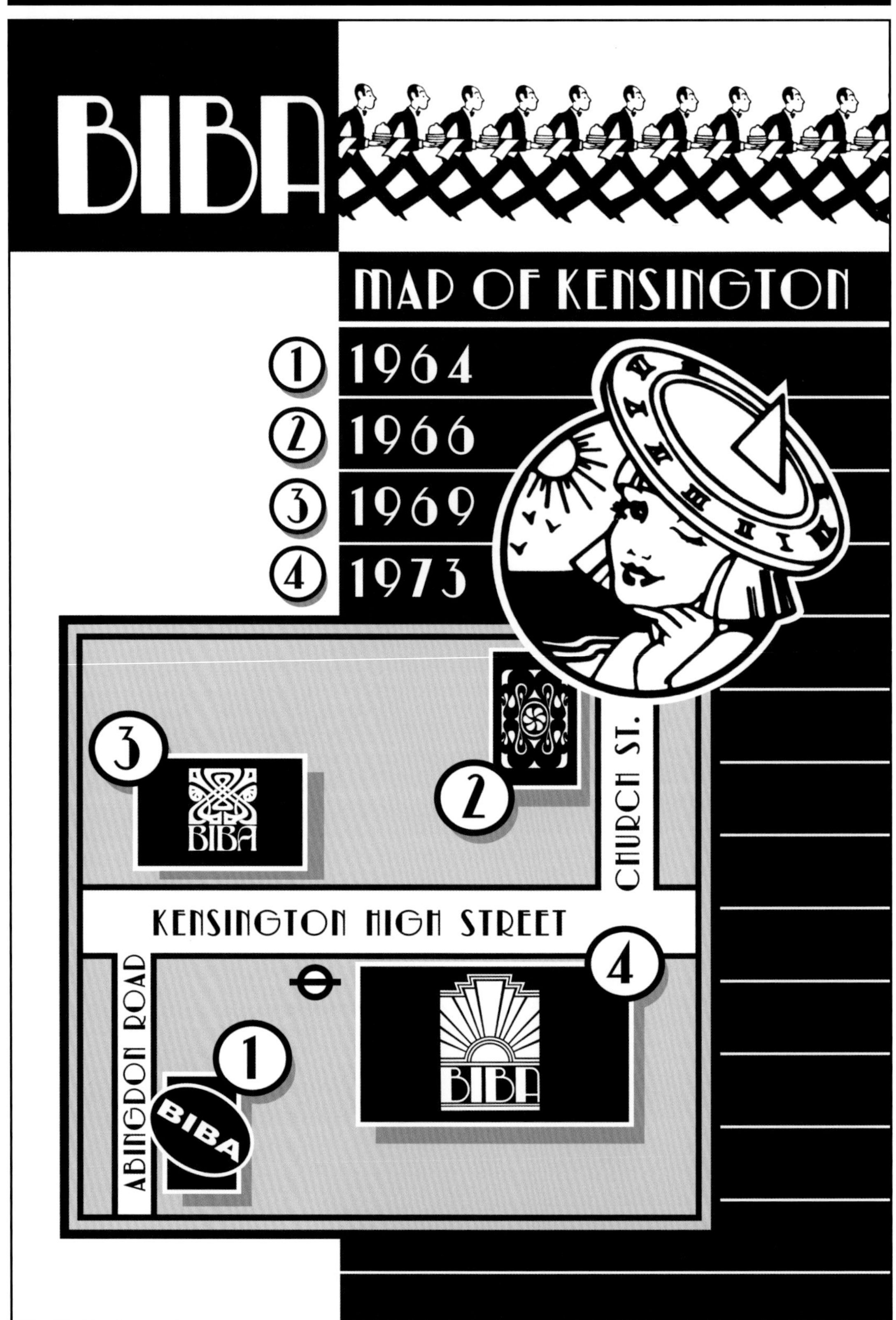
BIBA
MAP OF KENSINGTON
1 1964
2 1966
3 1969
4 1973
3
BIBA
2
CHURCH ST.
KENSINGTON HIGH STREET
ABINGDON ROAD
4
BIBA
1
BIBA

PROLOGUE

THE STORY SO FAR...

In 1963 fashion illustrator Barbara Hulanicki makes her first moves into fashion design, launching Biba's Postal Boutique, in collaboration with her husband, Stephen Fitz-Simon. It struggles to make any impact at all for the first few months, before things start to move...

May '64	Biba's Postal Boutique has its first success with a pink gingham dress offered in the *Daily Mirror*: 17,000 pieces are sold.
September '64	The first Biba boutique opens at 87 Abingdon Road, Kensington, helping to create a new market of fashion-conscious young women who desired access to couture but couldn't afford the entrance fee. 'I wanted to make clothes for people in the street,' Hulanicki was later to remark, 'and Fitz and I always tried to get prices down to the bare minimum.'
April '65	The *Daily Telegraph* calls Hulanicki one of the 'people who make London swing' in an article that started the re-branding of the city.
March '66	Biba moves from Abingdon Road to 19-21 Kensington Church Street, later to be described as 'the most exotic shop in London' by *Vanity Fair*.
April '66	International recognition of Swinging London as *Time* magazine crowns the capital as the 'city of the decade' – Biba is cited as 'the most in shop' for girls.
April '68	The first Biba mail-order catalogue is launched: five further catalogues are issued before the mail-order department is wound up.
September '69	Biba moves from Church Street to 124-126 Kensington High Street. Evening wear, menswear and household are added as Biba becomes a department store.
December '69	Formation of Biba Ltd, with Dorothy Perkins as the majority shareholder.
April '70	Launch of Biba Cosmetics.
February '71	A Biba boutique opens in the Bergdorf Goodman store, New York. Meanwhile Biba Cosmetics open stands in Au Printemps in Paris, Fiorucci in Milan, Tekano in Tokyo, Bloomingdale's in New York and the Judy's chain in California.
May '71	The Angry Brigade set off a bomb in Biba, issuing a statement that claims: 'If you're not busy being born, you're busy buying.'
June '71	Biba Cosmetics are introduced in more than 300 Dorothy Perkins stores nationwide.
December '71	A forthcoming move is announced to what is currently the Derry & Toms on the other side of Kensington High Street.
September '73	Biba opens its final incarnation in what had previously been the Derry & Toms department store on Kensington High Street. In the space of nine years, it has grown from a crowded corner-shop into a fully fledged department store: seven storeys of own-brand goods on a scale not attempted before or since. It was, as the press dubbed it, the Superstore Boutique. Big Biba had arrived.

NOW READ ON...

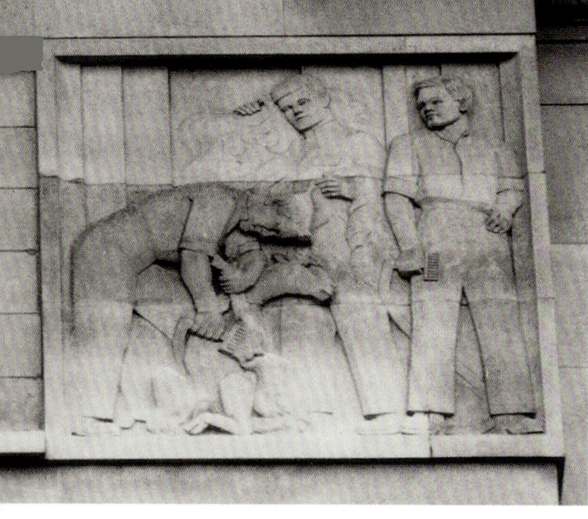

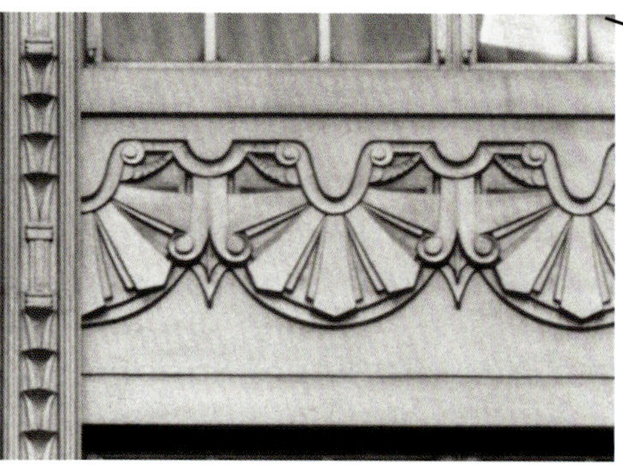

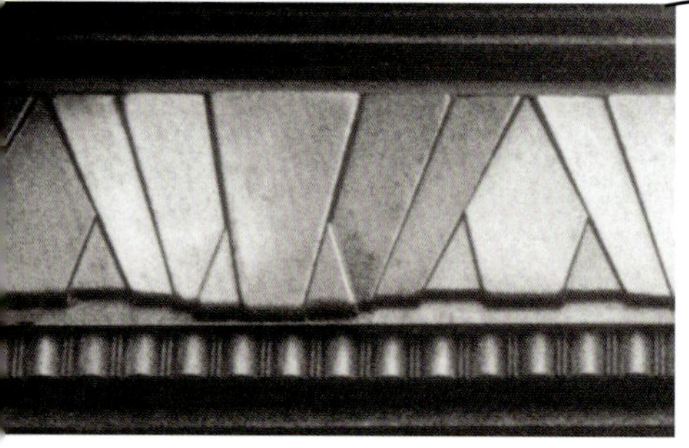

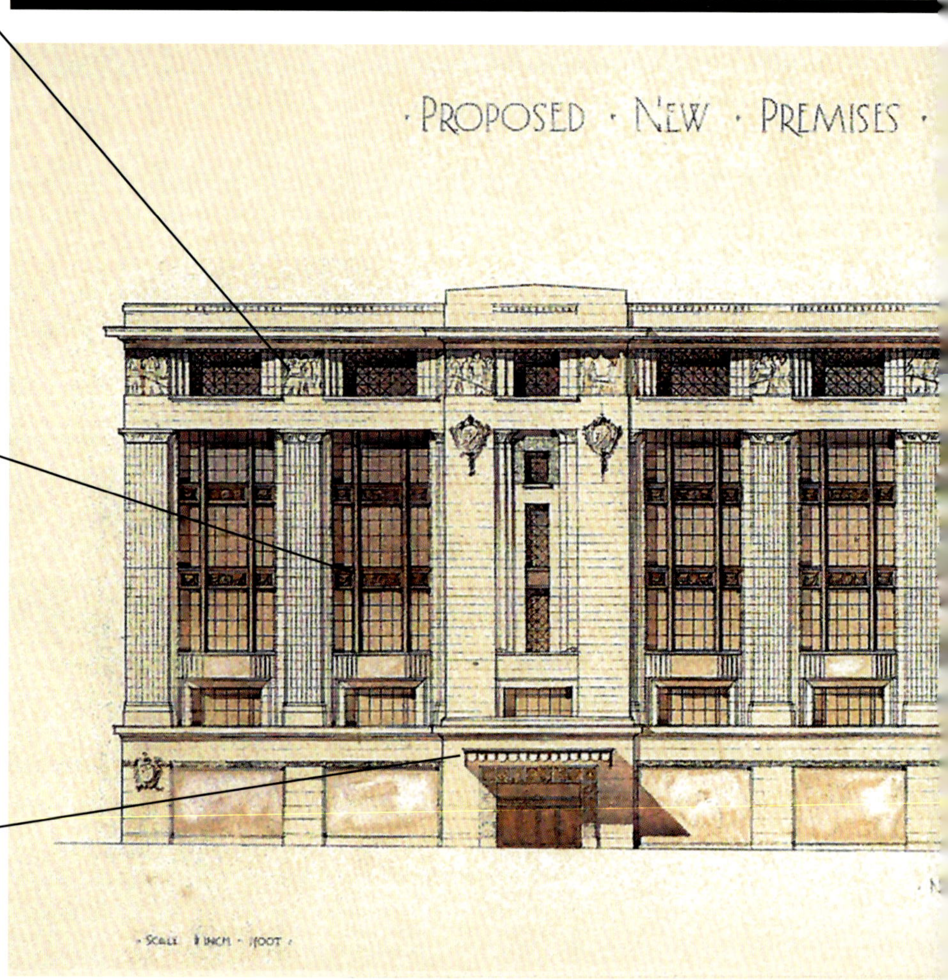

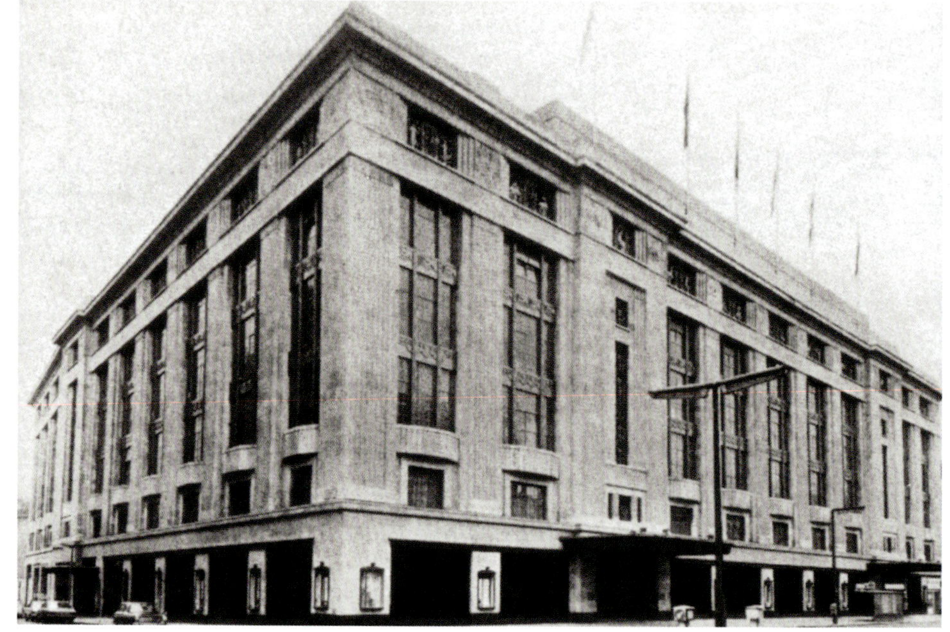

The Derry & Toms building at 99-119 Kensington High Street was opened in 1933, a statement of optimism in the wake of the First World War and the Great Depression.

Among the casualties of the times had been the store itself, which, despite antecedents going back to the 1820s, had been bought up by its neighbour, John Barker & Co. It was that company's architect, Bernard George, who designed the new building.

External metalwork (including cast-iron grilles of the signs of the zodiac) was by Walter Gilbert, and under the eaves was a series of reliefs in Portland stone by CJ Mabey depicting scenes of labour and technology.

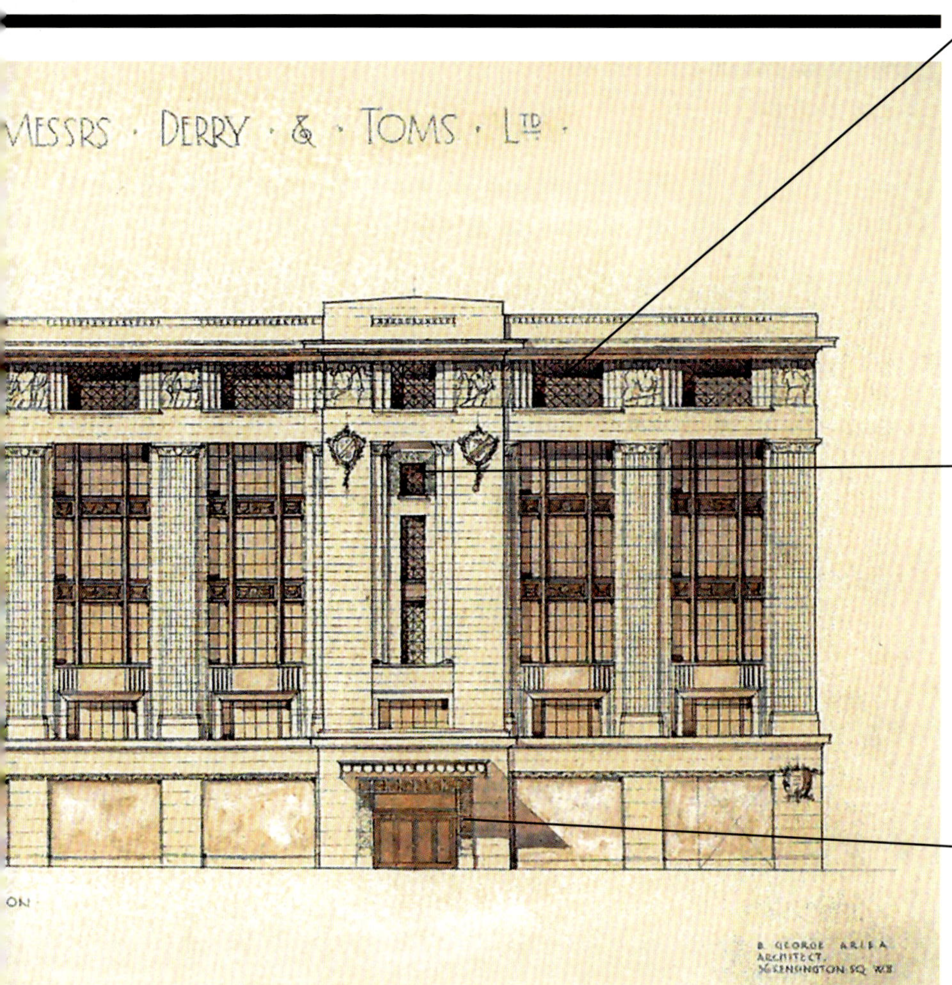

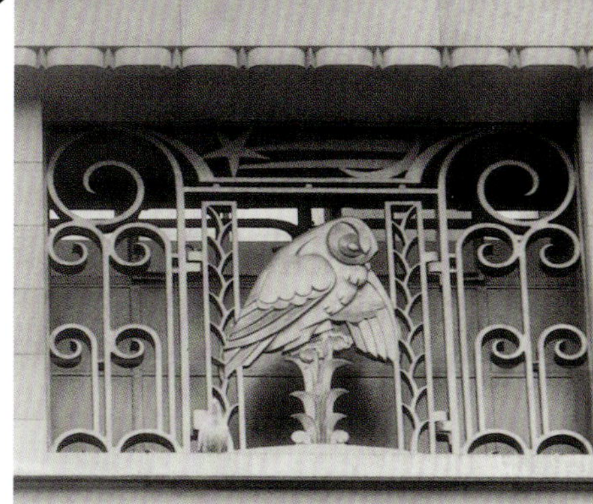

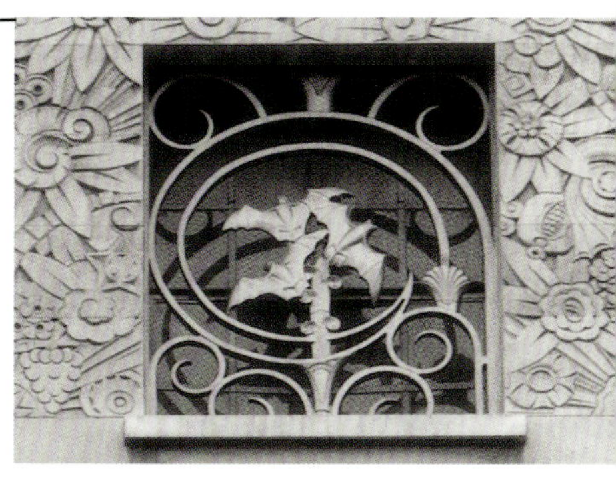

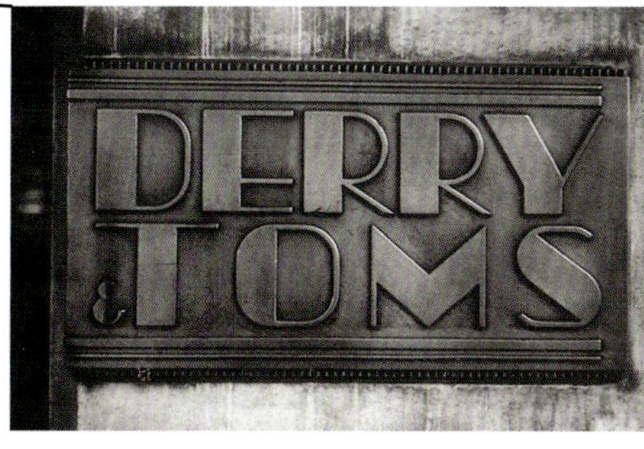

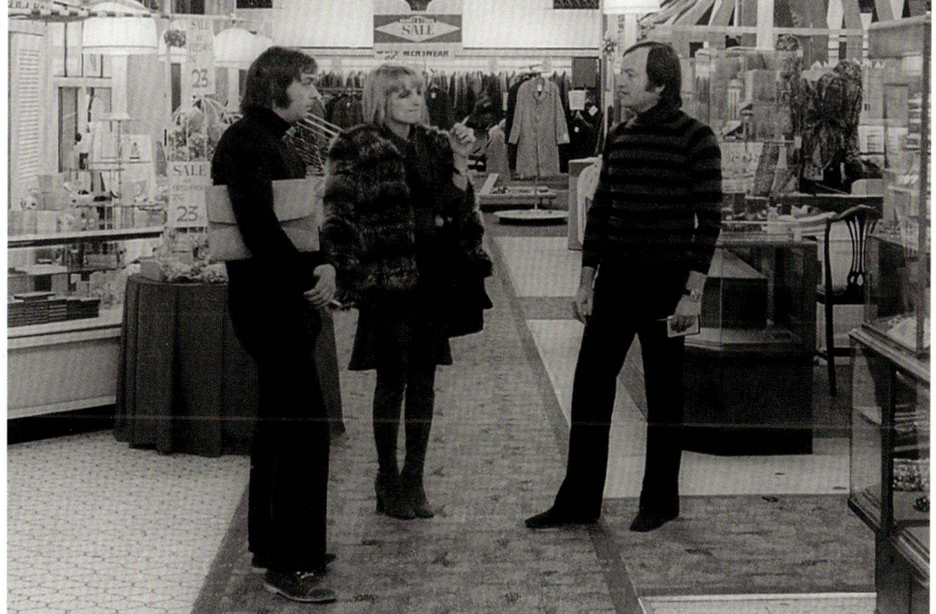

Architecturally the building was a confidently understated piece of art deco, its open-plan floors without central stairwells quietly revolutionary for a London store.

Derry & Toms closed in January 1973. 'By the time it closed its doors,' said the *New Yorker*, 'Derry & Toms was reduced to sorely faded glory.' Biba's task, Barbara Hulanicki explained, was simply to 'bring it back to its original splendour'.

Left to right: Tim Whitmore, Barbara Hulanicki, Stephen Fitz-Simon in the original Derry and Toms store, Christmas 1971. Photograph: Steven Thomas

OPENING ADS

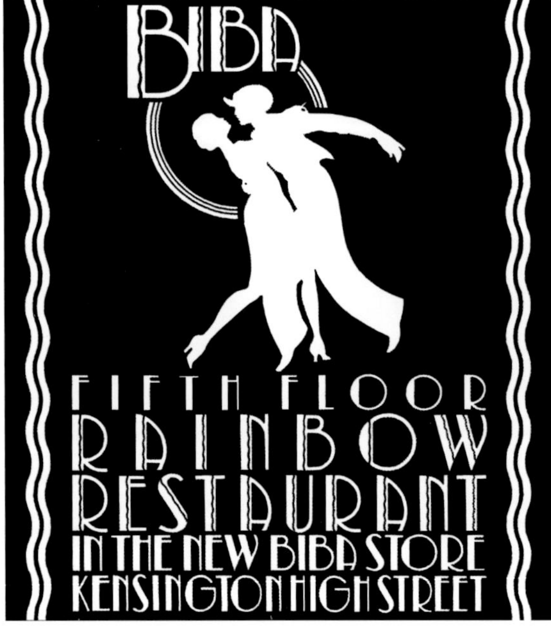

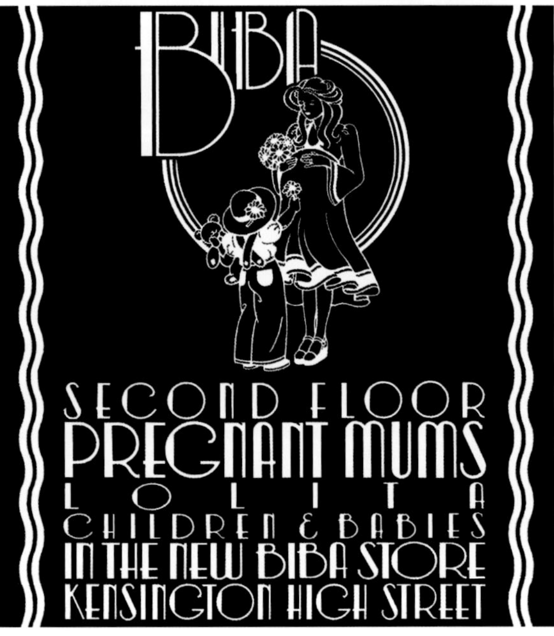

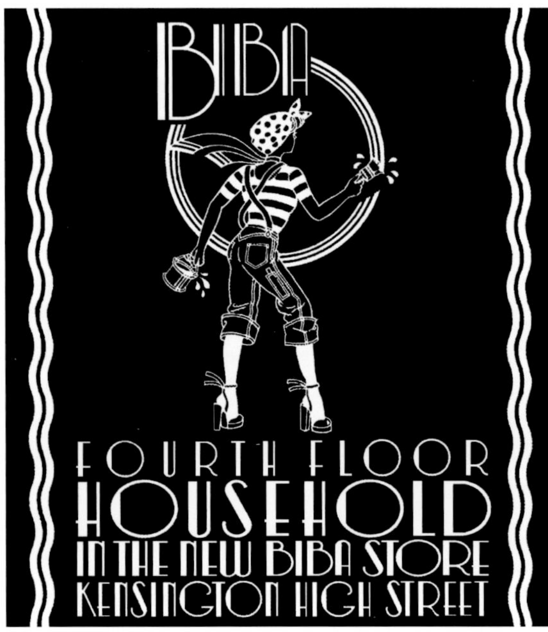

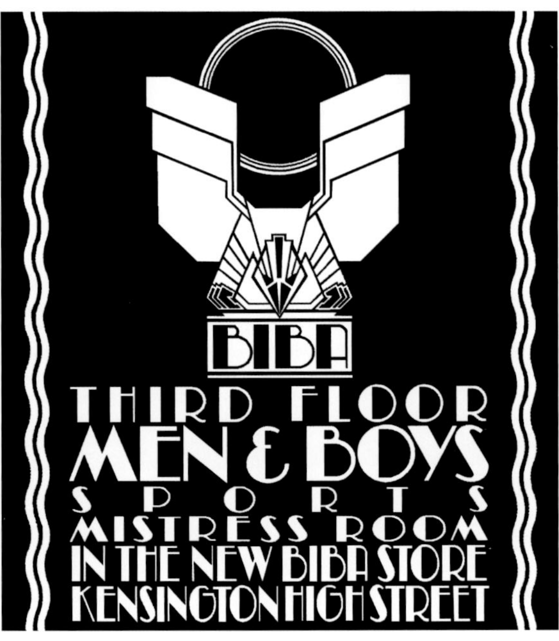

With the exception of a few notices in the fashion press for the mail-order catalogues, Biba had never advertised itself, relying on word of mouth and media endorsements.

Big Biba was different: a series of teaser ads and a quarter-page advert (opposite) were taken in national newspapers leading up to the opening of the store.

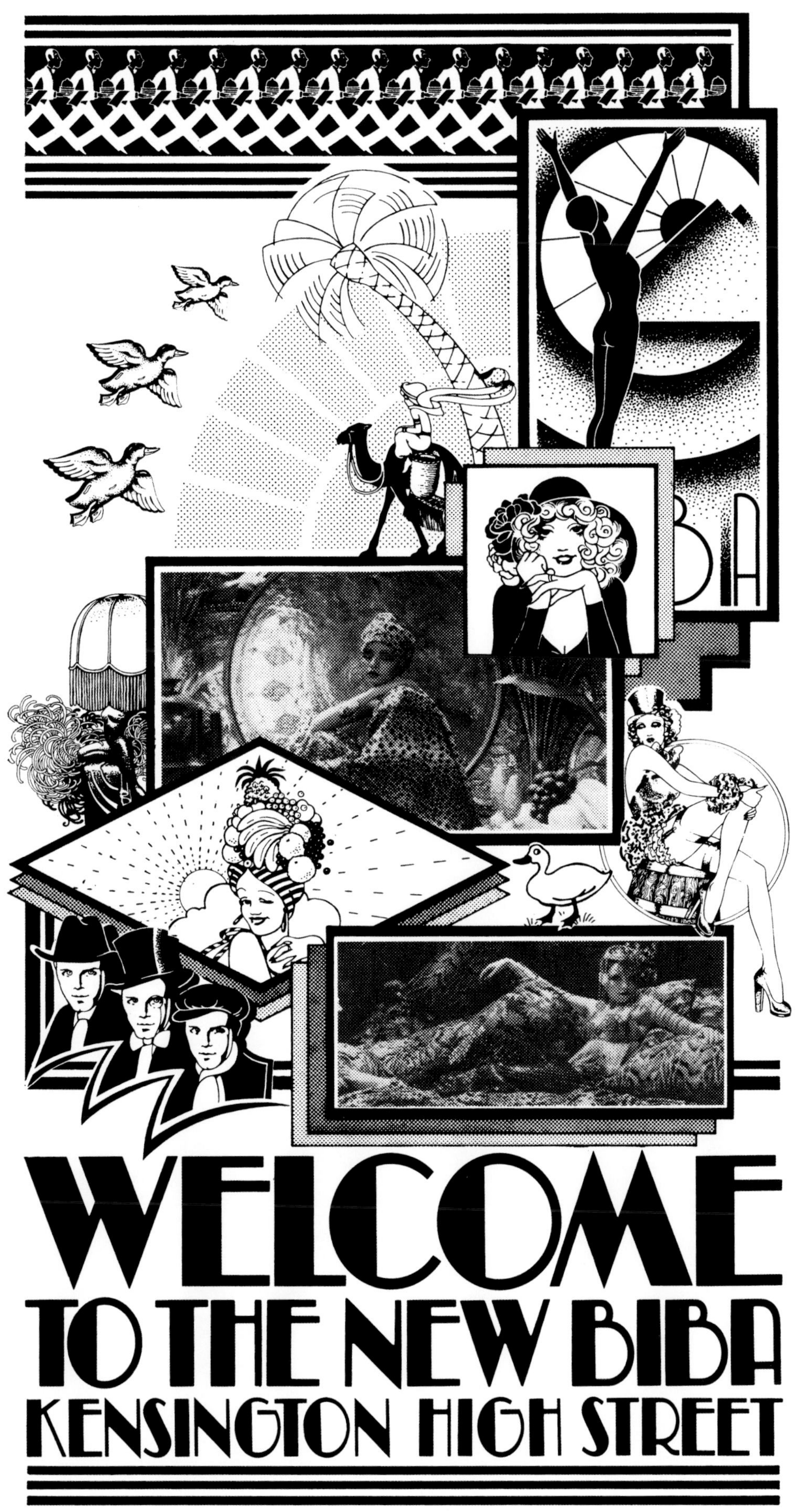
BIBA
WELCOME
TO THE NEW BIBA
KENSINGTON HIGH STREET

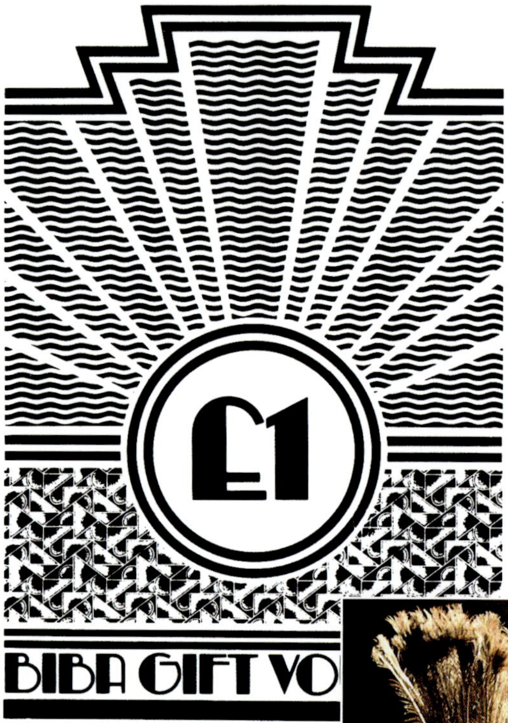

At twenty times the size of the previous store, Big Biba was a massive leap for Hulanicki and Fitz-Simon, though they claimed to be unfazed by the prospect: 'It sounds a big jump, but funnily enough it isn't. We've got 100,000 a week store-traffic at Biba now, with too little space to display the right quality of merchandise.' Having already achieved sales four times higher than the average for department stores (calculated in turnover per square foot), confidence was high.

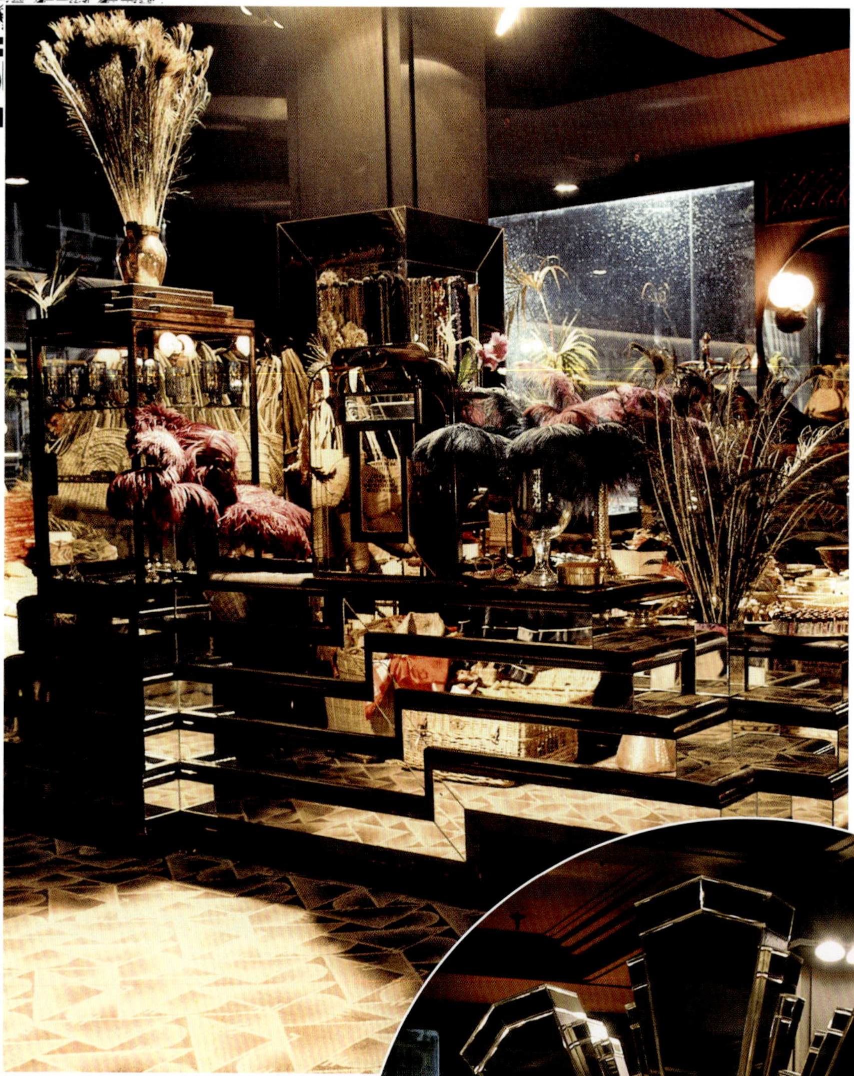

For years Biba had been in the business of fantasy, transforming every Eliza Doolittle who crossed its threshold into a gorgeous, vampish queen of the night. Now it sought to build a stage that would be worthy of the High Street stars it had created.

Everything was on a scale that had hitherto only existed in imagination. This was to be 'more like a Busby Berkeley film set than a department store,' said the *Observer*, and from the graphics upwards there was a sense of imperial grandeur: each of the fifteen departments had its own logo, while seven new typefaces were designed, one for each floor.

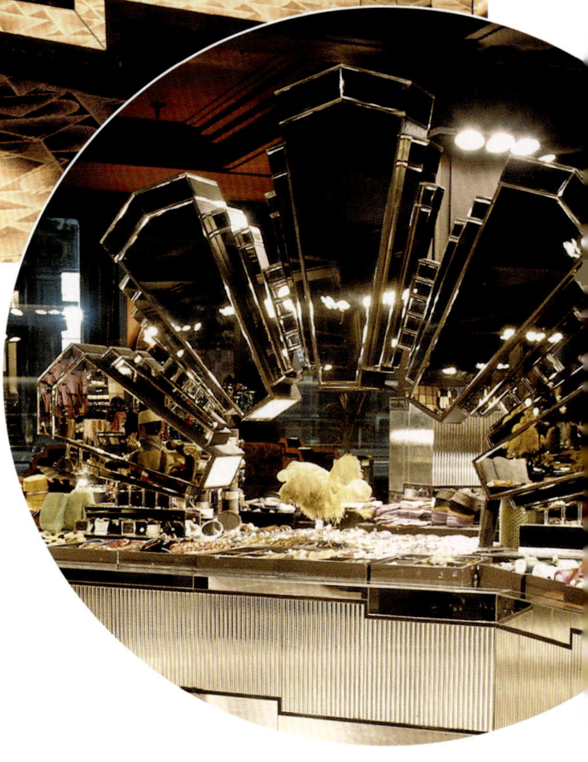

Left to Right: Ground floor gift voucher logo; detail of the exotic Casbah unit; the fan-shaped back unit to the jewellery counter inspired by the window decoration (see page 8); the original lift surrounds in bronze, copper and marble designed by Walter Gilbert; mannequin on the ground floor books unit; and the ground floor gift voucher, one of the four varients used throughout the store.

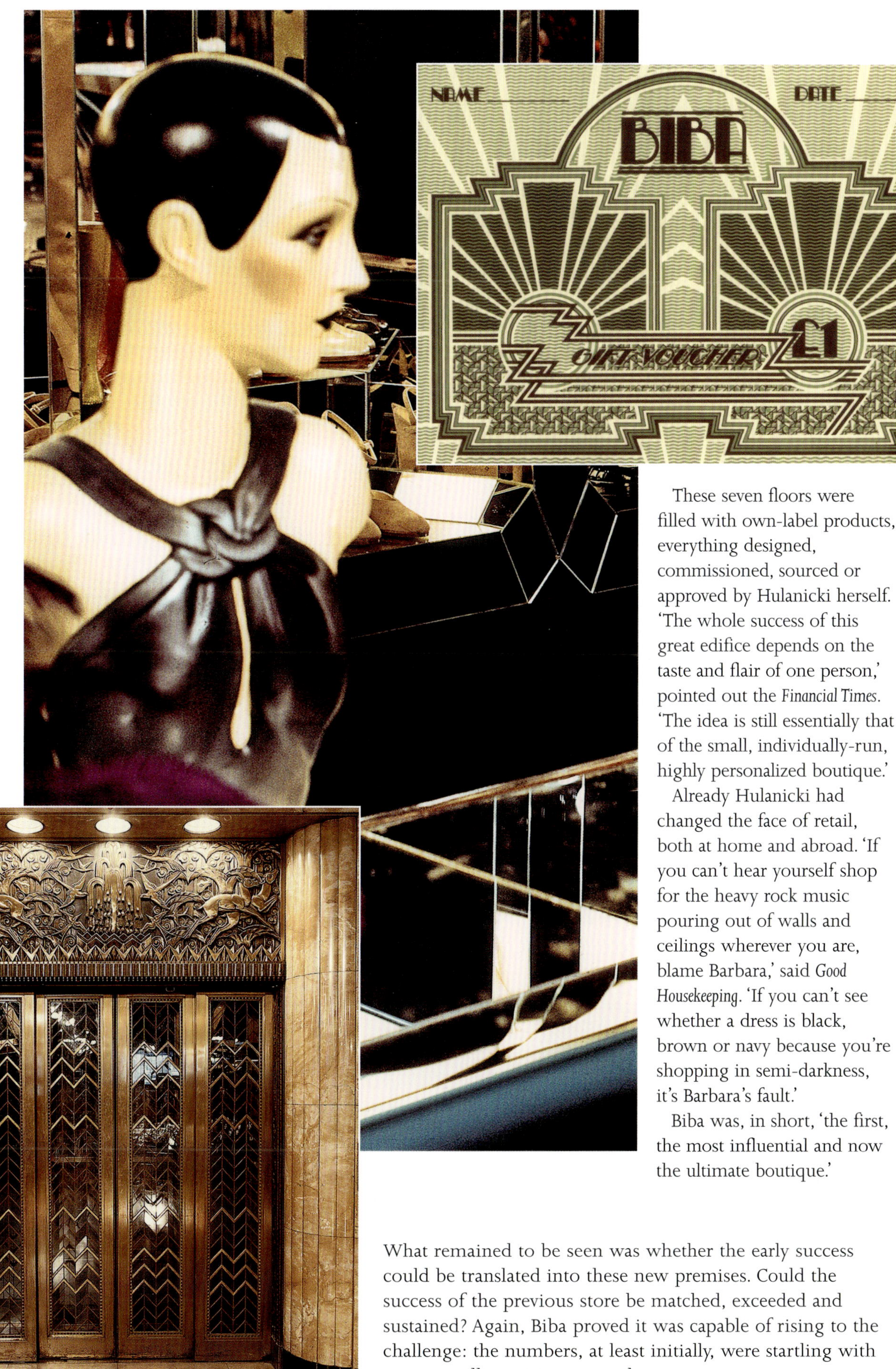

These seven floors were filled with own-label products, everything designed, commissioned, sourced or approved by Hulanicki herself. 'The whole success of this great edifice depends on the taste and flair of one person,' pointed out the *Financial Times*. 'The idea is still essentially that of the small, individually-run, highly personalized boutique.'

Already Hulanicki had changed the face of retail, both at home and abroad. 'If you can't hear yourself shop for the heavy rock music pouring out of walls and ceilings wherever you are, blame Barbara,' said *Good Housekeeping*. 'If you can't see whether a dress is black, brown or navy because you're shopping in semi-darkness, it's Barbara's fault.'

Biba was, in short, 'the first, the most influential and now the ultimate boutique.'

What remained to be seen was whether the early success could be translated into these new premises. Could the success of the previous store be matched, exceeded and sustained? Again, Biba proved it was capable of rising to the challenge: the numbers, at least initially, were startling with up to a million visitors a week.

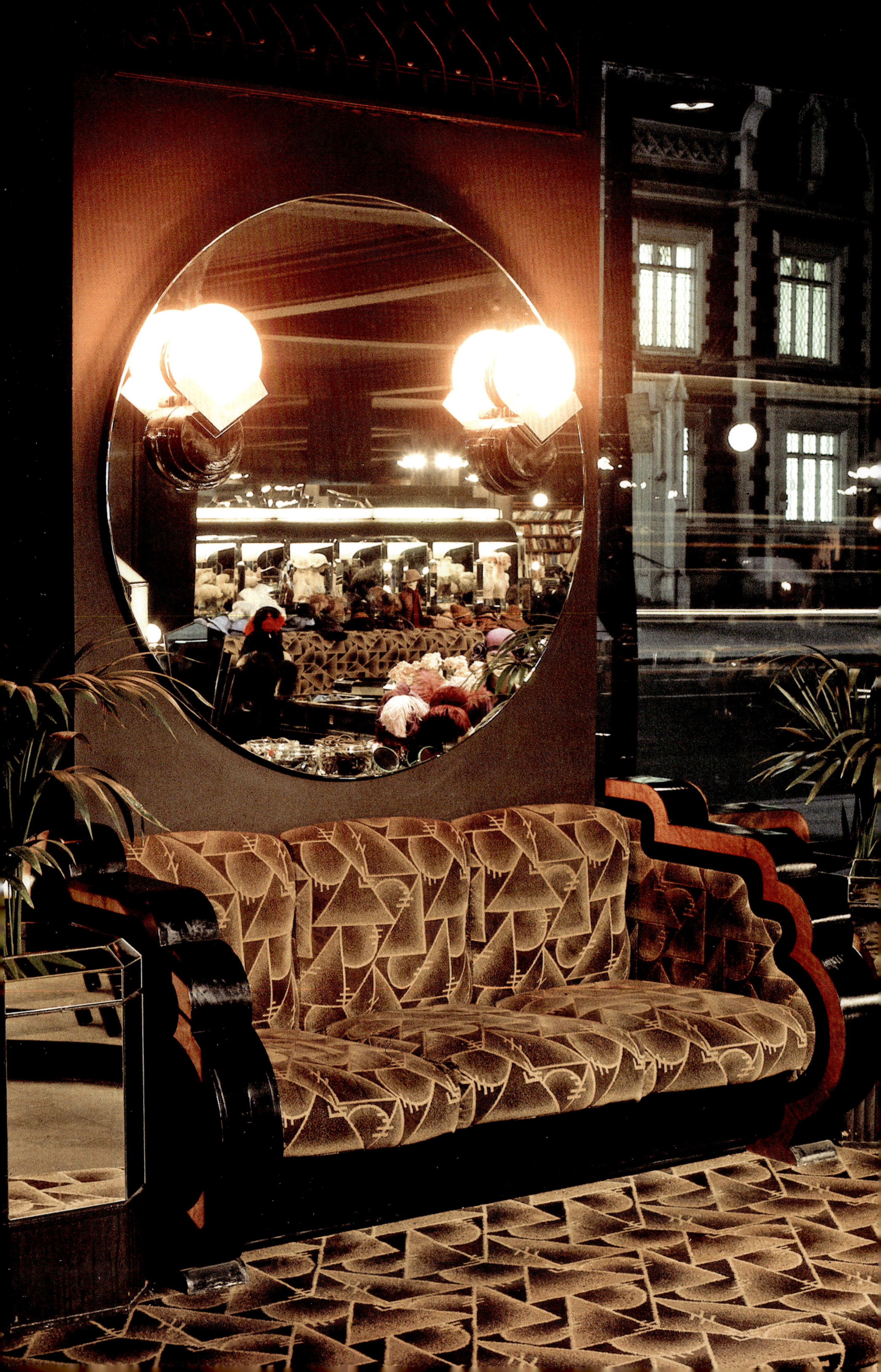

GROUND FLOOR

It was the size that made the first impression, the sheer scale of the enterprise, the space as well as the range of goods for sale. For those who had grown up in the crowded, conspiratorial atmosphere of the first boutiques, even for those who had frequented the most recent incarnation, this was a Biba beyond imagining, a Biba run riot in what *Vogue* called 'a palace of apricot marble, coloured counters and fake leopard-skin walls; seven floors of fantasy.'

For those who were counting, there were over 20,000 mirrors in the shop, 8000 square feet of narcissistic nirvana. Meanwhile, the marble flooring – 26,000 square feet of it on the ground floor alone – came from Portugal, exhausting supplies and still demanding more. As one entered, broad boulevards swept around the various counters and departments, directing the hordes of Bibaphiles to the lifts and the wonderlands beyond.

And hordes there were, with the store rapidly attracting a million visitors a week. What looked, in the absence of customers, like vast empty spaces became crowded thoroughfares, filled with such throngs that the most common complaint was the difficulty of finding a shop assistant to sell you anything.

The ground floor comprised the accessories department, 'things you come in for when you're in a hurry'. This is where records and magazines, stationery, leather goods, boots and shoes, jewellery, knitwear, sweaters and more were to be found. Familiar features from earlier shops were present in gloriously exaggerated forms, as seen in the tights counter (pp.26-27), which displayed only what was considered a basic range of everyday wear – the main lingerie department was upstairs on the first floor. Similarly, the t-shirt counter (pp.30-31) had over a thousand separate pigeon-holes to accommodate a series of styles that came in three sizes and any of 24 colours. Most of these colours were customized and manufactured to Biba's own requirements.

Other areas were entirely new, such as the book shop (pp.24-25), a deco dream of a library specializing in art and design volumes.

Here too was an area called the Casbah, selling goods sourced from Morocco to China, via Turkey and India, and a florist's shop, which revealingly sold many more artificial flowers than fresh blooms.

But above all, there was the space, the sense of drama that left commentators reaching for cinematic comparisons: 'a grand, almost Hollywood environment' as the architectural press put it. It was, said the *Sunday Times*, 'the most beautiful store in the world.'

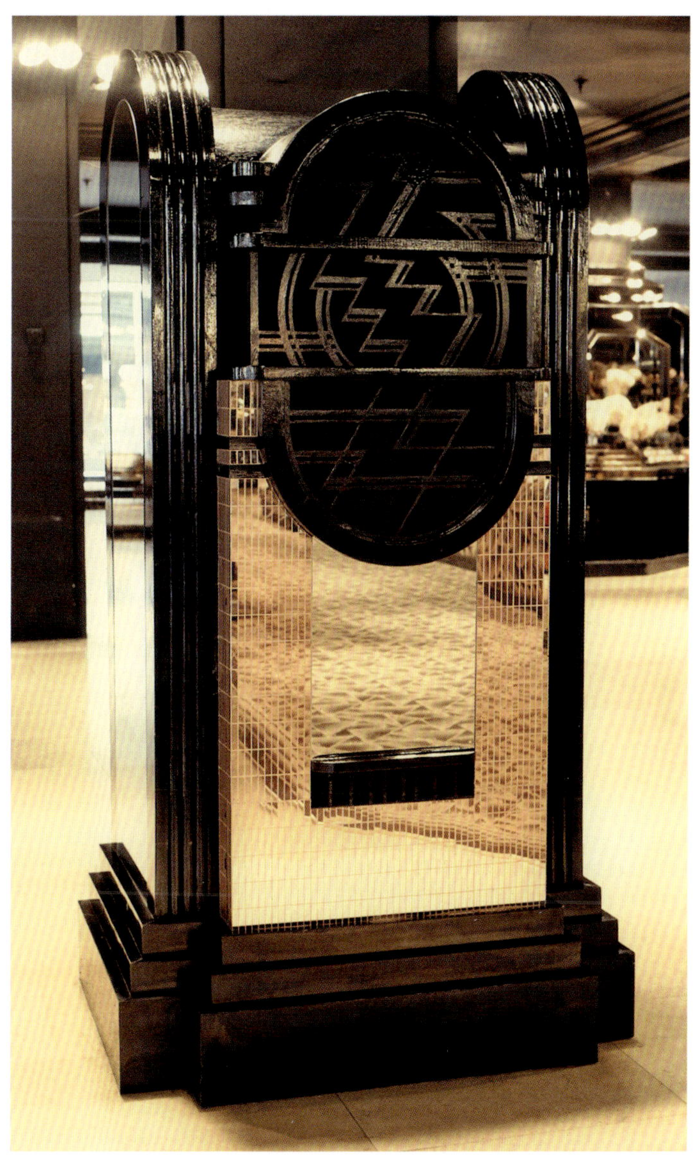

Opposite page: Biba didn't do windows and never had. From Abingdon Road onwards, there had been a refusal to advertise the wares in the window, though seats were provided for those who wished to sit and watch the world go by. Confronted with 226 feet of frontage on a busy shopping street, the attitude was defiantly unchanged, except that a great many more sofas were provided: indeed there was more seating on the ground floor alone than there was on Euston station. The speaker (above) was one of twelve on the ground floor.

COSMETICS

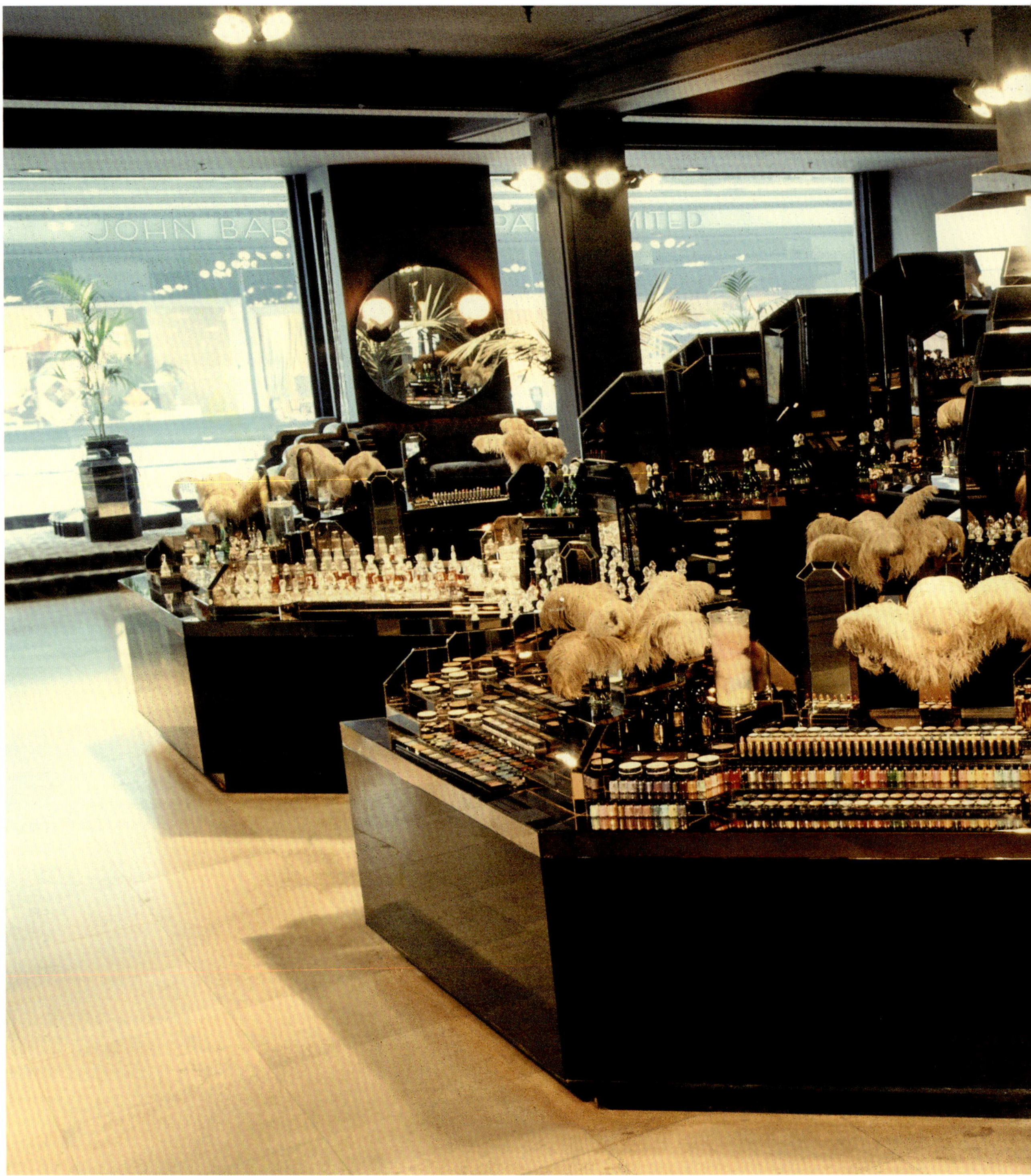

The flagship department on the ground floor of Big Biba centred on a cruciform display unit in black glass and specially made peach mirror, with a tester counter at the end of each arm. It was calculated that, averaged across the week, one piece was sold here every seven seconds.

Biba launched its make-up range in 1970. The colours that had become associated with the fashion – dark-brown, plum, mulberry, mahogany, even black – now appeared in lipstick, eye shadow and nail polish, creating a distinctively decadent look that became *de rigueur* in glam circles. The likes of Lou Reed and Freddie Mercury were enthusiastic customers, and the influence continued into the next generation, as future goth star Siouxsie Sioux remembered in John Robb's oral history of *Punk Rock*: 'Once I started going to Biba on my own, and discovered rust colours for the eyes, I really got quite heavily into wearing red eye shadow.'

Biba Cosmetics took Hulanicki's vision out beyond the confines of West London to the rest of the

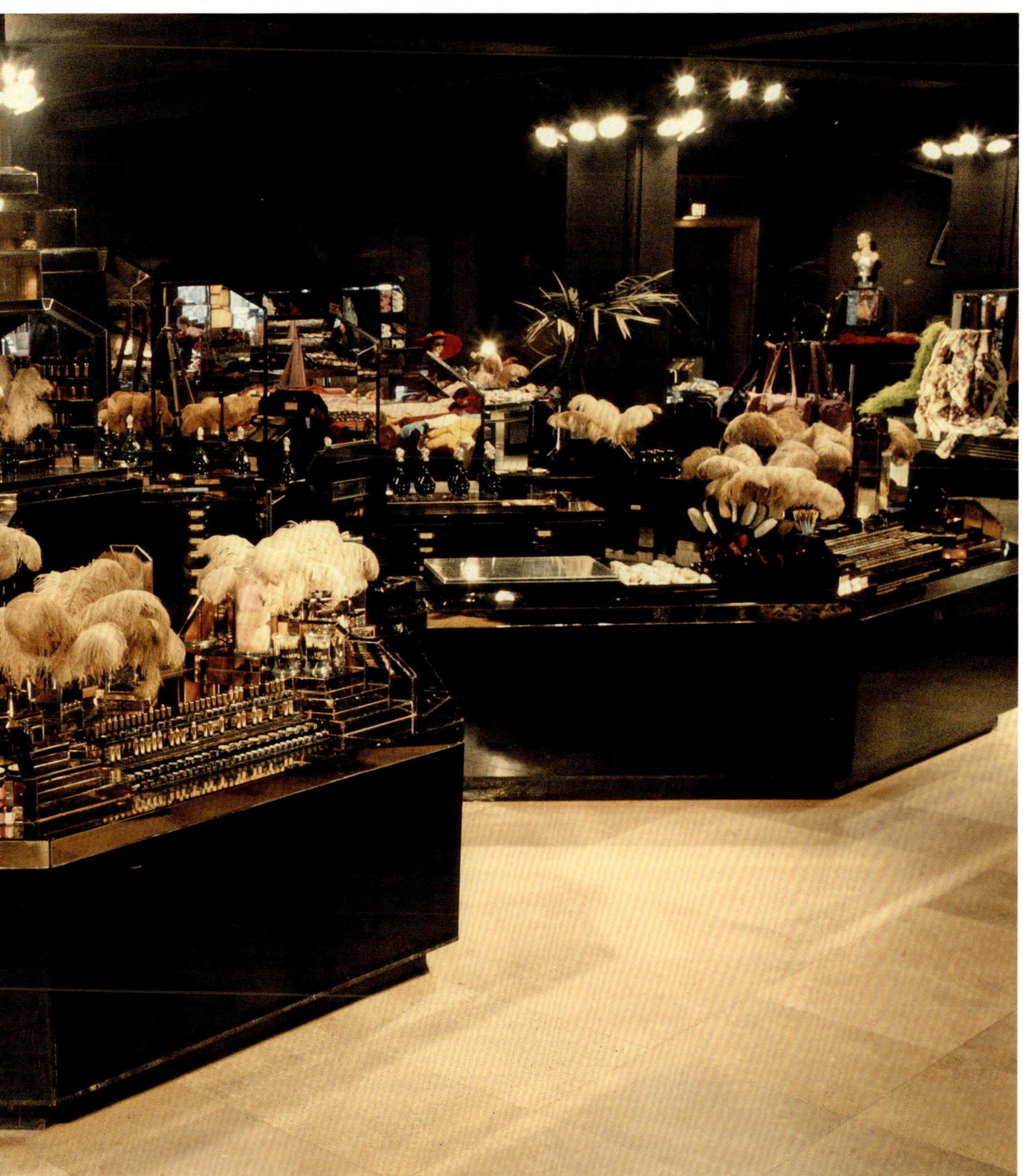

country, via the Dorothy Perkins chain of shops.

The old-fashioned pots and bottles, their shapes evoking apothecaries past, were dressed in black-and-gold livery and sold on display units designed by Whitmore-Thomas. For thousands, this was their first exposure to Biba, and it became the most successful venture for the firm.

As a separate company, it also survived the closure of the store itself: indeed, even as the closure was being announced, Biba Cosmetics was branching into yet another new territory with an outlet in Washington, DC. By that stage the range was available in fifteen countries, sold not only in New York, Milan and Paris, but also in Japan, Scandinavia and the Middle East.

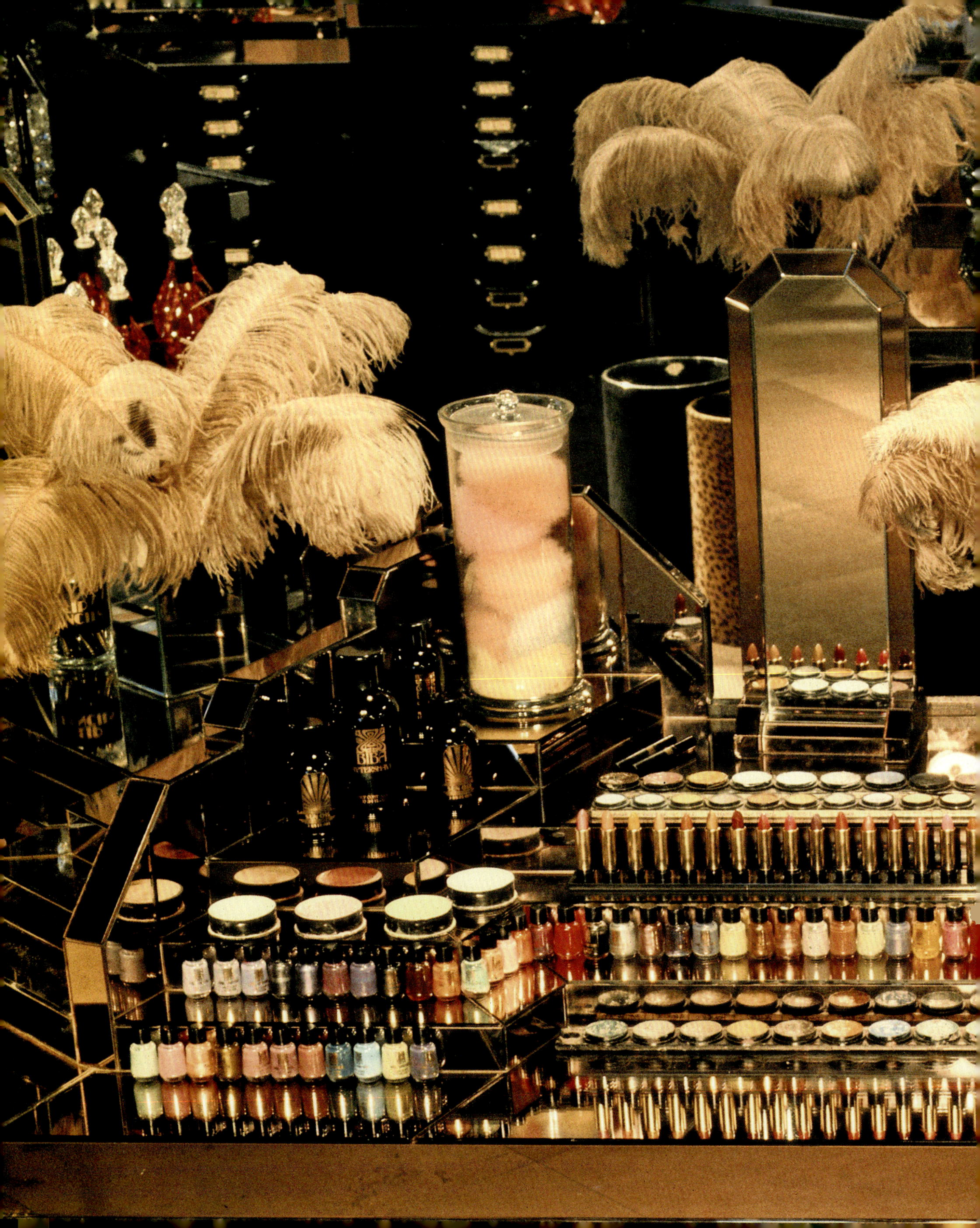
BIBA

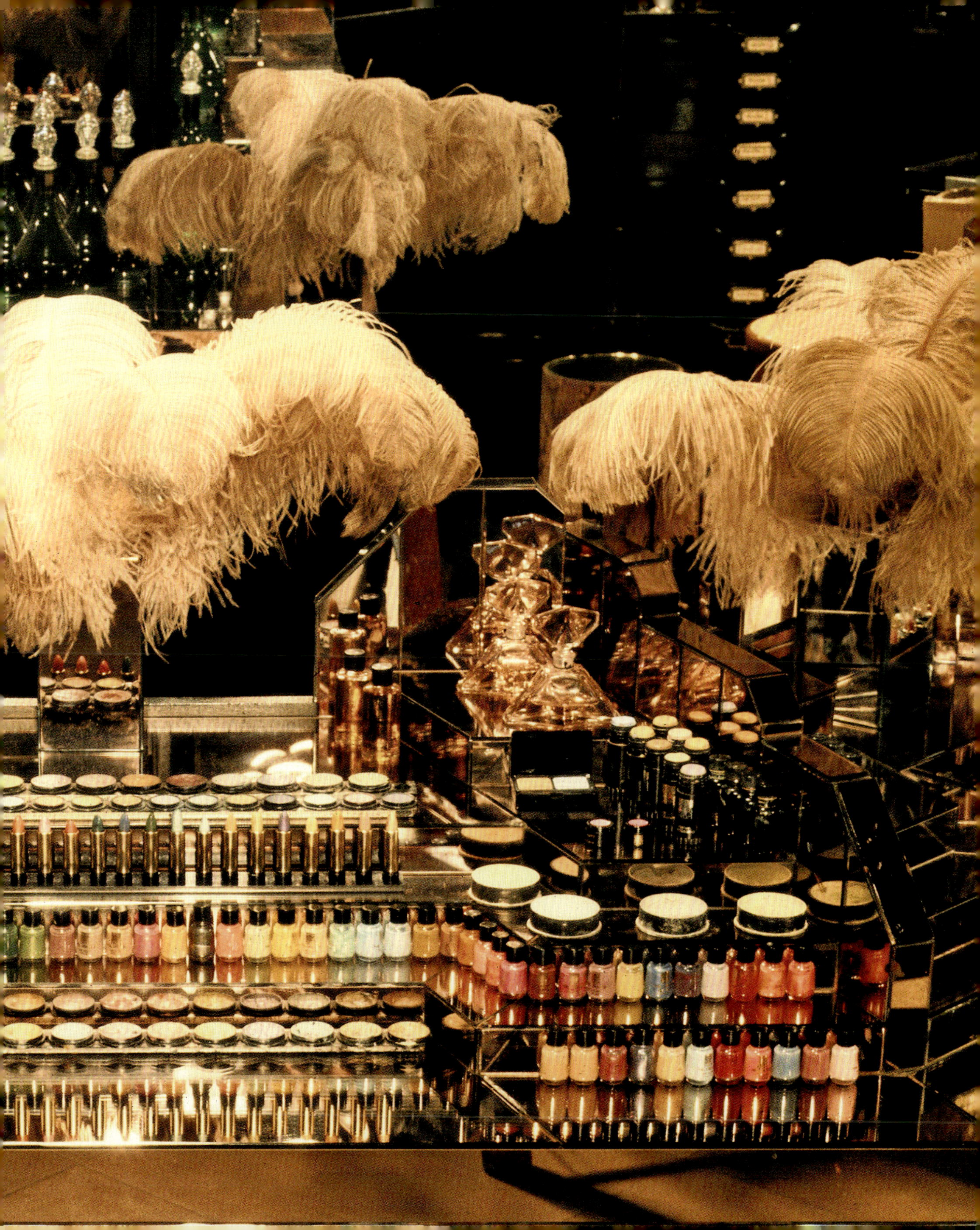

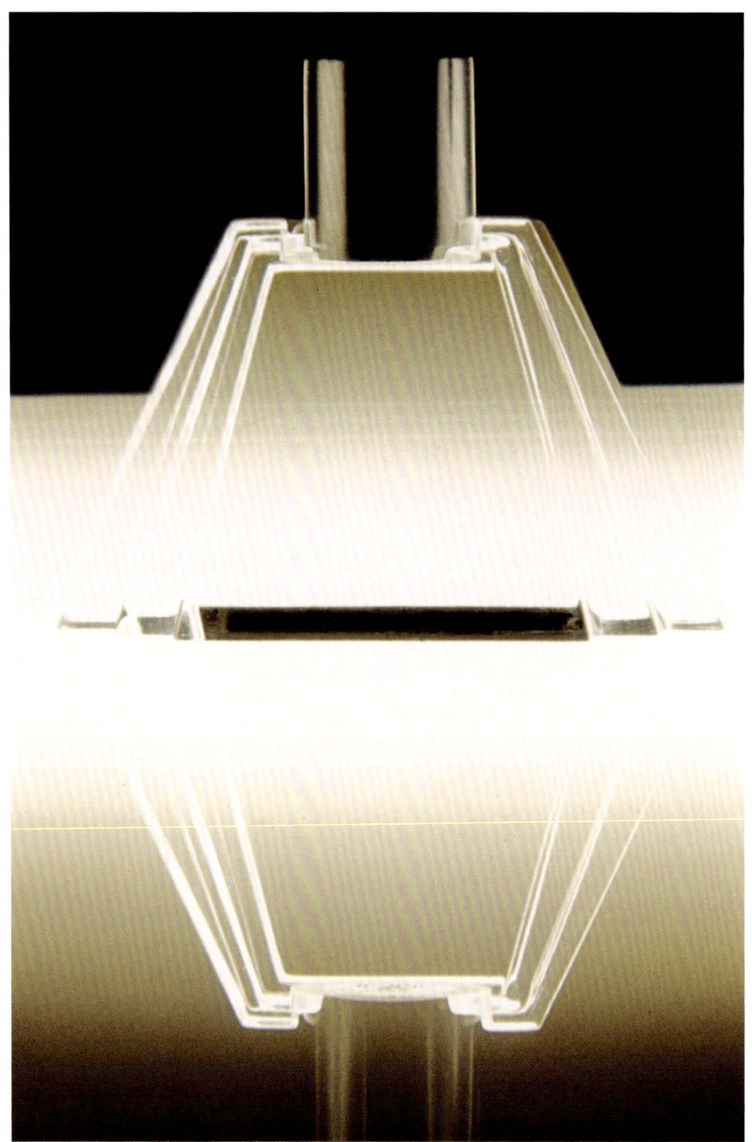

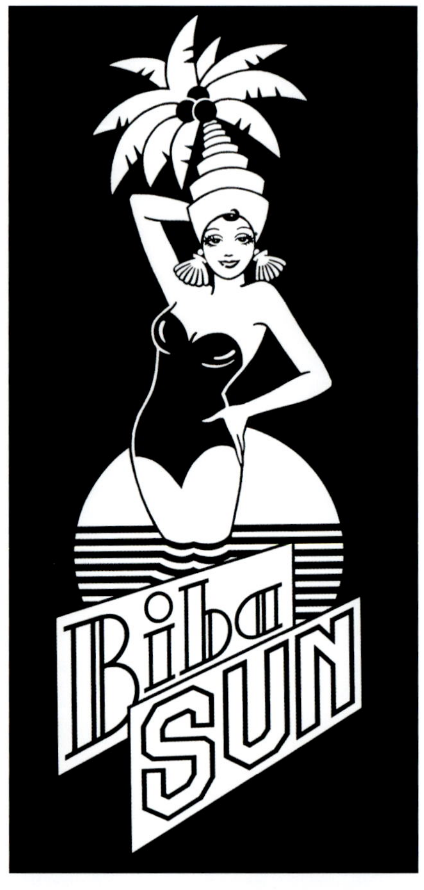

This page: *A flacon designed for Biba scent but never actually manufactured; the logo for the holiday skin-care collection; part of the health-care range for women.*

Opposite: *This poster won a British Poster Design Award. Designed by Steven Thomas; photography by Sarah Moon; model Ingrid Boulting.*

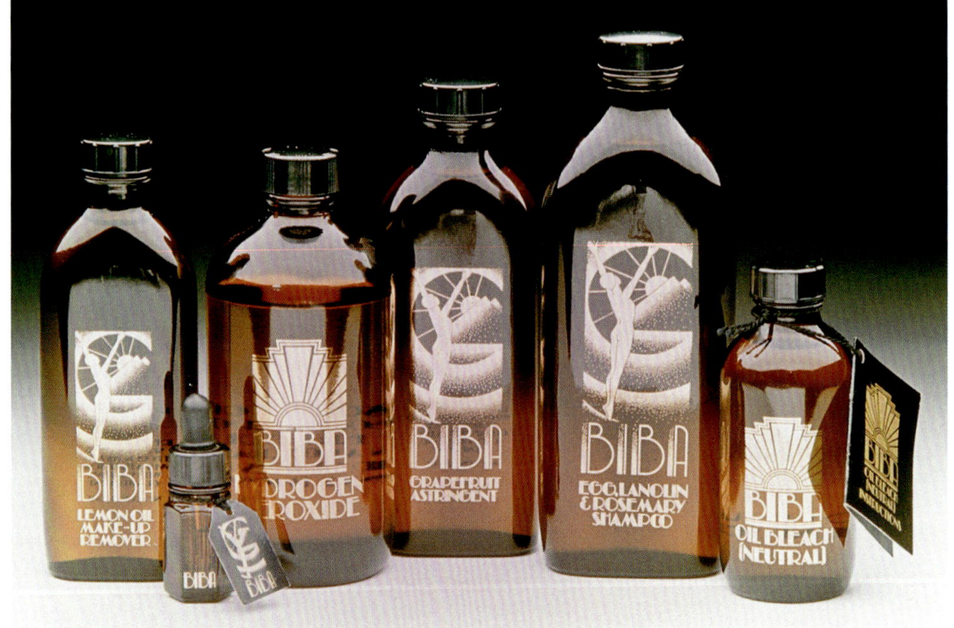

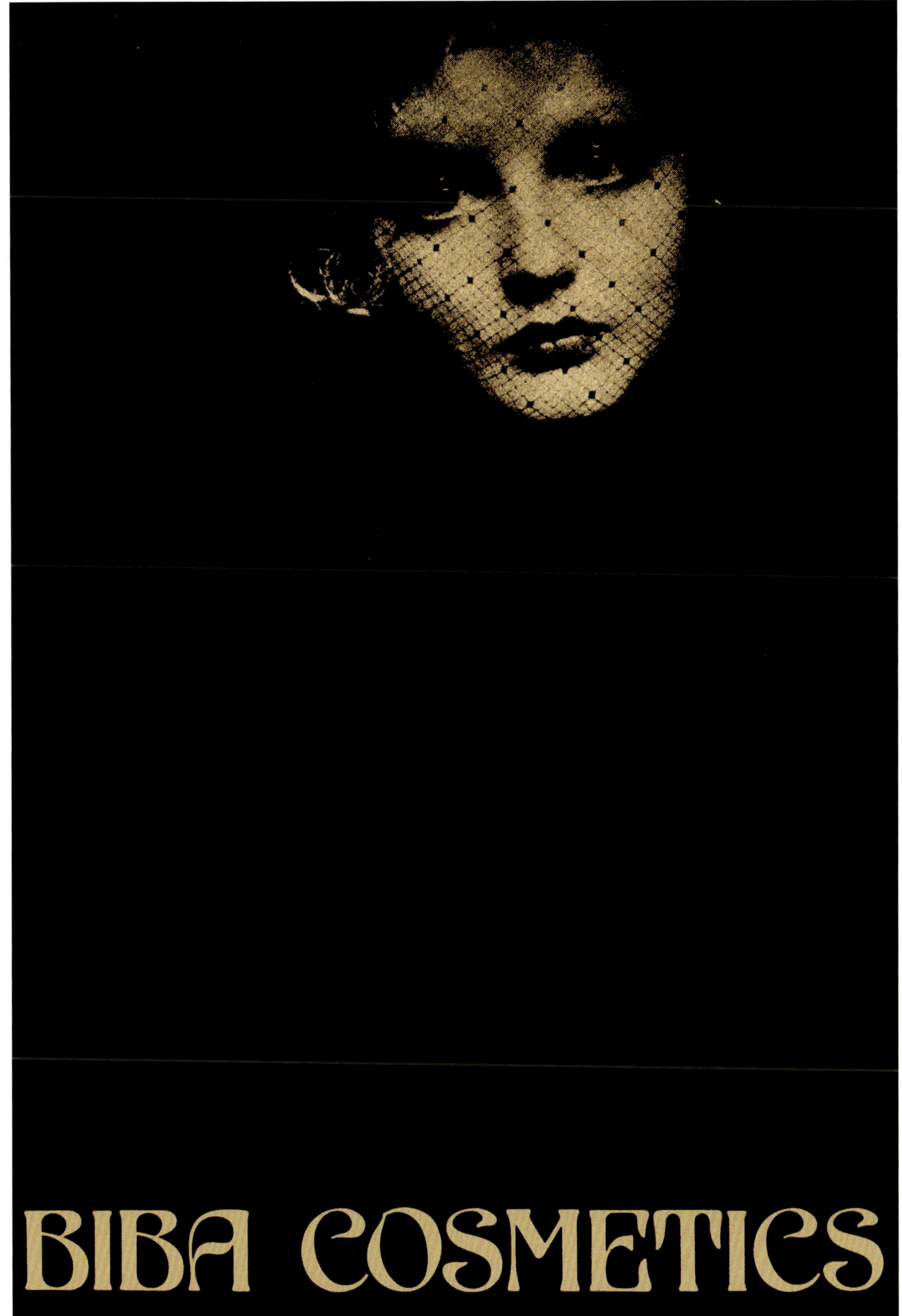
BIBA COSMETICS

LEATHER

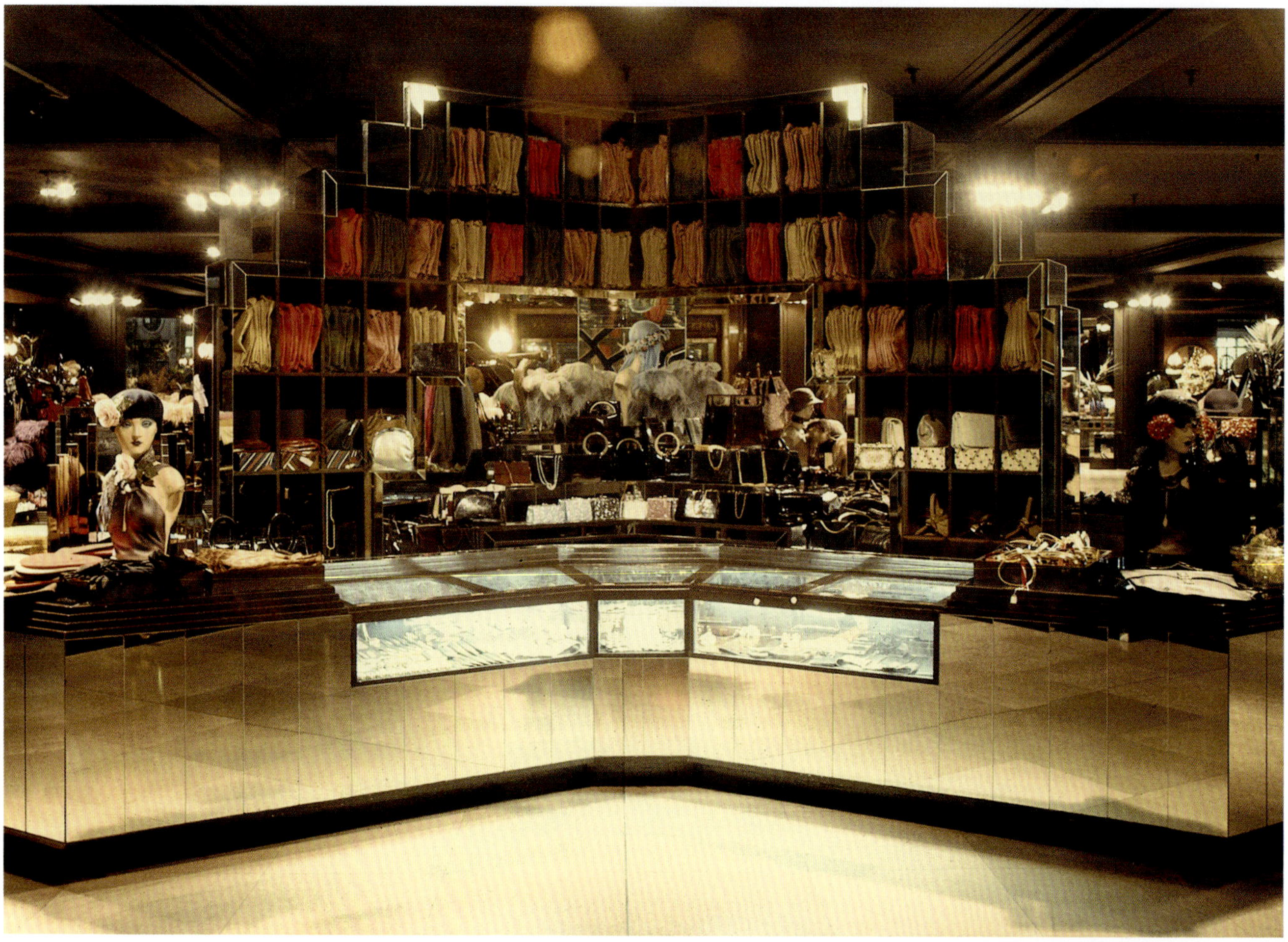

The leather unit on the ground floor comprised three arched arms that met over a hollow centre, and sold wallets, key-fobs, chequebook covers and belts, as well as Biba leopard-skin luggage, a range that went all the way up to cabin trunk size.

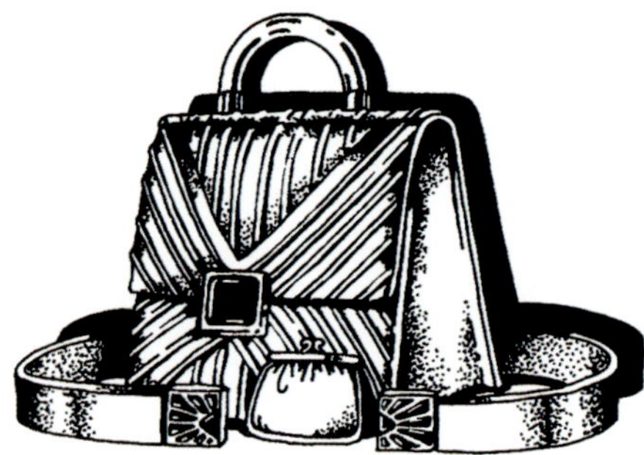

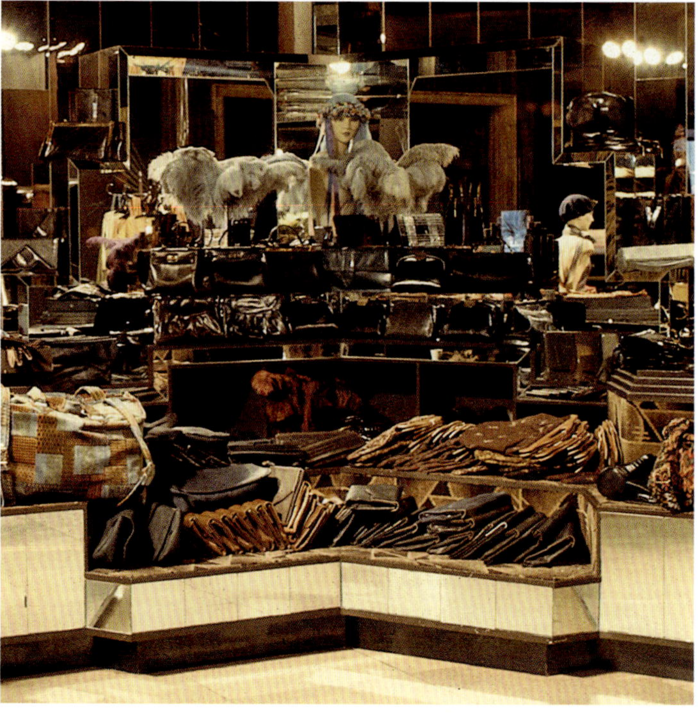

Opposite: Boots and shoes had been one of the great successes of the previous store, literally provoking fights when a new delivery of Biba boots was delivered. 75,000 pairs of these boots were said to have been sold within three months of their launch.

SHOES

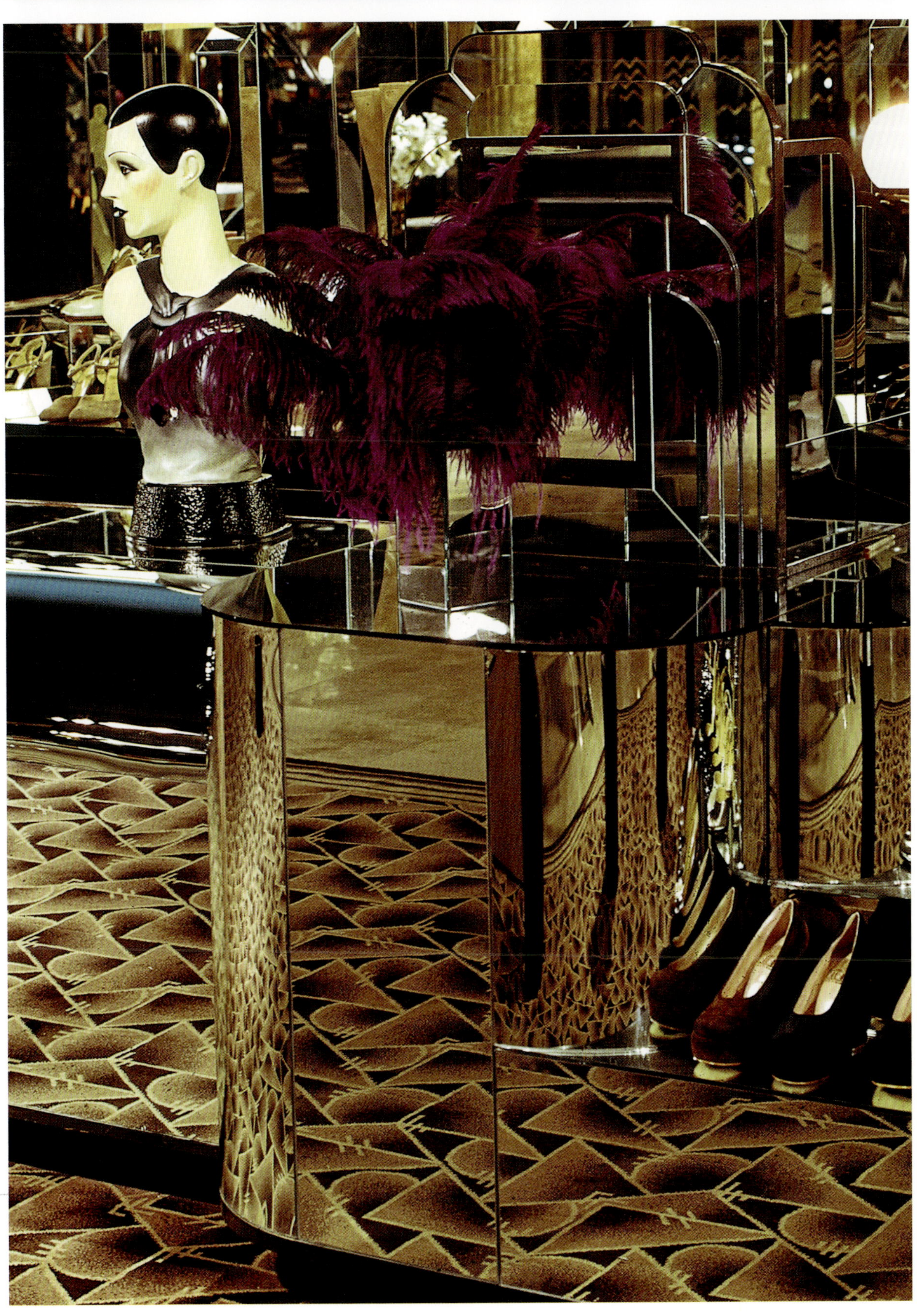

THE BOOK SHOP

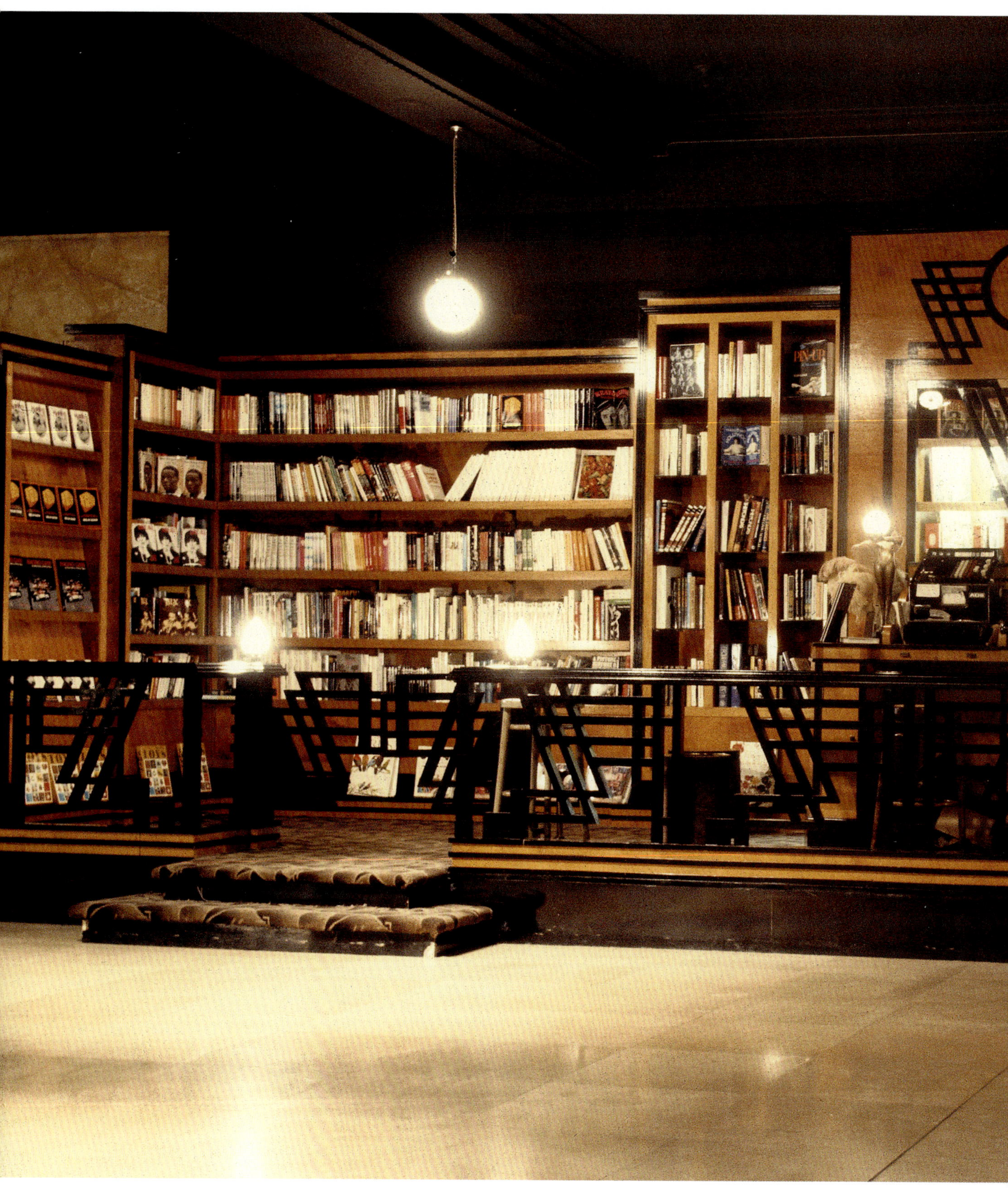

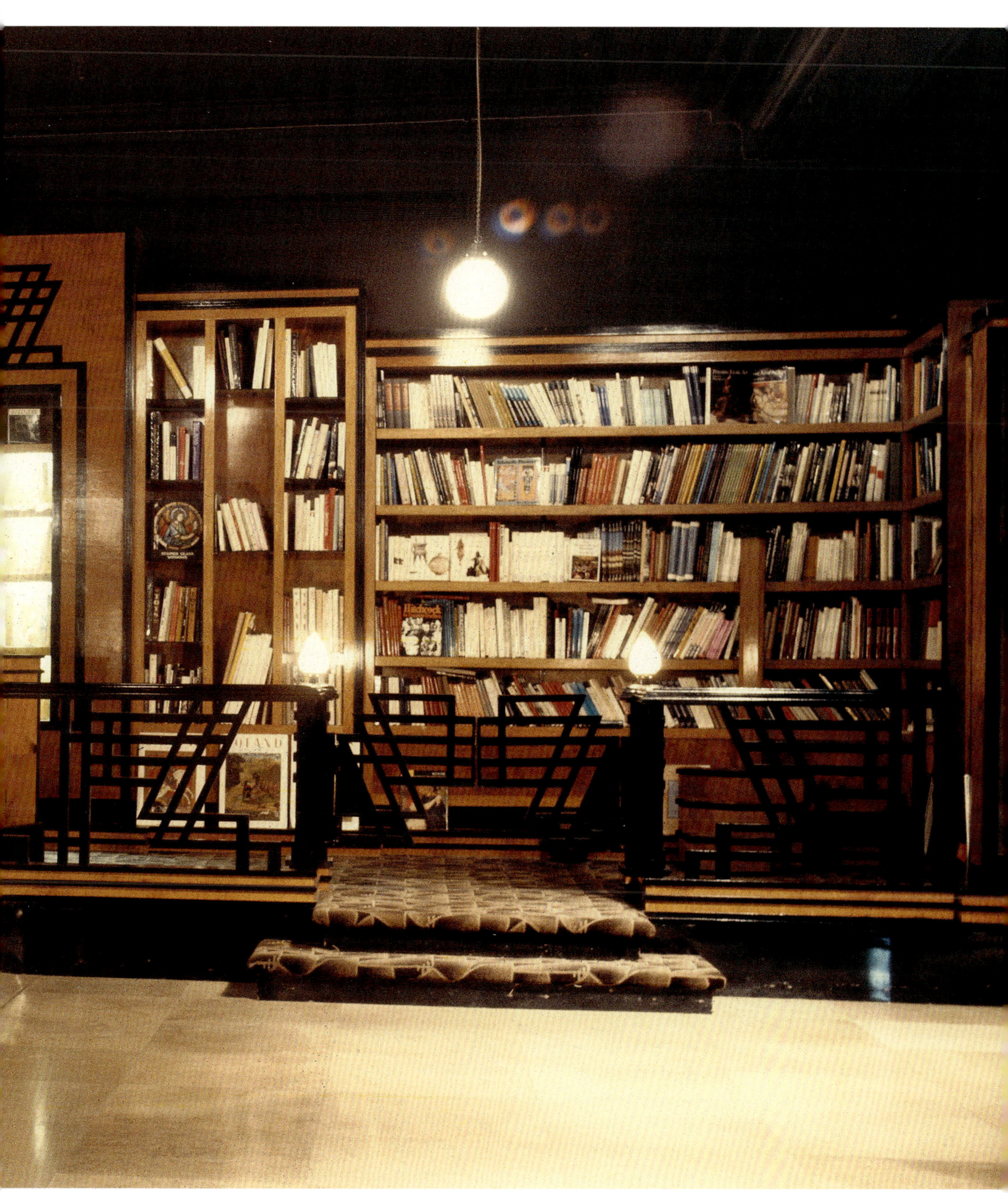
Hitchcock

TIGHTS

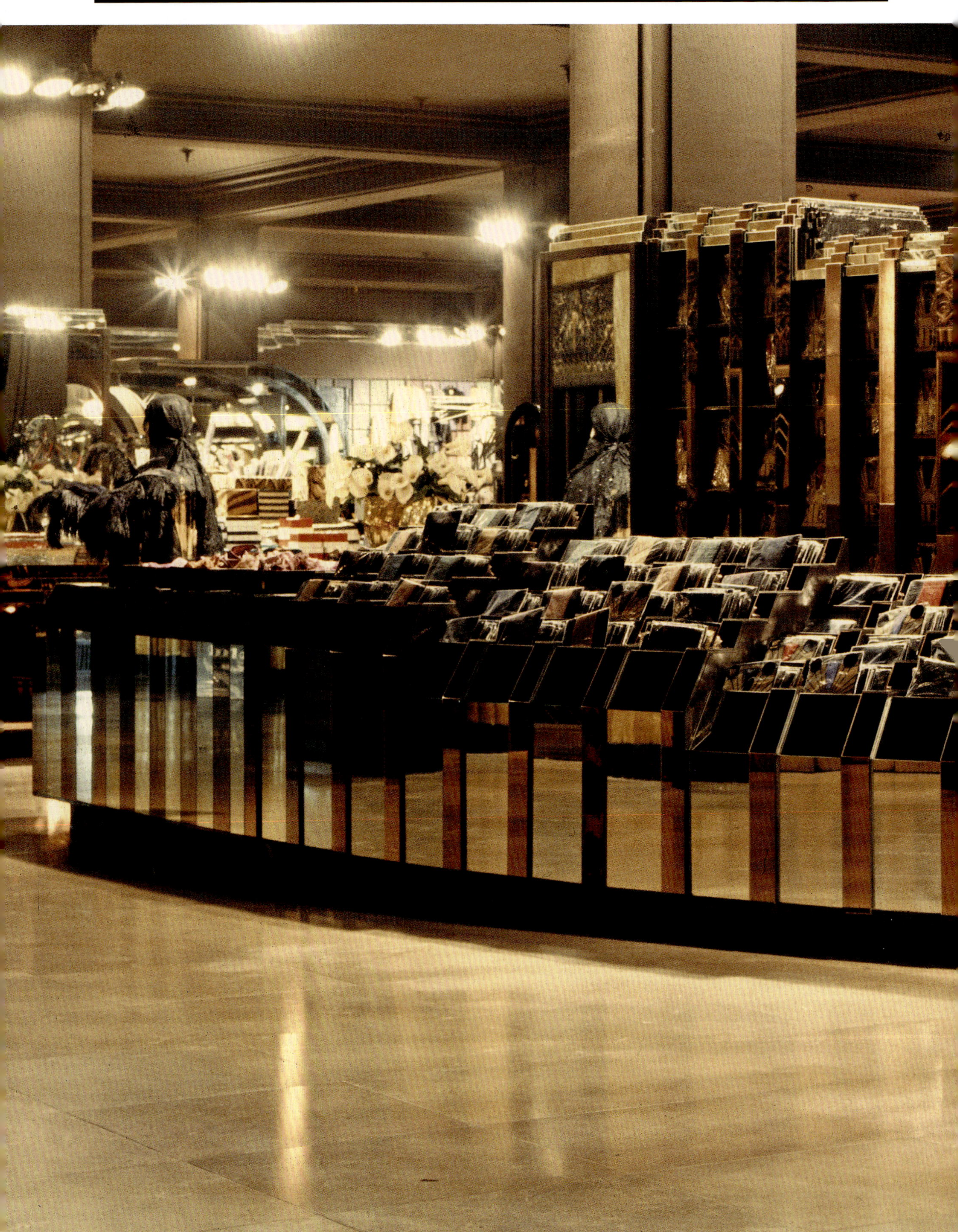

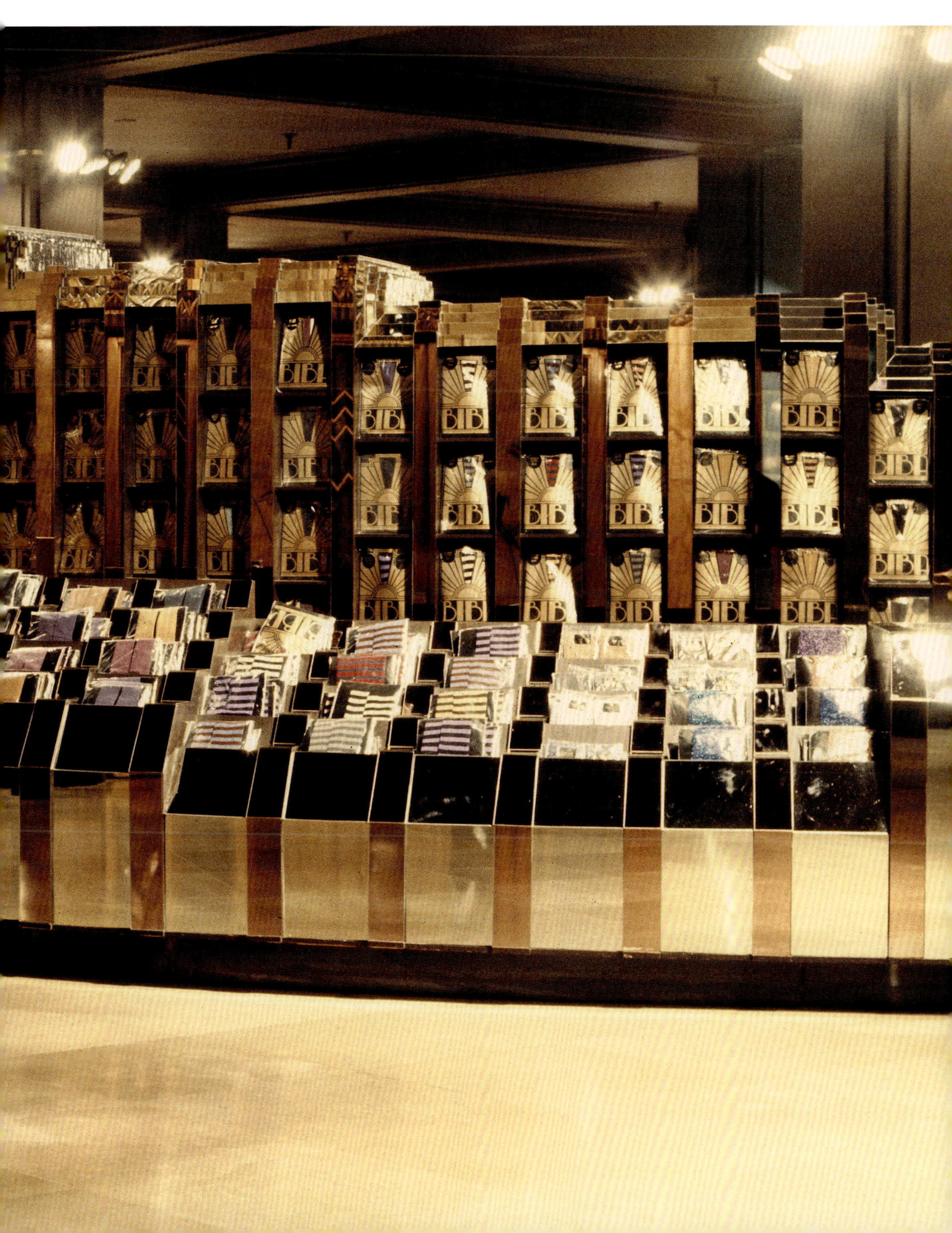

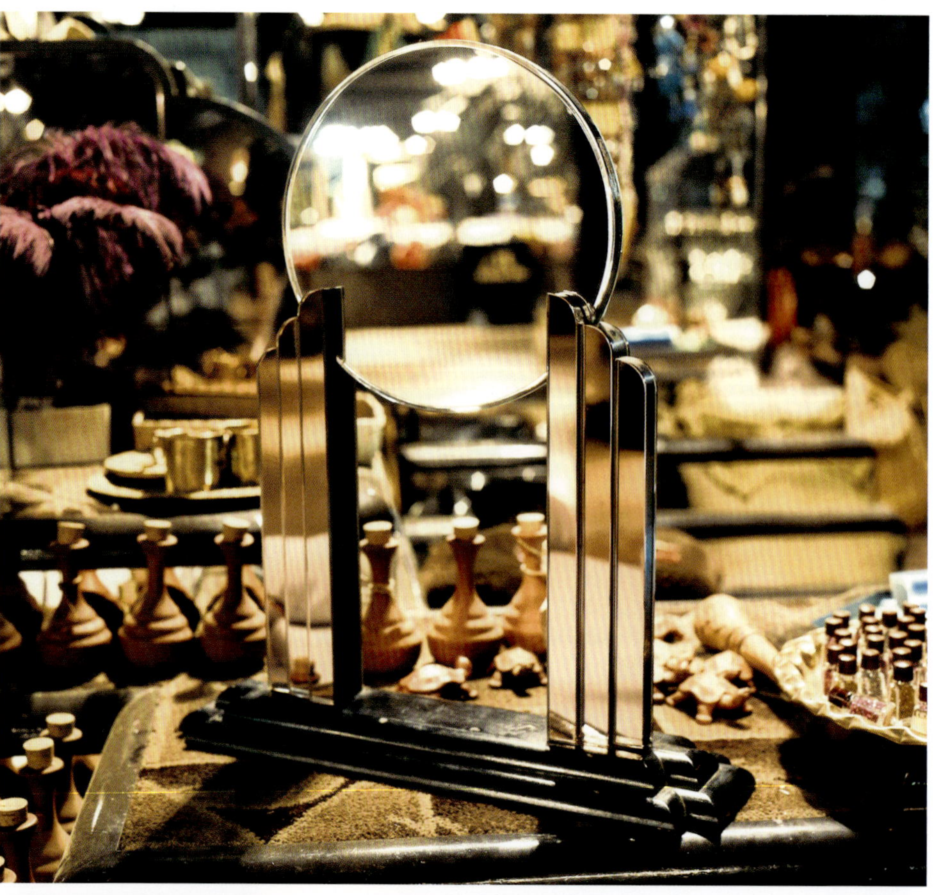

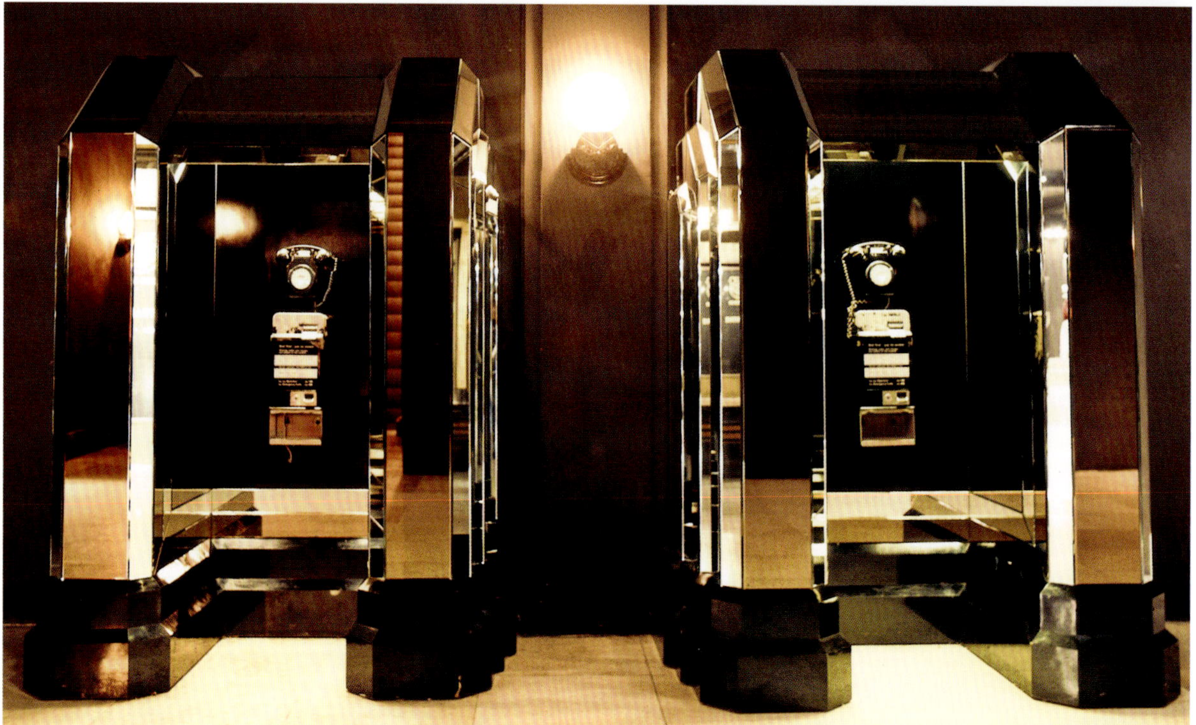

Big Biba had the first computerised till system of any major store in Britain, supplied by the German firm, Anker. The technical limitations imposed by such early technology created one of the most severe logistical problems encountered in the 16-week contract to refit the store, but once installed did enable continual monitoring of stock movement.

Meanwhile, the sheer size of the equipment required the creation of till cosies to conceal the hardware, three of which are shown opposite. Three designs of counter mirror were created, this example coming from the Exotics Unit. The telephone-boxes above were glazed in hundreds of pieces of polished and bevelled mirror.

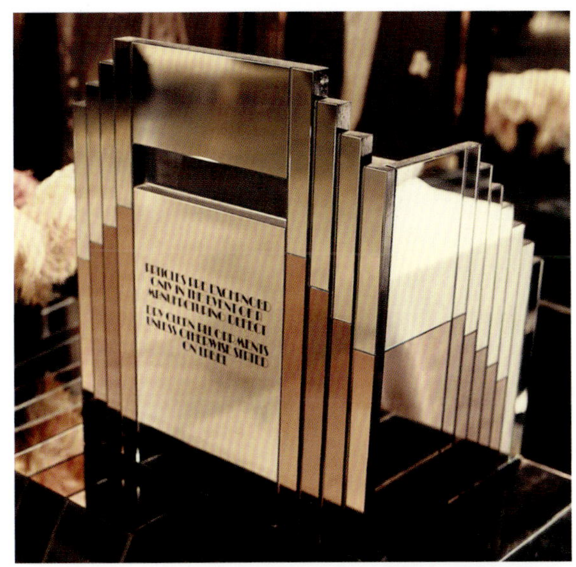

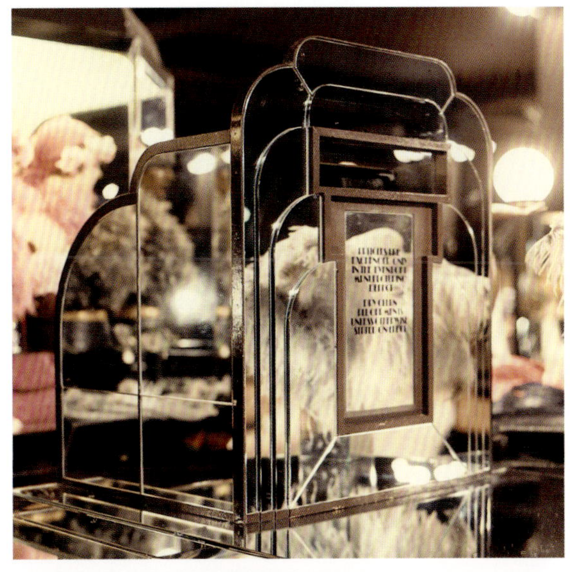

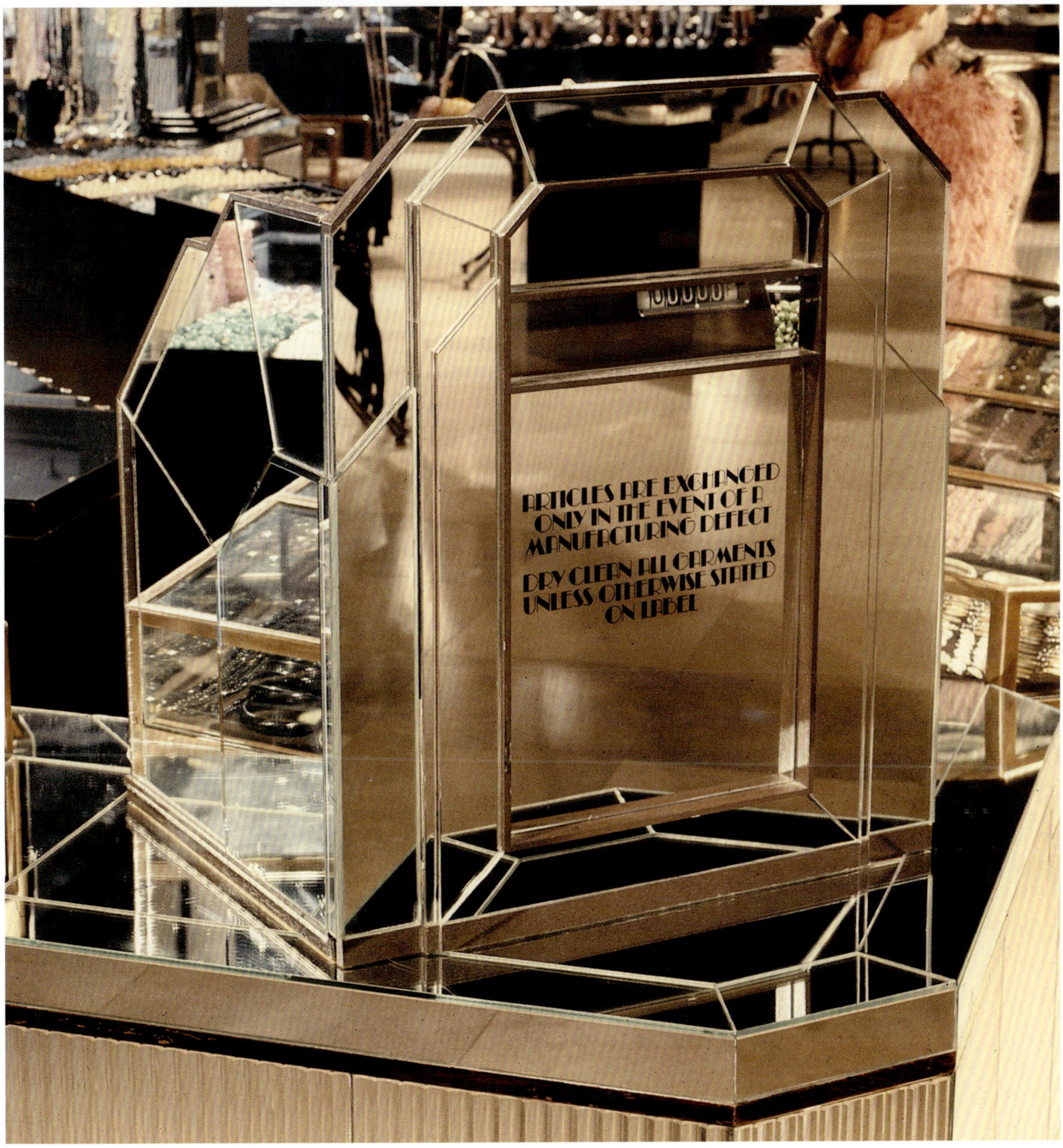

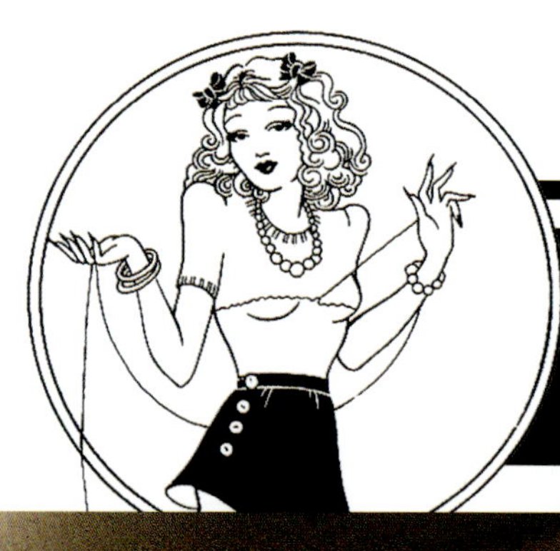

T-SHIRTS

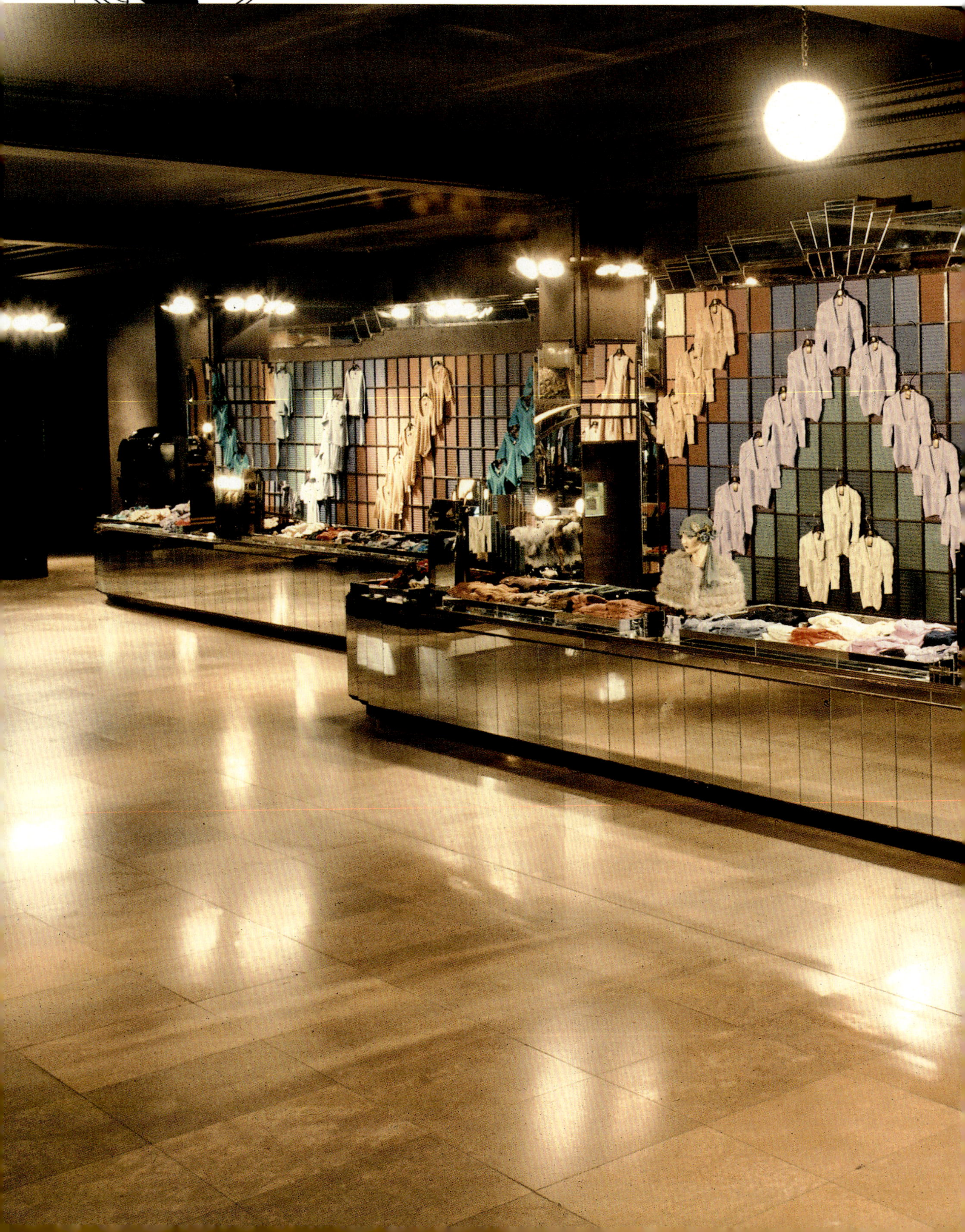

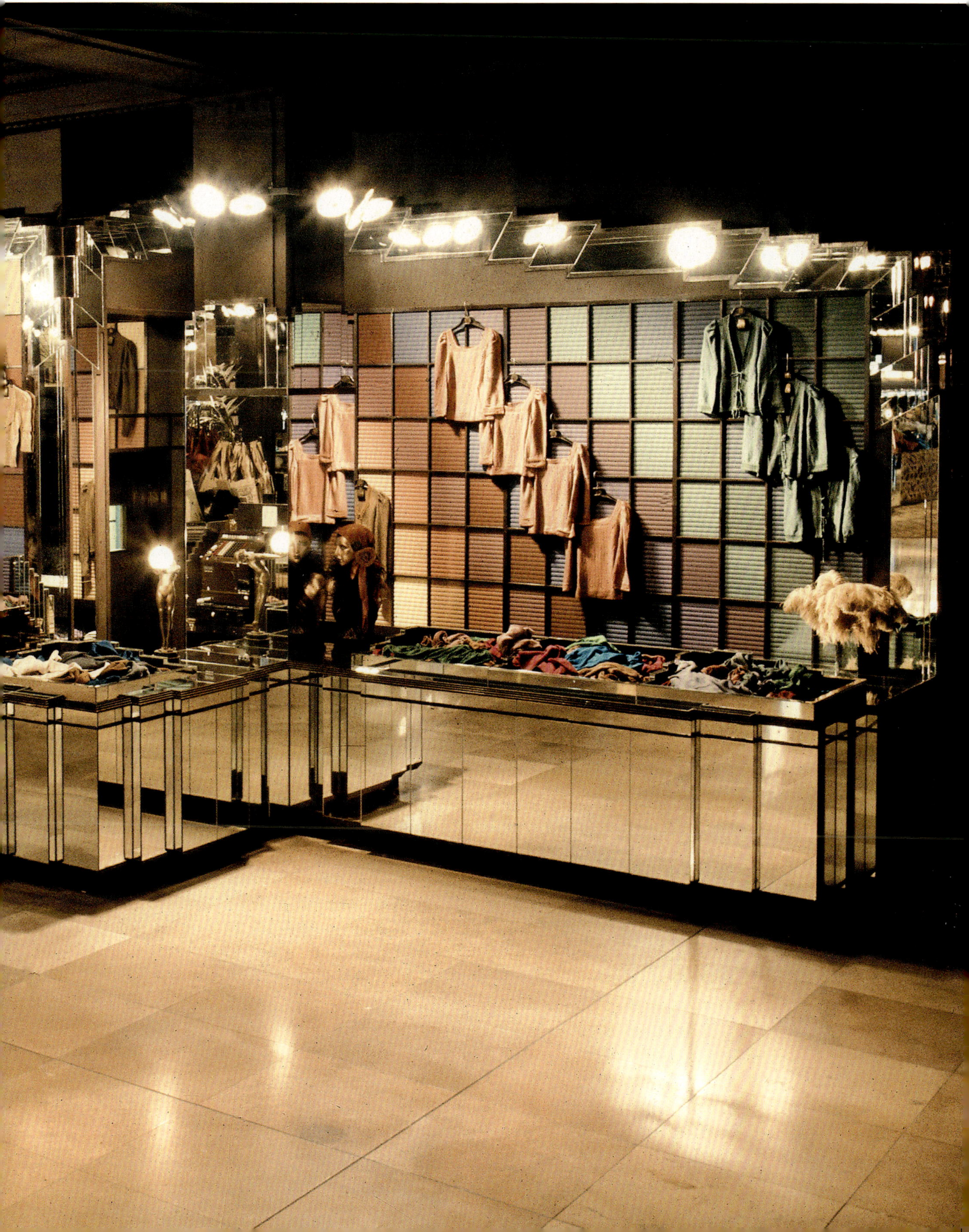

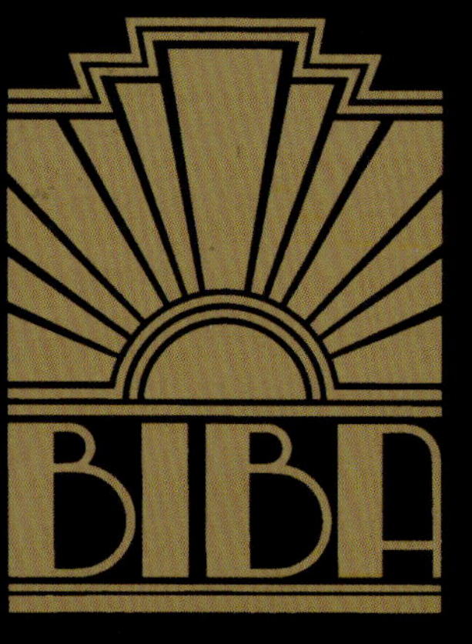

THE LOGO SHOP

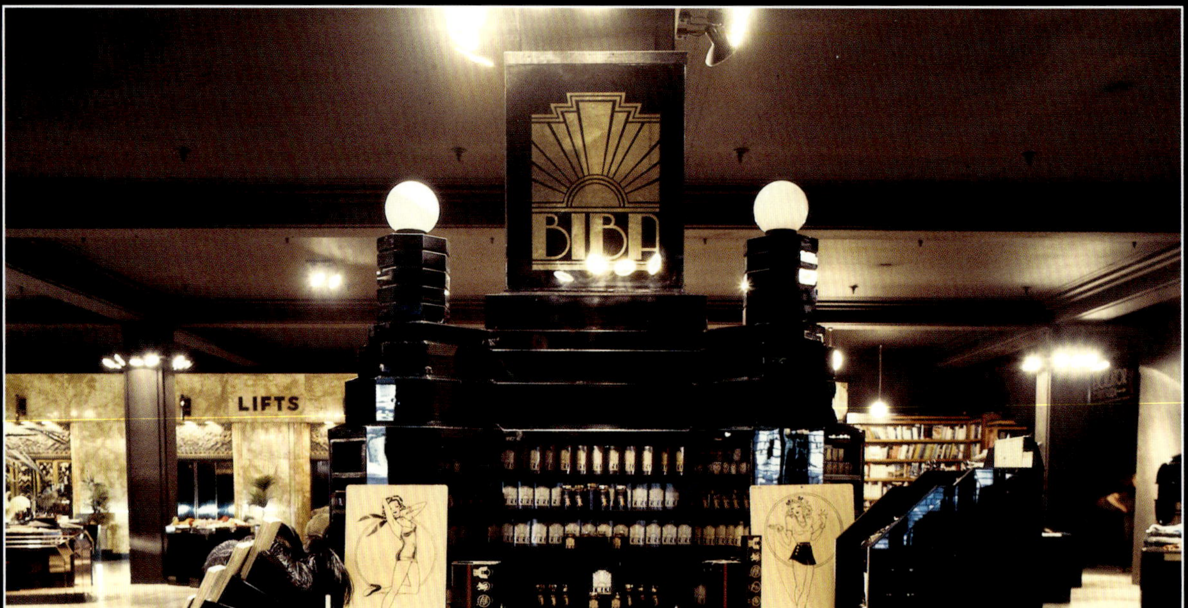

Biba was the first High Street store to recognize the power of branding, and it celebrated the fact with glee. As long ago as 1966 a diary and calendar had been adorned with the Biba logo; now, in the words of the opening newspaper: 'there are Biba posters, playing cards, greetings cards, balloons, chocolates, matches, ashtrays…'

In the Logo Shop there were also fountain pens, propelling pencils, watches, cigarette cases and lighters. Everything, in fact, except the Biba cigarettes and cigars, which – though proposed – never materialized.

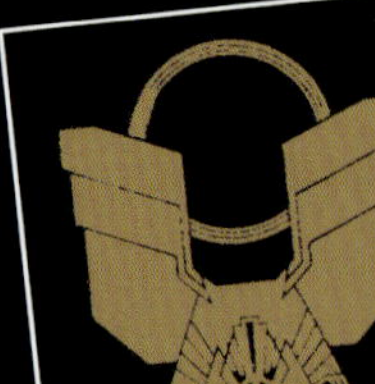

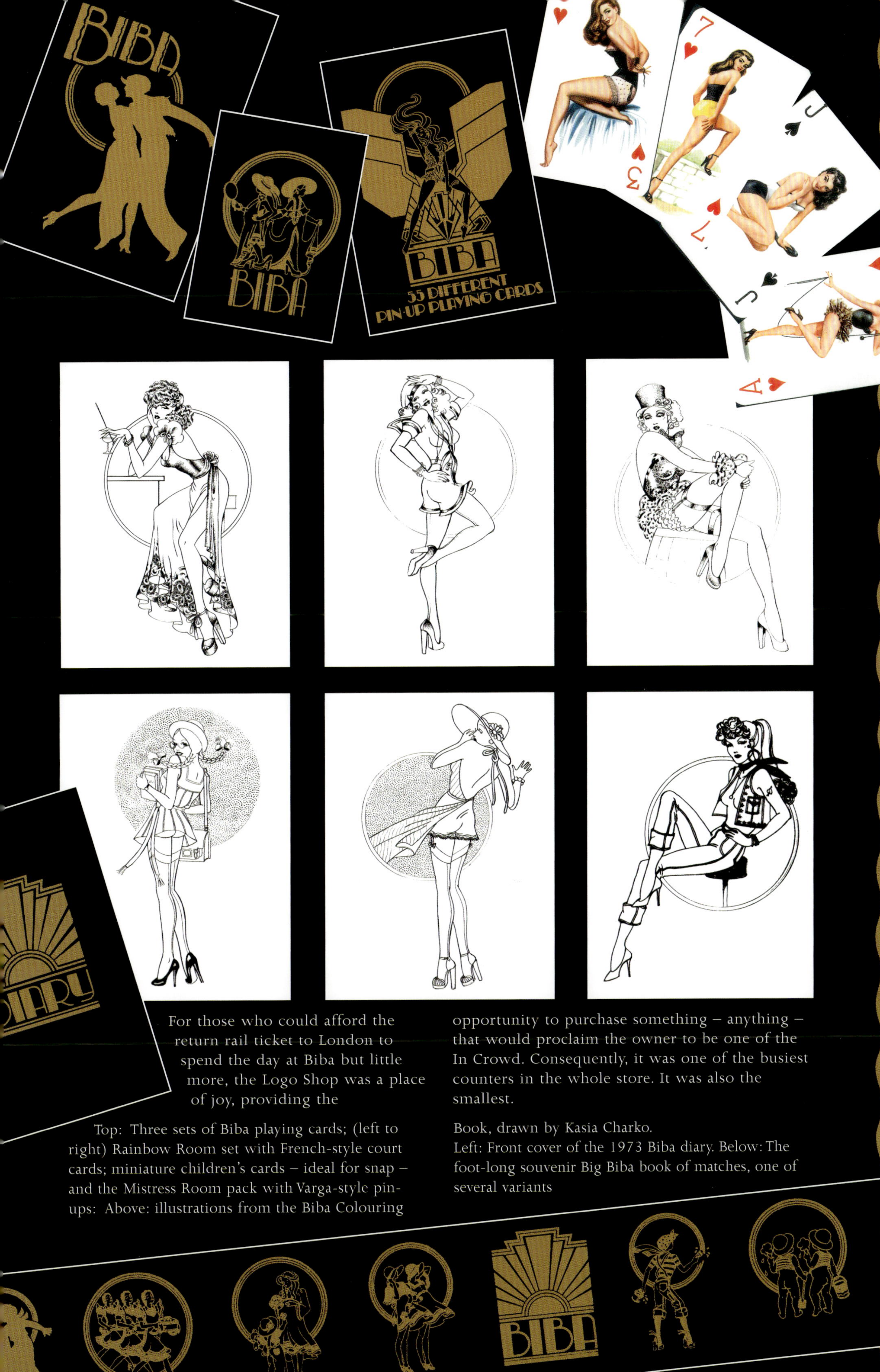

For those who could afford the return rail ticket to London to spend the day at Biba but little more, the Logo Shop was a place of joy, providing the opportunity to purchase something – anything – that would proclaim the owner to be one of the In Crowd. Consequently, it was one of the busiest counters in the whole store. It was also the smallest.

Top: Three sets of Biba playing cards; (left to right) Rainbow Room set with French-style court cards; miniature children's cards – ideal for snap – and the Mistress Room pack with Varga-style pin-ups: Above: illustrations from the Biba Colouring Book, drawn by Kasia Charko.
Left: Front cover of the 1973 Biba diary. Below: The foot-long souvenir Big Biba book of matches, one of several variants

FOOD HALL

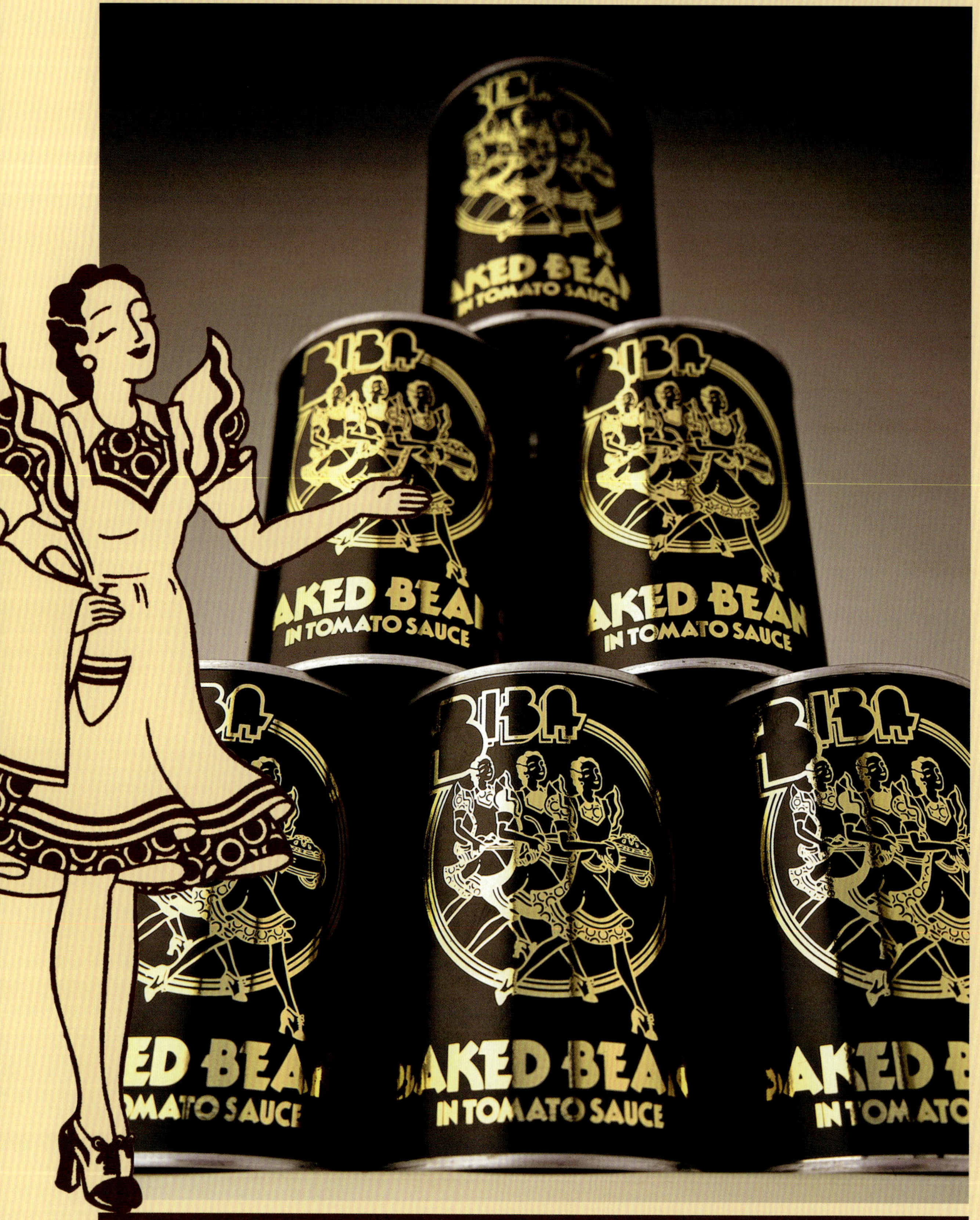

The basement represented the biggest departure from the established aesthetic. Biba had evolved from a crowded Victorian clutter to an embrace of the art nouveau revival of the late-1960s, and Big Biba extended this development to incorporate the deco theme of the Derry & Toms building. The Food Hall, however, designed by Steven Thomas, took off in an entirely new direction, with a witty celebration of pop art.

Where Andy Warhol had celebrated commercial design by putting the image of a Campbell's soup tin on a gallery wall, Biba now repaid the compliment by returning his work to the supermarket shelves, turning it indeed into the shelving itself, with a giant display unit for tinned soup labelled Warhol's Condensed (pp.40-41). Alongside were oversized cans of Heinz Baked Beans, tinned ham and sardines (with the key the wrong way round), together with the jokily self-referential Whitmore's Frankfurters and Thomas's Baked Beans. Lord of his domain was a huge incarnation of Hulanicki's Great Dane named Othello, inside whose stomach were stacked tins of dog-food (p.43).

Although some of the stock was bought in (including 'the best that Smithfield, Billingsgate and Covent Garden have to offer'), the core of the Food Hall was a range of 350 own-brand products, everything from wine to ice cream, from baked beans to soap suds.

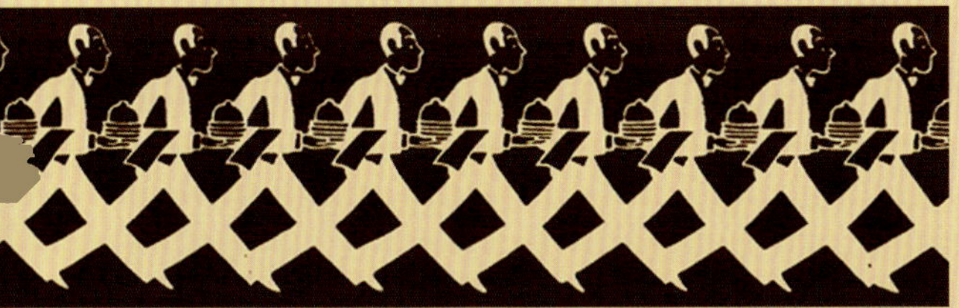

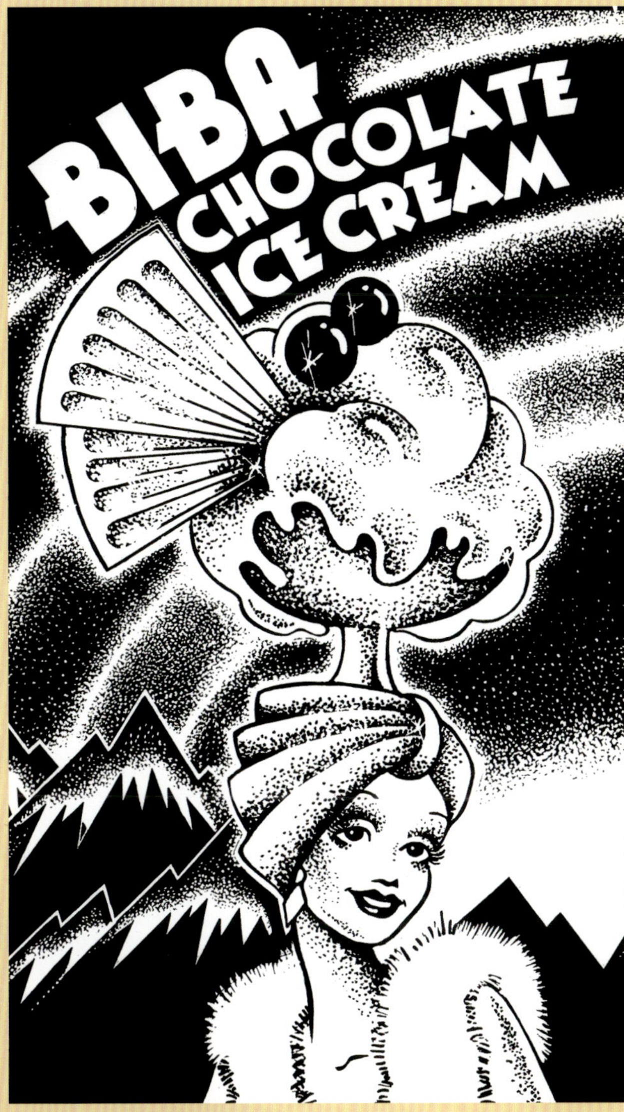

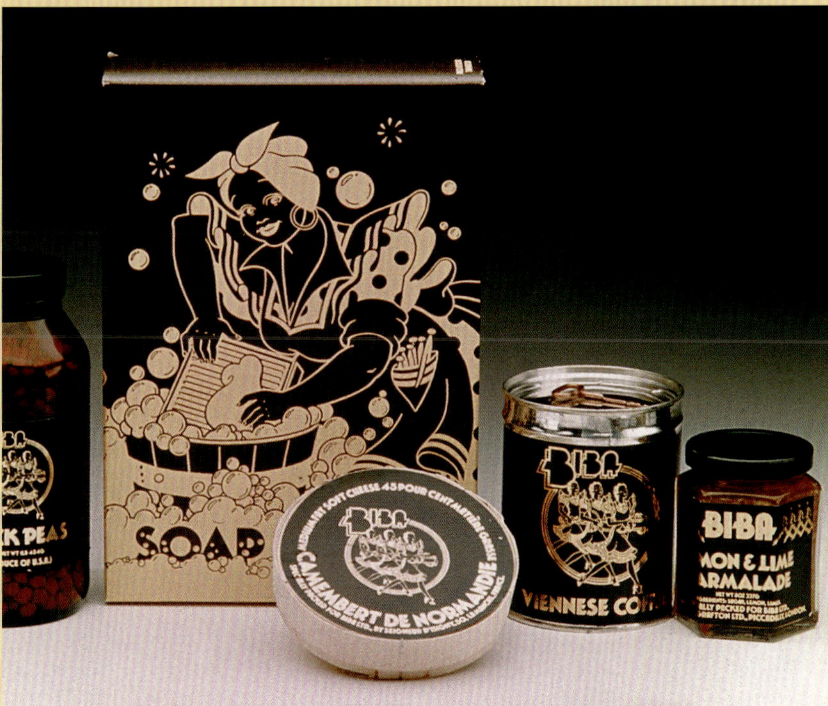

These were lines intended for display in one's kitchen: canned goods to be cherished for the sheer style of their packaging. They also hoped to enlarge the horizons of British shoppers: just as Biba had democratised fashion, so the Food Hall made available to the general public a breadth of products more associated with Fortnum & Mason than with a typical High Street supermarket.

Above all, there was humour, from the Carmen Miranda design on the yoghurt pots to the understated claims for the soap powder: 'Try it – it washes quite white'.

FRUIT & VEG

TINNED Fruit
Fresh Fruit
JARLSBERG
CAERPHILLY
DOLCELATTE
BEL PAESE
GJETOST
GRUYERE
EMMENTAL
PARMESAN
DANISH BLUE
LEIDEN
BRIE
FETA

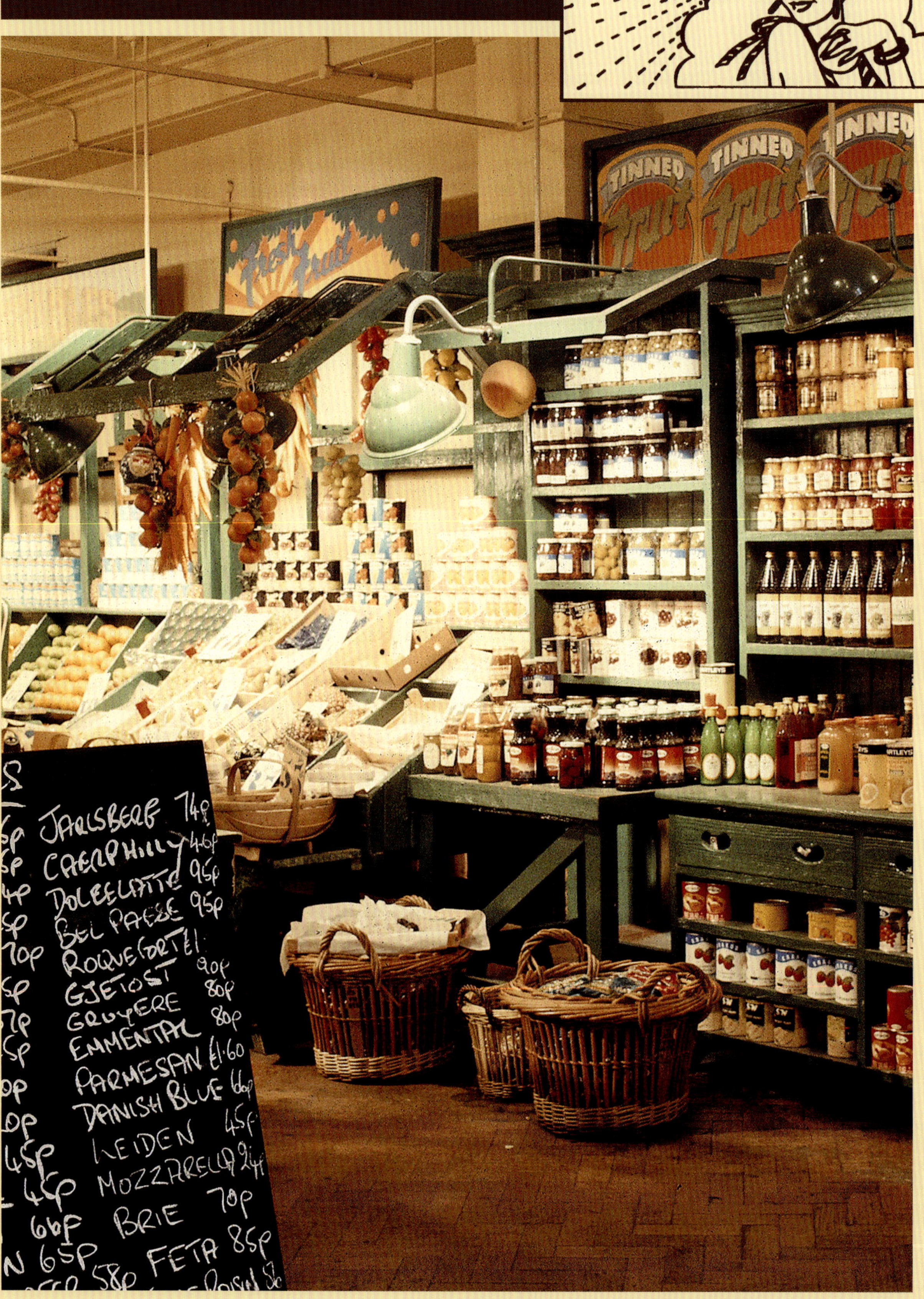

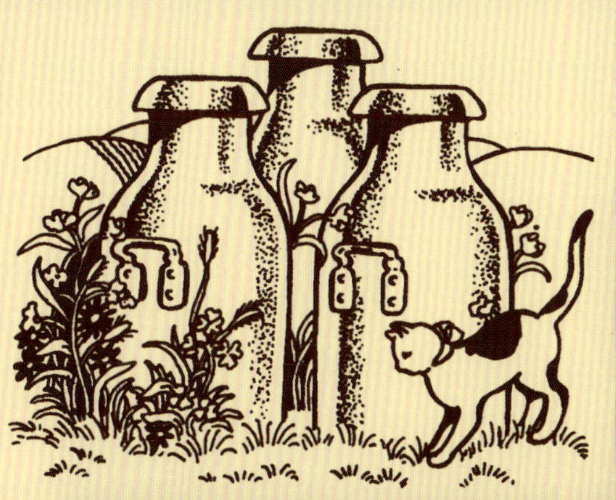

THE DAIRY

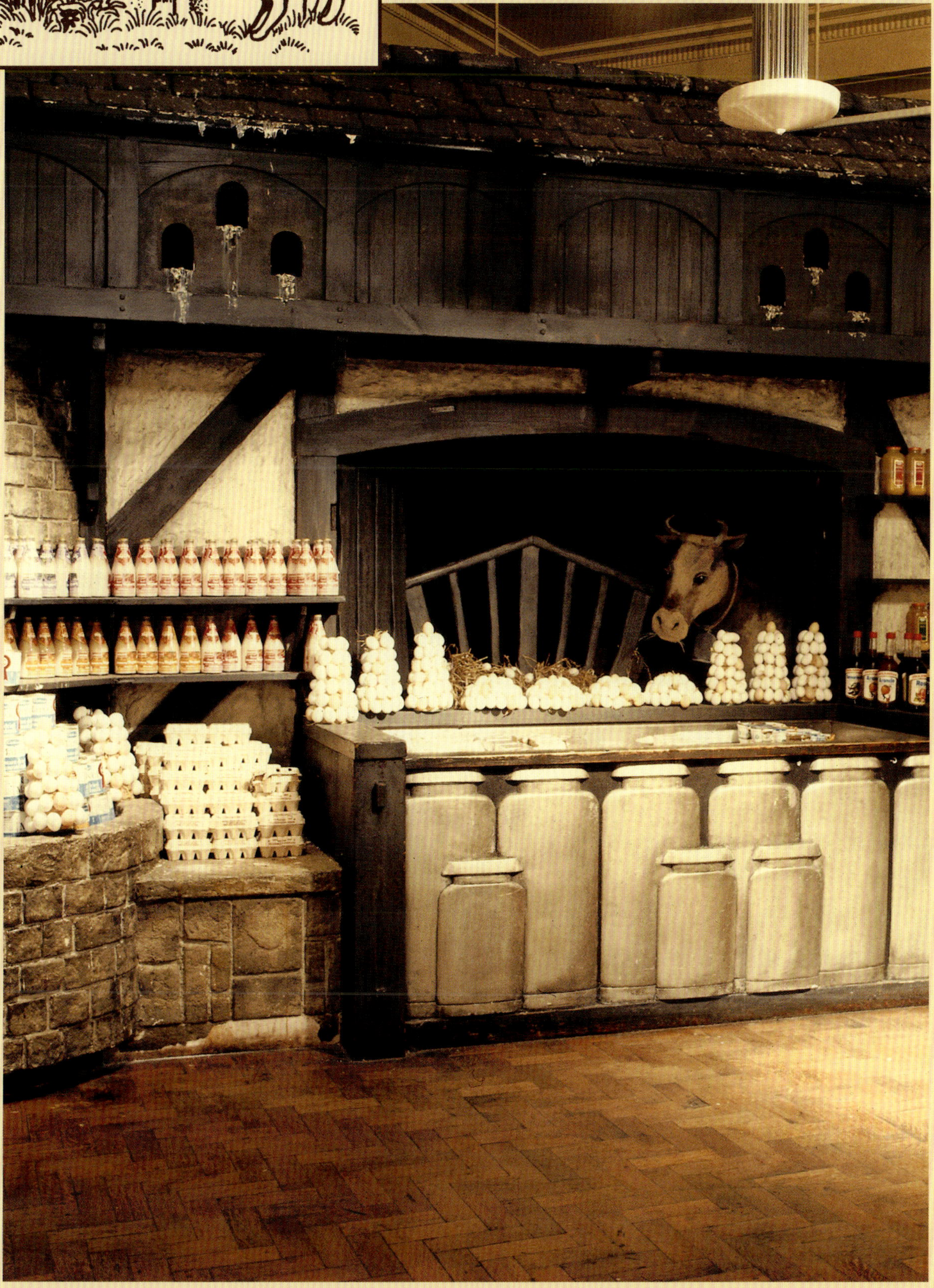

WINE, FISH & BREAD

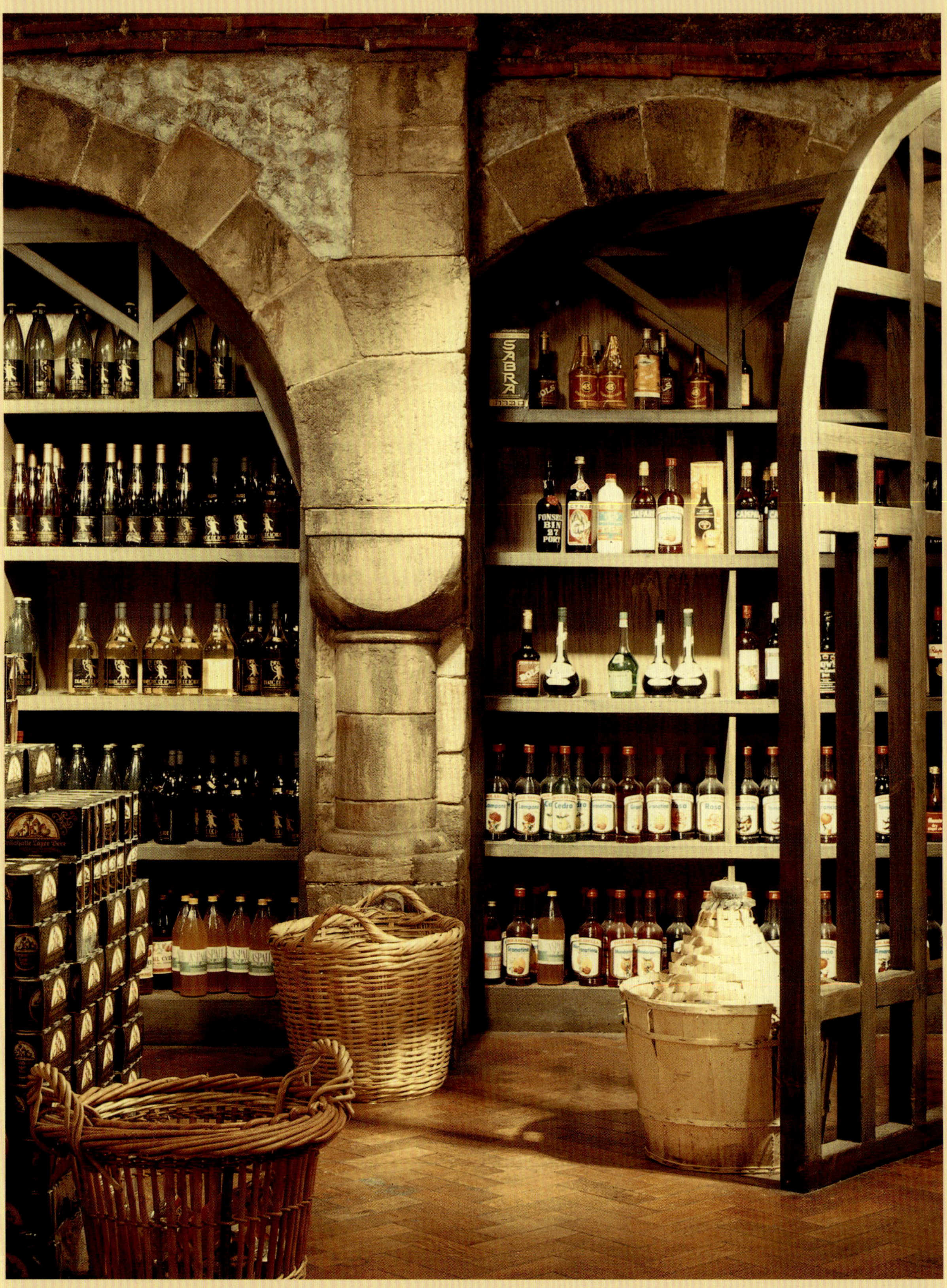

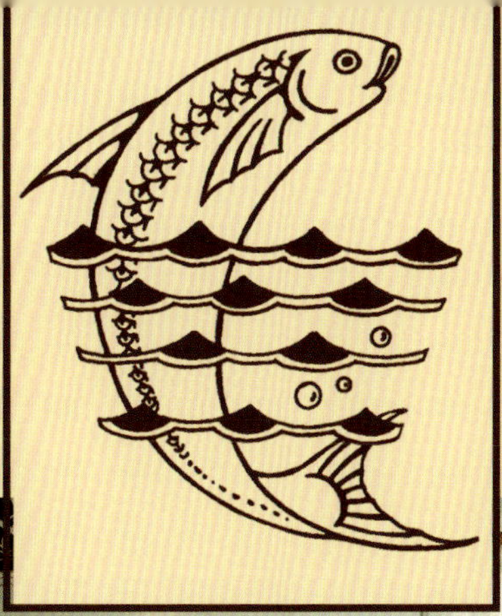

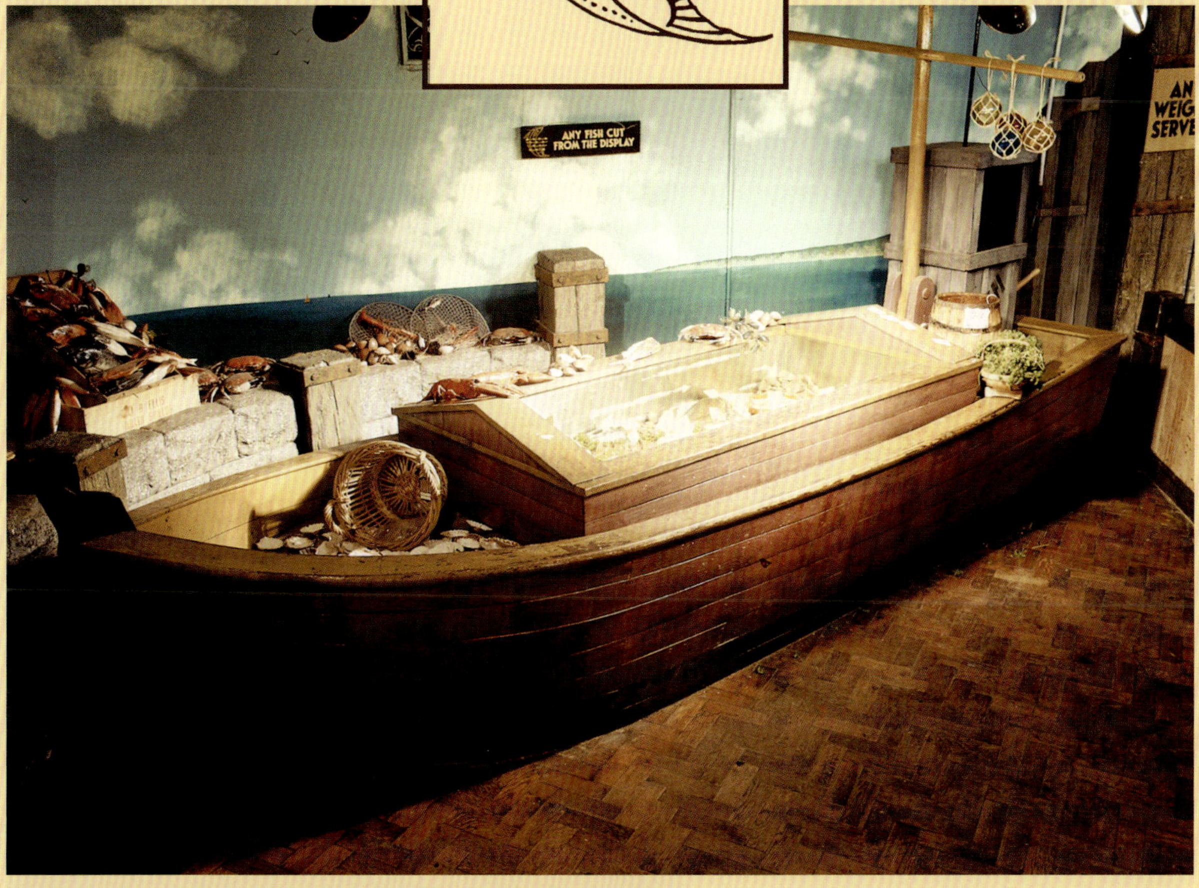

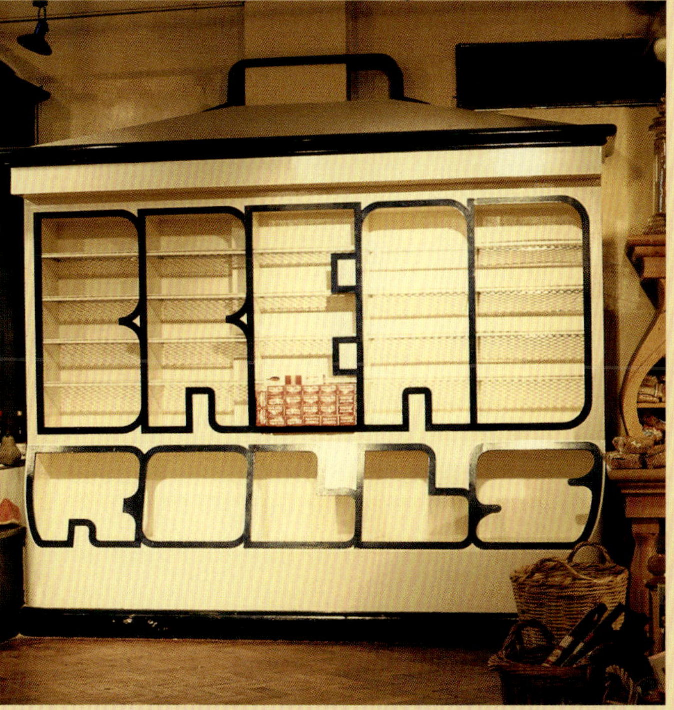

The barge selling fresh fish was accompanied by a tape of sound effects of waves, seagulls and the creaking of a ship's timbers, while the bread was stored in a giant Victorian bread-bin, and the wine-shop – replicating the cellar of a Chateau – came complete with an iron-grille door and cobwebs.

Elsewhere, the fresh fruit and vegetables were displayed in a recreation of a traditional market (p.36), and the Breton dairy came with careful reproduction of dove-droppings (p.37). One pot of yoghurt in the chiller cabinet was placed on a touch-sensitive pad, so that when the pot was lifted, it made the sound of a cow mooing.

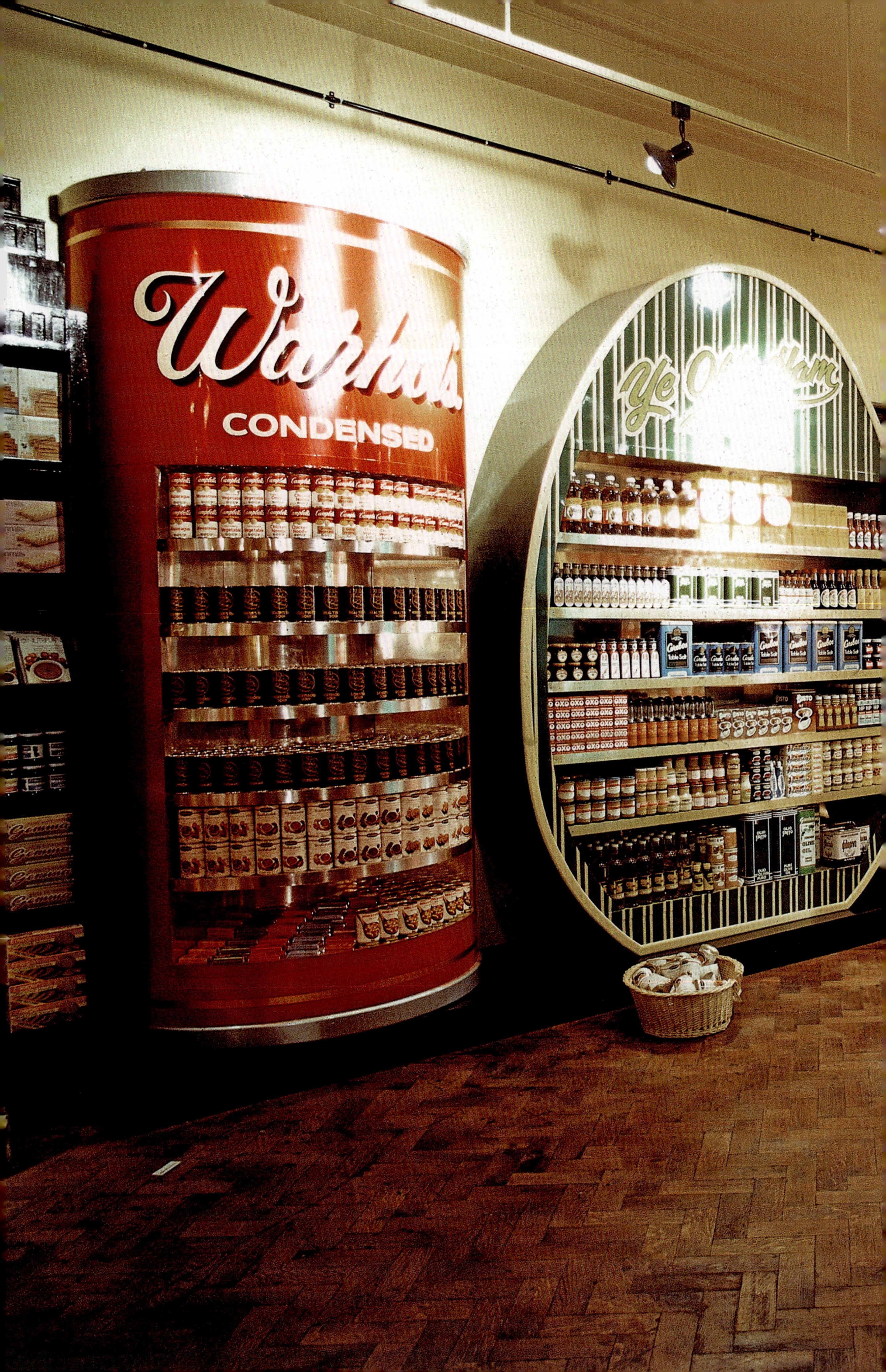
Warhol's
CONDENSED

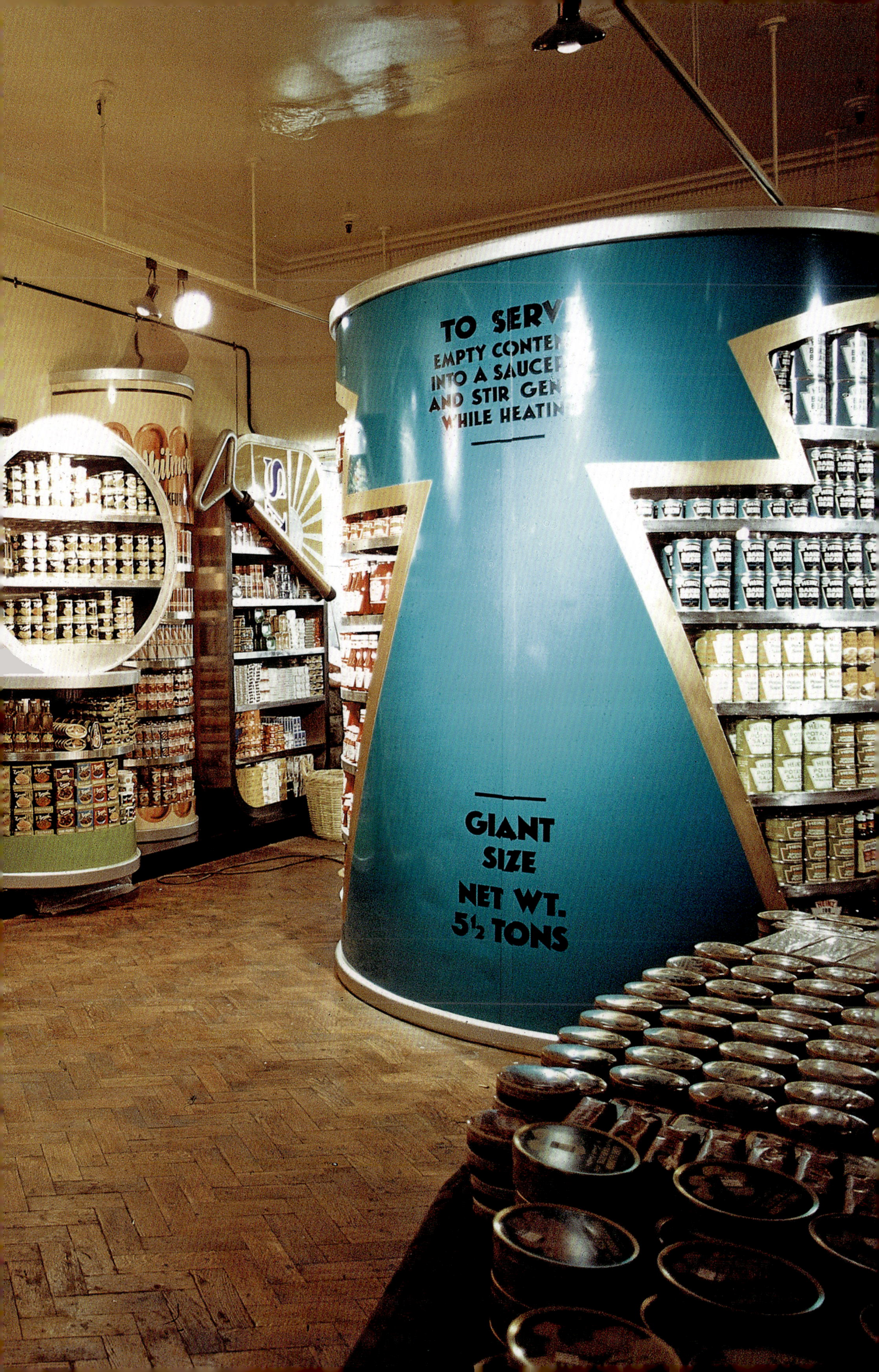
TO SERV
EMPTY CONTEN
INTO A SAUCEP
AND STIR GEN
WHILE HEATIN
GIANT
SIZE
NET WT.
5½ TONS

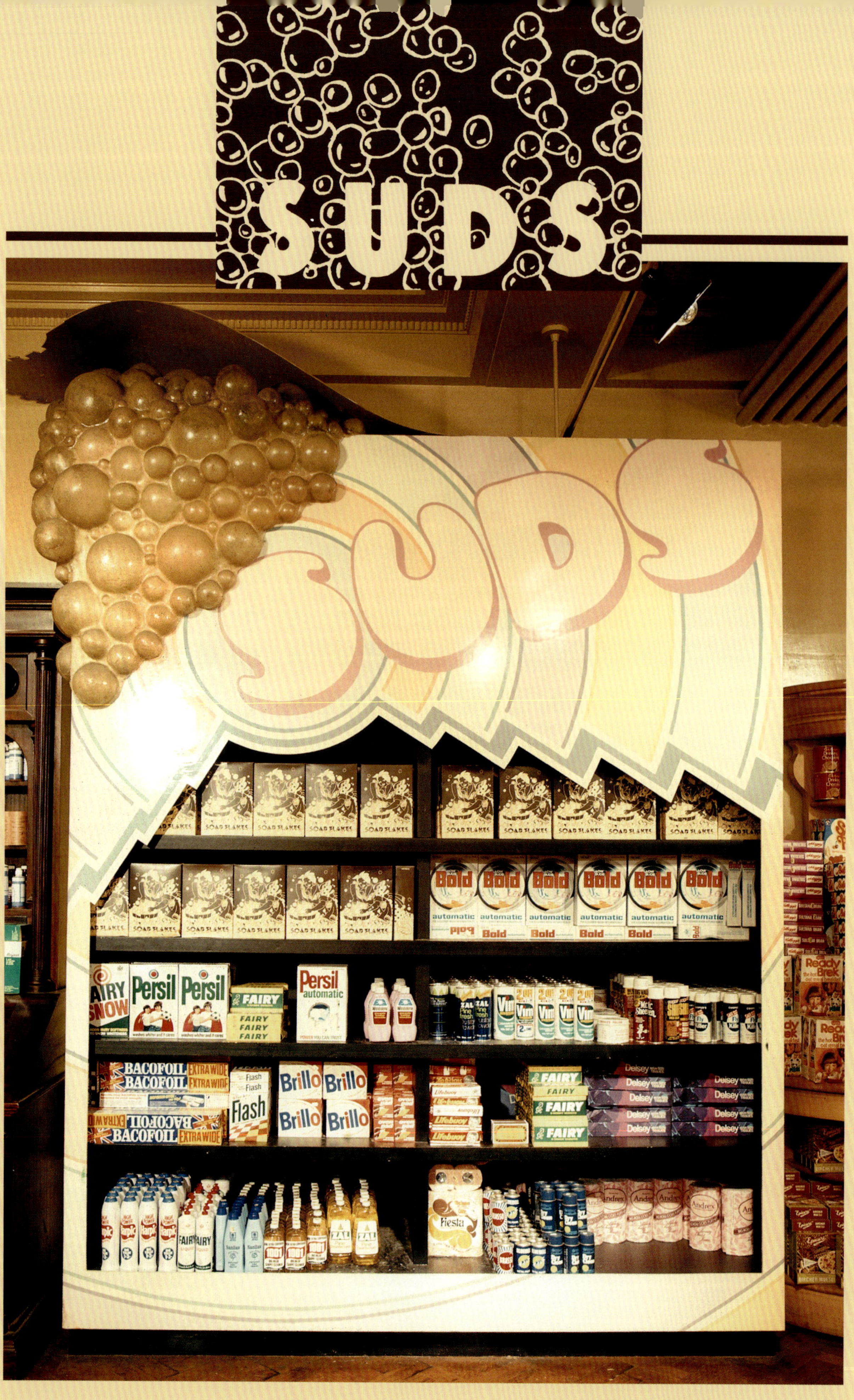
SUDS
SUDS
SOAP FLAKES
Bold
automatic
Persil
Persil automatic
FAIRY SNOW
FAIRY
Vim
BACOFOIL EXTRA WIDE
Flash
Brillo
Lifebuoy
Delsey
Fiesta
Ready Brek

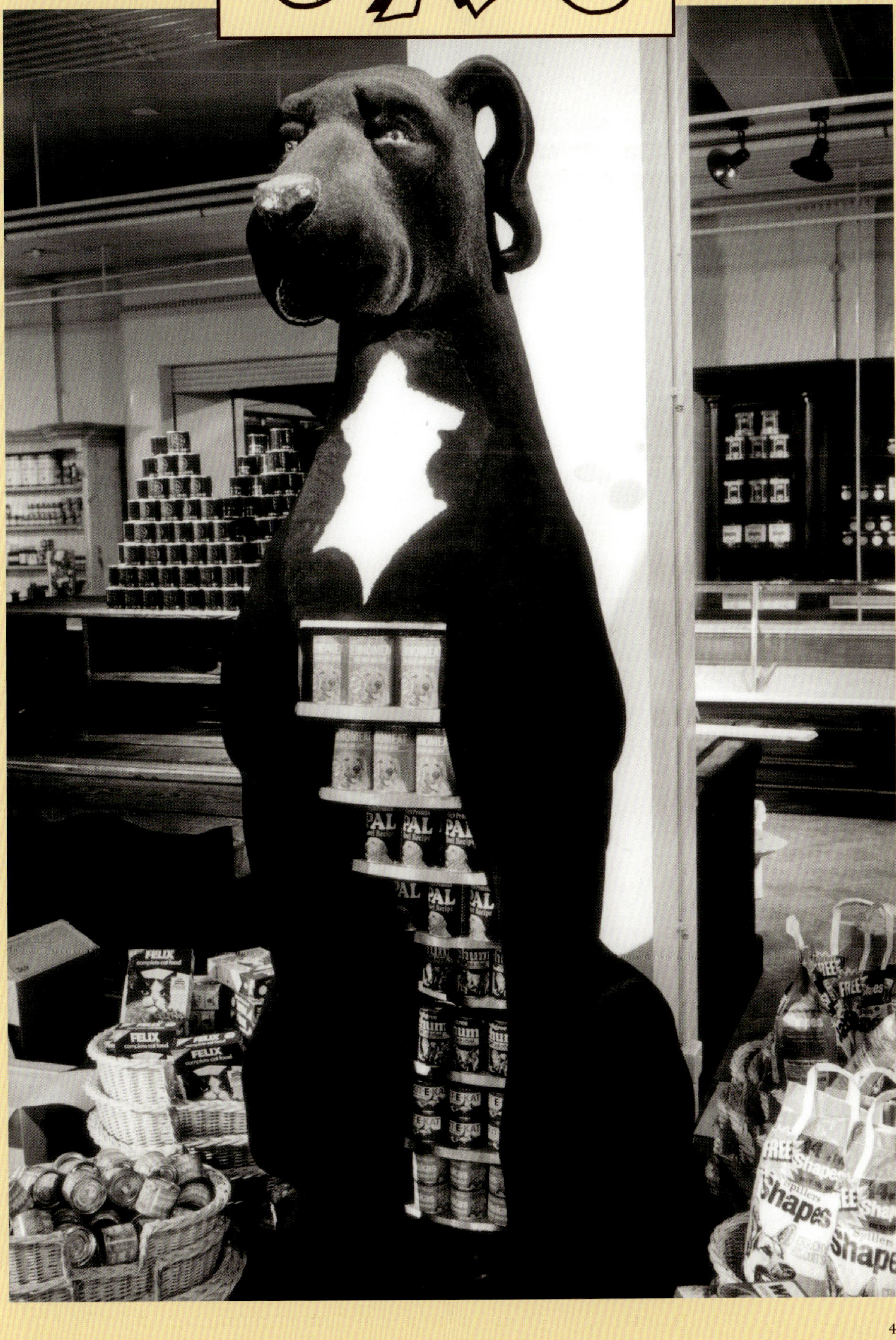

FASHION

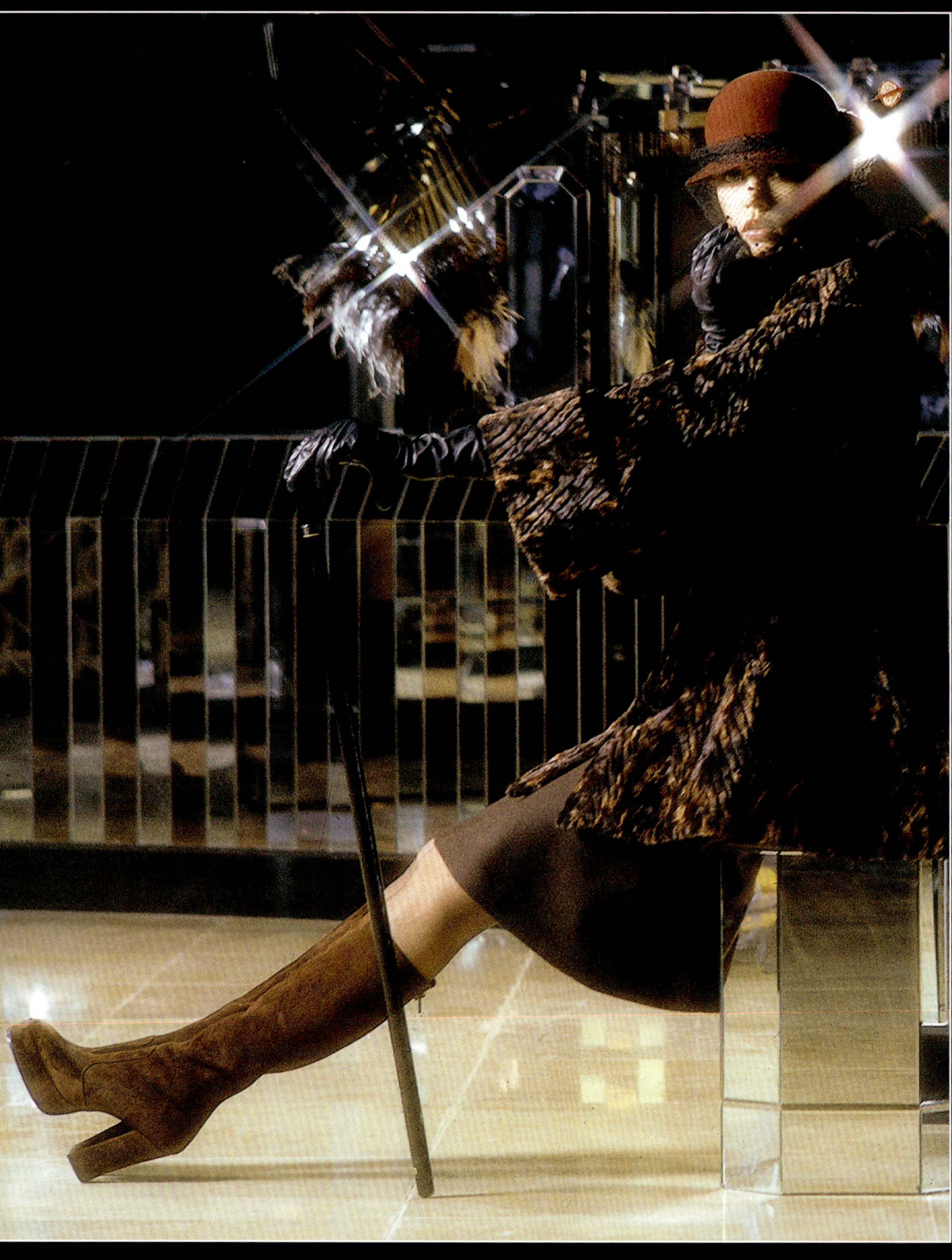

The photographs on the following pages were taken by John Bishop on the day before the store opened, and show pieces from the first Autumn collection at Big Biba. Commissioned by Norma Moriceau, fashion editor of 19 magazine, the photo-feature ran in October 1973 and featured the model Mouche, who had been pictured lying naked on a divan of cushions in one of the most famous Biba posters.

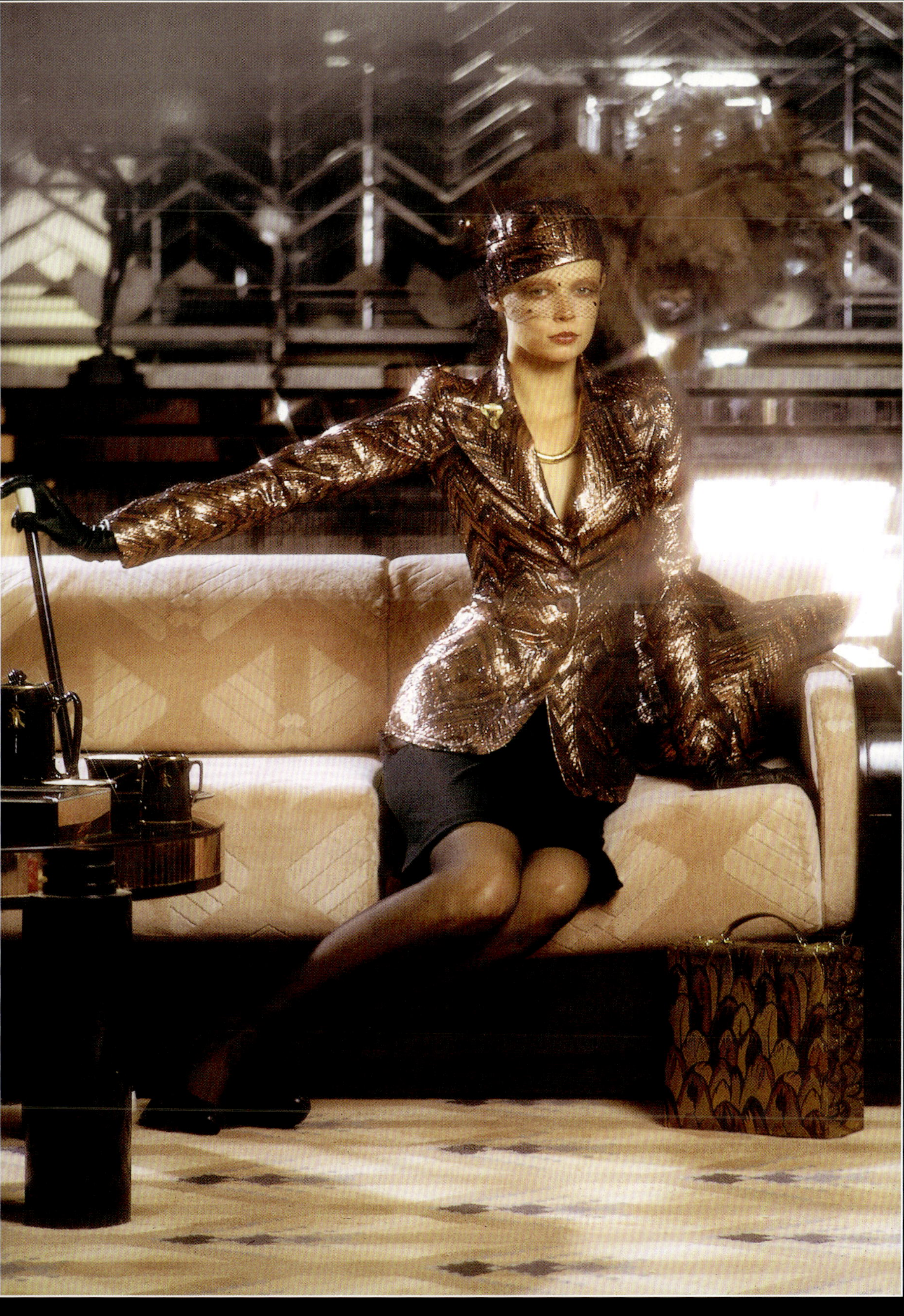

Opposite: Faux fur zip-front coat with expansive cuffs, jersey skirt, tights and suede zipped boots, all in brown. Black leather gloves and black cane with mock ivory head. The rust felt hat was from the Lolita department. Location: ground floor tights unit.

This page: Matching pill-box hat and jacket in rust, gold and black lurex brocade. Black jersey pencil skirt, sheer tights and suede court shoes. Gloves and cane as on opposite page. The black veiling cost 35p a yard. Location: reception area of the Rainbow Room

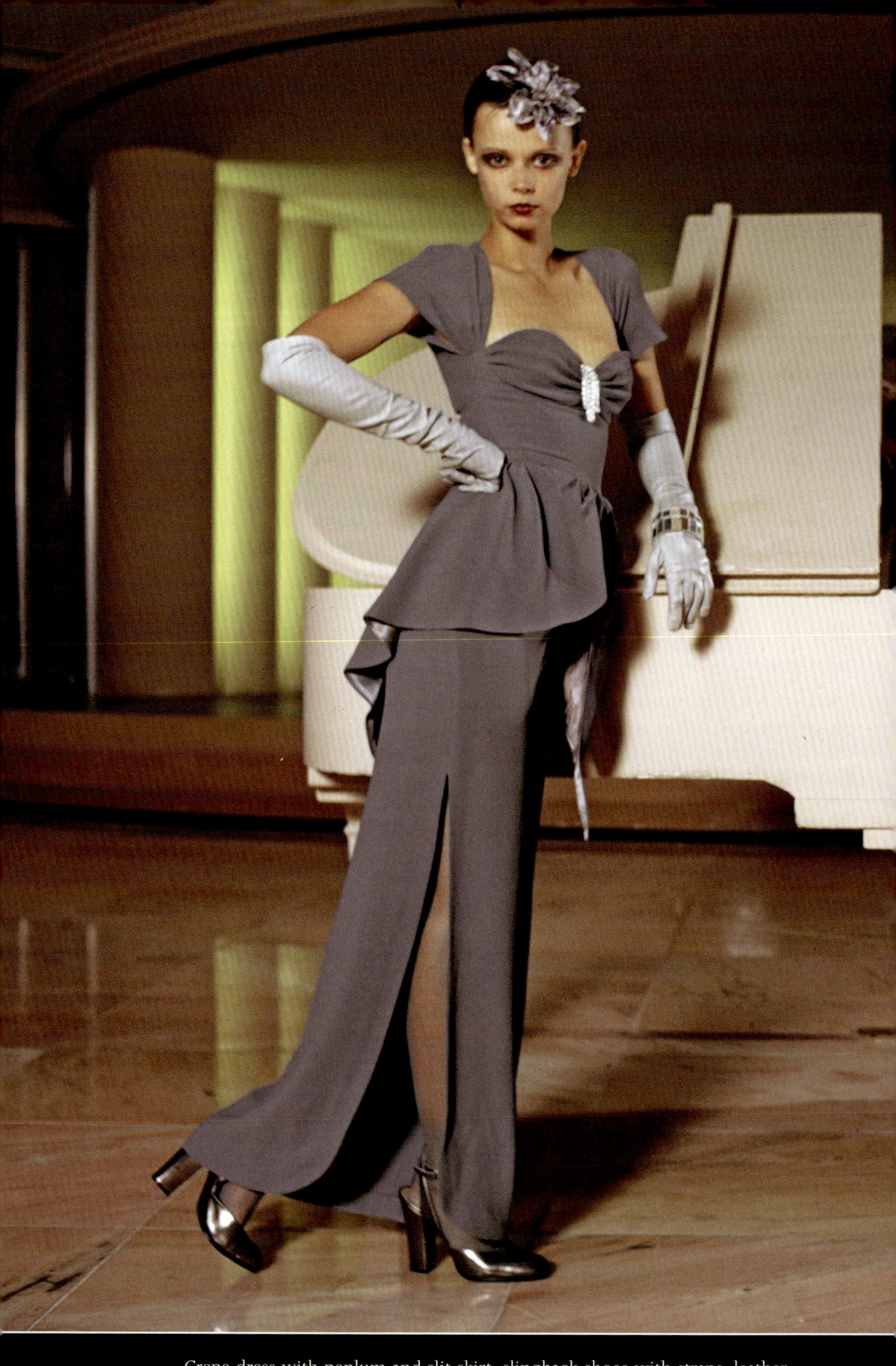

Crepe dress with peplum and slit skirt, slingback shoes with straps, leather gloves – all in grey. Zip-front cape and trousers in black velvet, with black patent leather boots. Location: the Rainbow Room proscenium arch

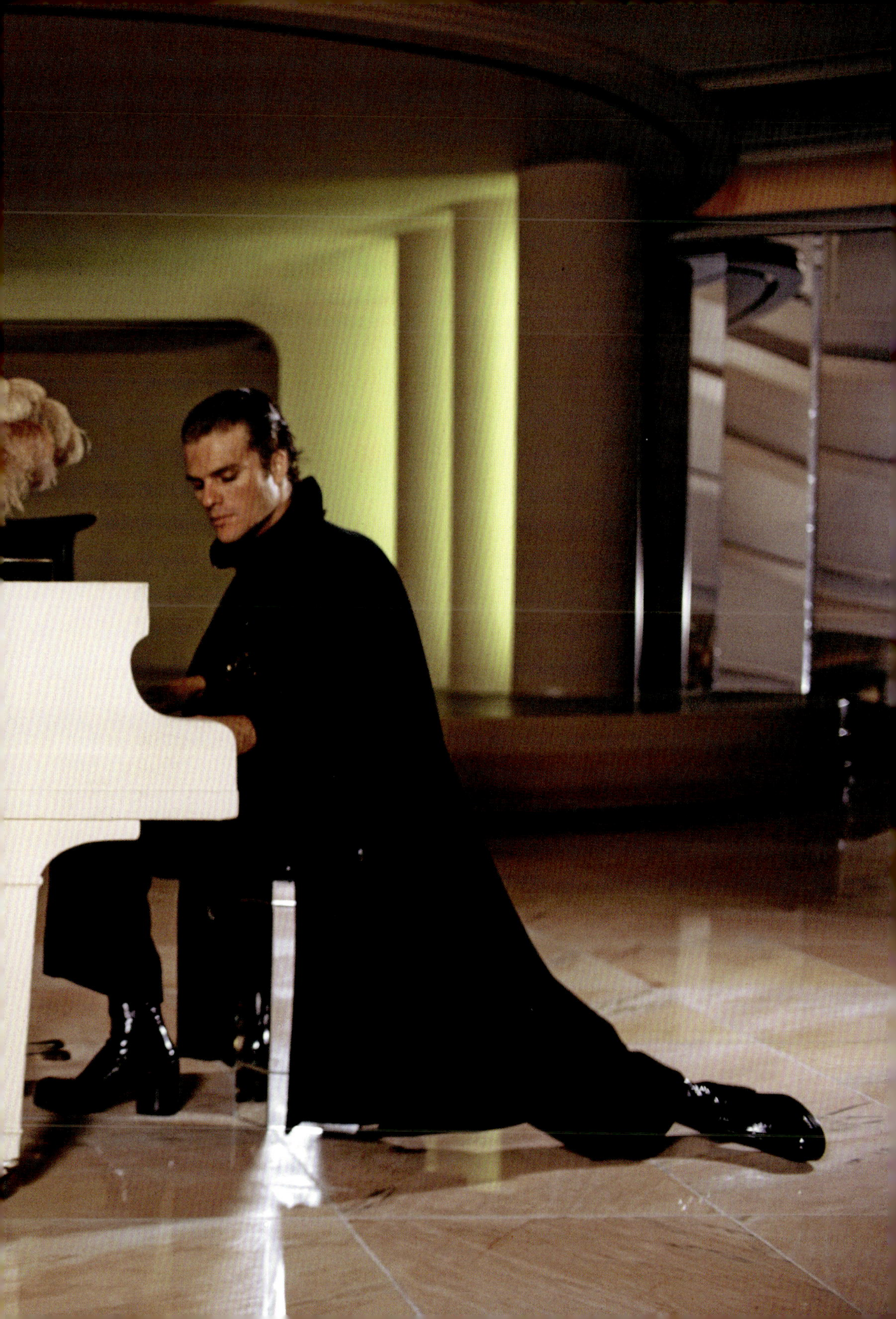

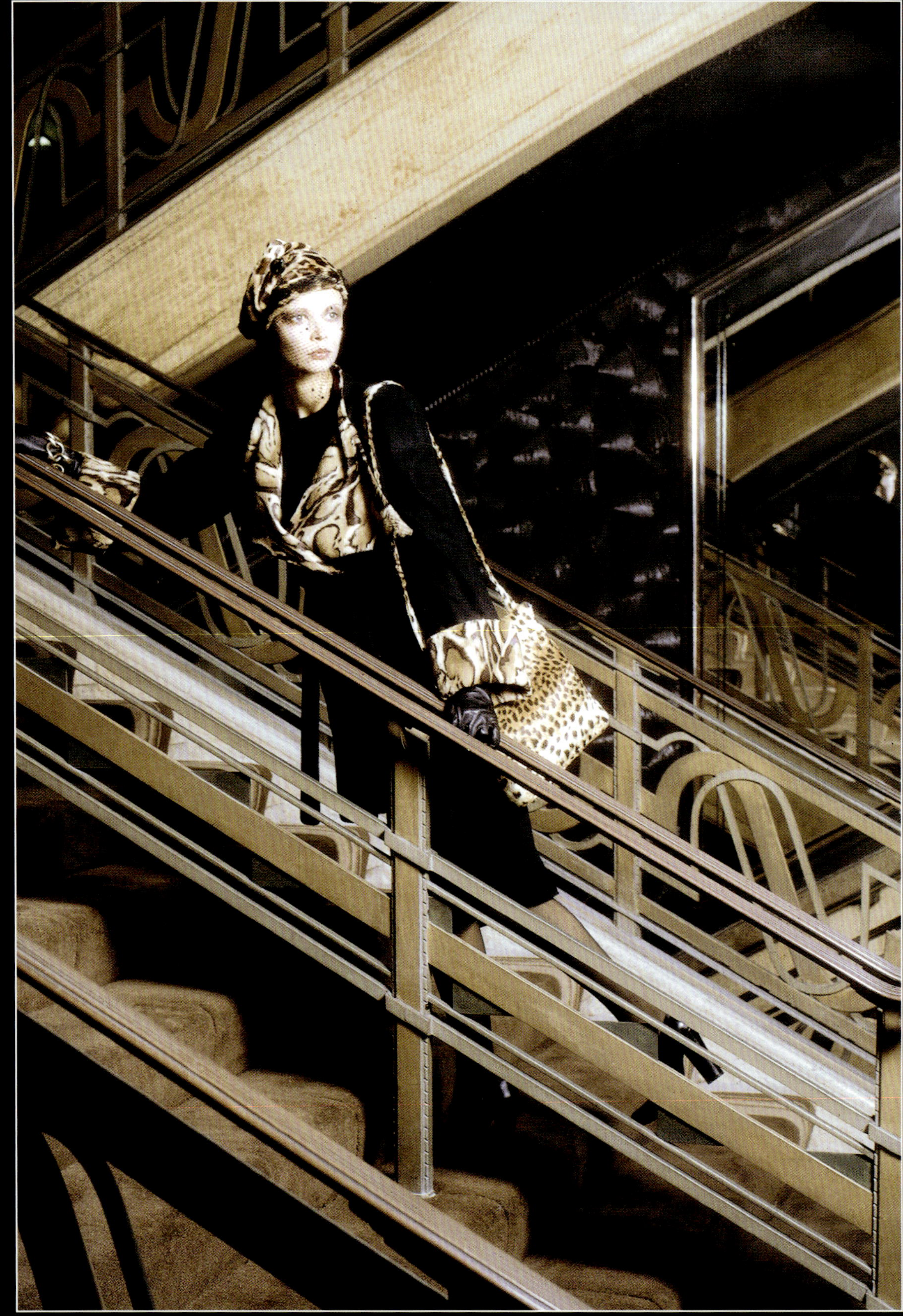

Black jersey jacket with tiger-print trim; banlon halter-neck, pencil skirt, leather gloves, tights and shoes – all in black. Shoulder bag and hat in mock ocelot. Location: one of the main staircases.

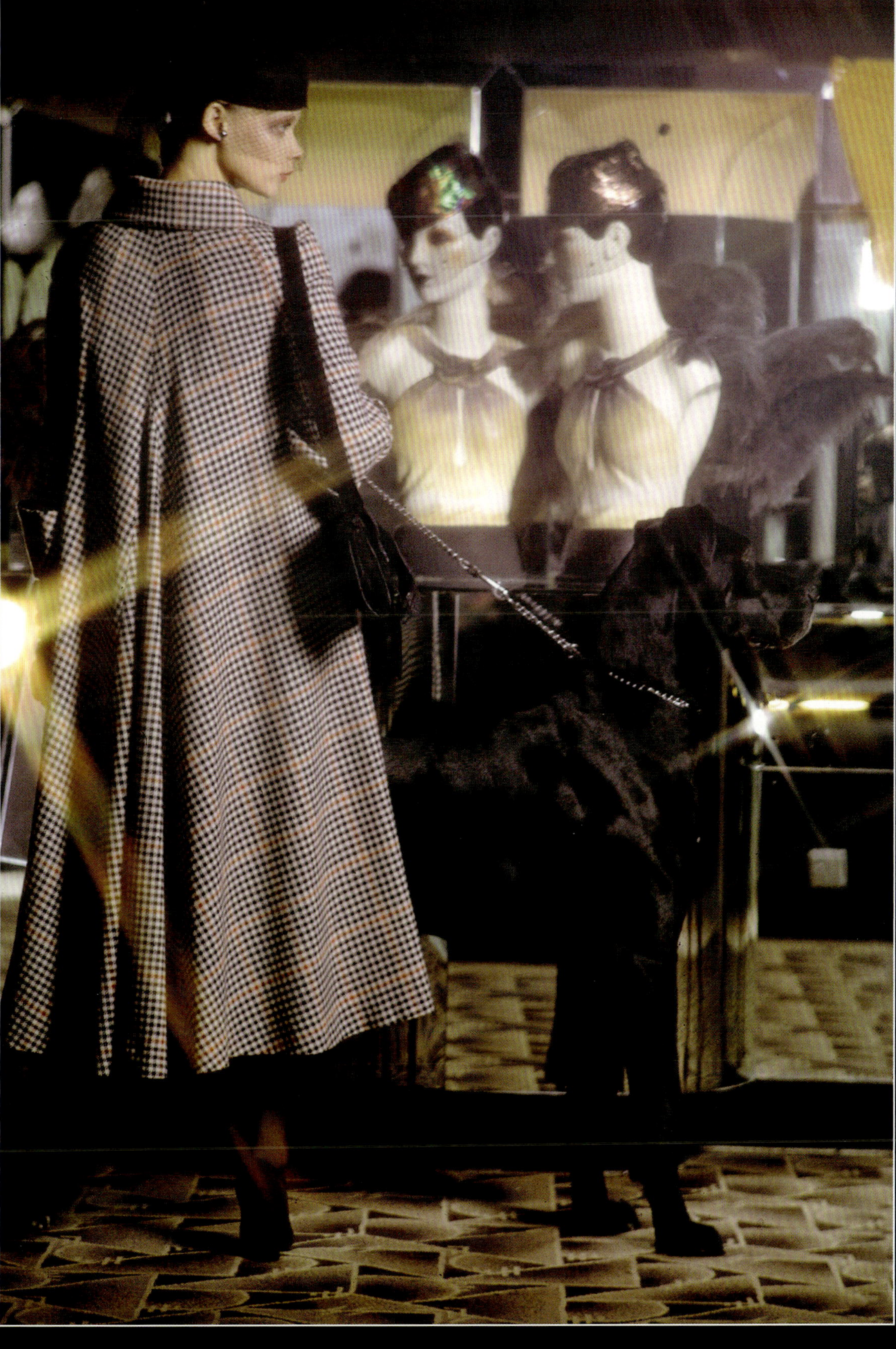

Swagger coat in black, cream and red check with three buttons; tights, suede

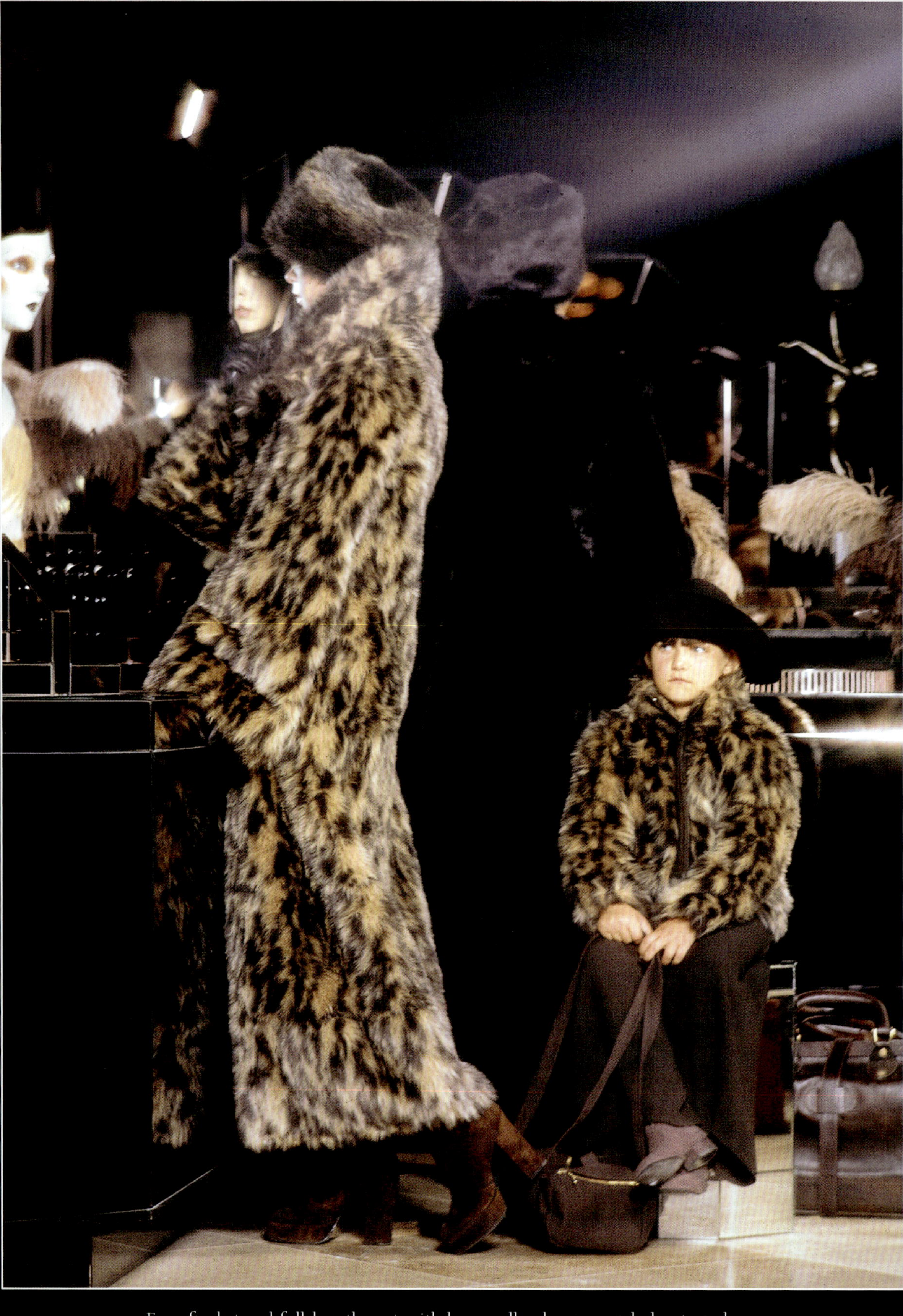

Faux fur hat and full-length coat with large collar, brown suede boots and brown leather gloves. Faux fur Cossack hat and full-length coat. Faux fur zip-front jacket; felt hat, crepe trousers, canvas boots and canvas shoulder-bag –

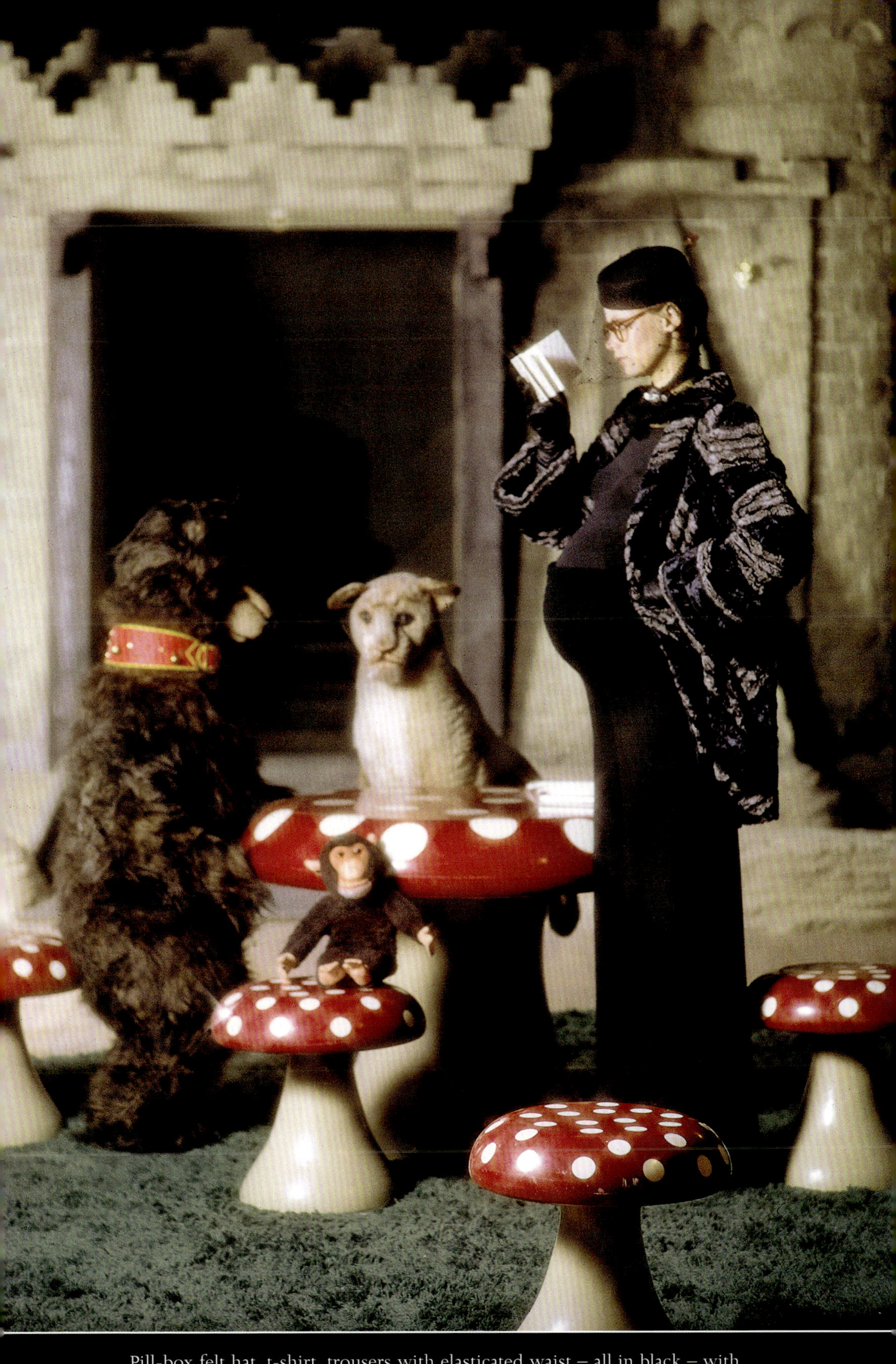

Pill-box felt hat, t-shirt, trousers with elasticated waist – all in black – with black and grey jacket. All pieces from the pregnant mums' department, photographed just across from the castle on the children's floor

THE BIBA FLOOR

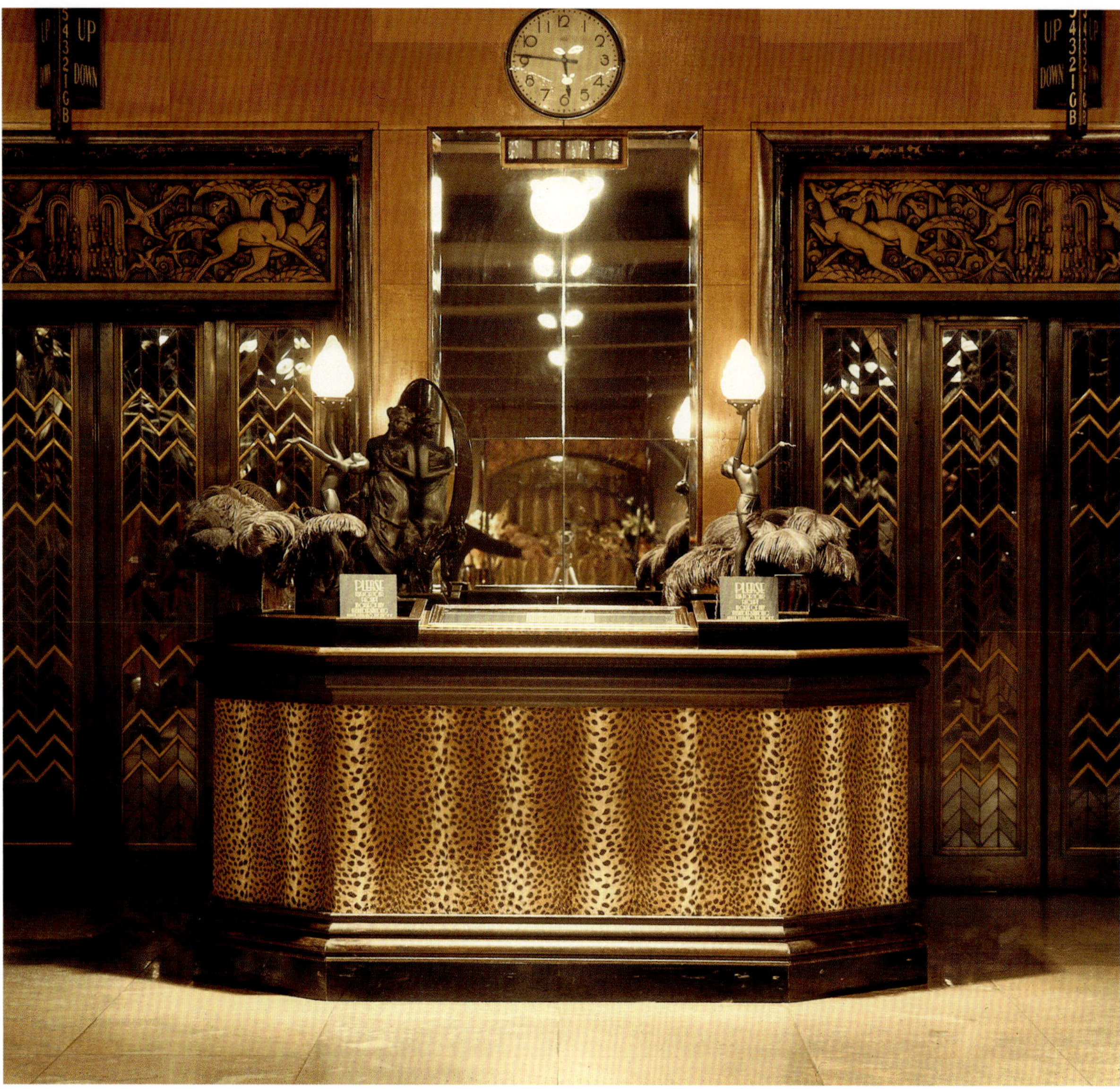

Despite gleeful diversions into other fields, the heart and soul of Biba remained where the adventure had begun, in women's clothes. The first floor of Big Biba – where these were now housed – was larger than all three of the previous shops put together, but it endeavoured to keep the spirit of the boutique alive.

Accessed by stairs, by lifts and – in the one major structural change to the existing building – by escalator, the Biba floor retained the nouveau ambience of the last store.

The Victorian bentwood hat-stands that had been adopted in Abingdon Road days as a cheap alternative to display rails were also retained, though the sheer number now involved (over 200 of them) meant that they were no longer vintage pieces picked up on street markets, but made specially in Czechoslovakia. These were placed in the centre of the floor, a forest of hat-stands on islands of patterned carpet, through which wound marble paths.

Music too had been a part of the Biba experience since the very first days: 'The mothers of the girls who hung out at Biba used to attack us because it was such a dark place,' reminisced Hulanicki, 'and the clothes were dark and the music was loud.' Again this theme was reproduced here on a grand scale: each floor had specially designed speakers (p.54) with the tapes controlled from Fitz's office (the Hallelujah Chorus was particularly impressive when heard on the stairs). The sound system was designed by Colin Howard.

Colours were, of course, matched across the floor – and indeed the store – with the opening collection including electric blue, camellia pink, tobacco, army and camel. 'Biba's autumn fashion look is sophisticated 1930s,' noted the *Sunday Times*. 'Marlene Dietrich would feel at home. Sweaters are fuzzy, coats are tweed and colours are dark and muted.'

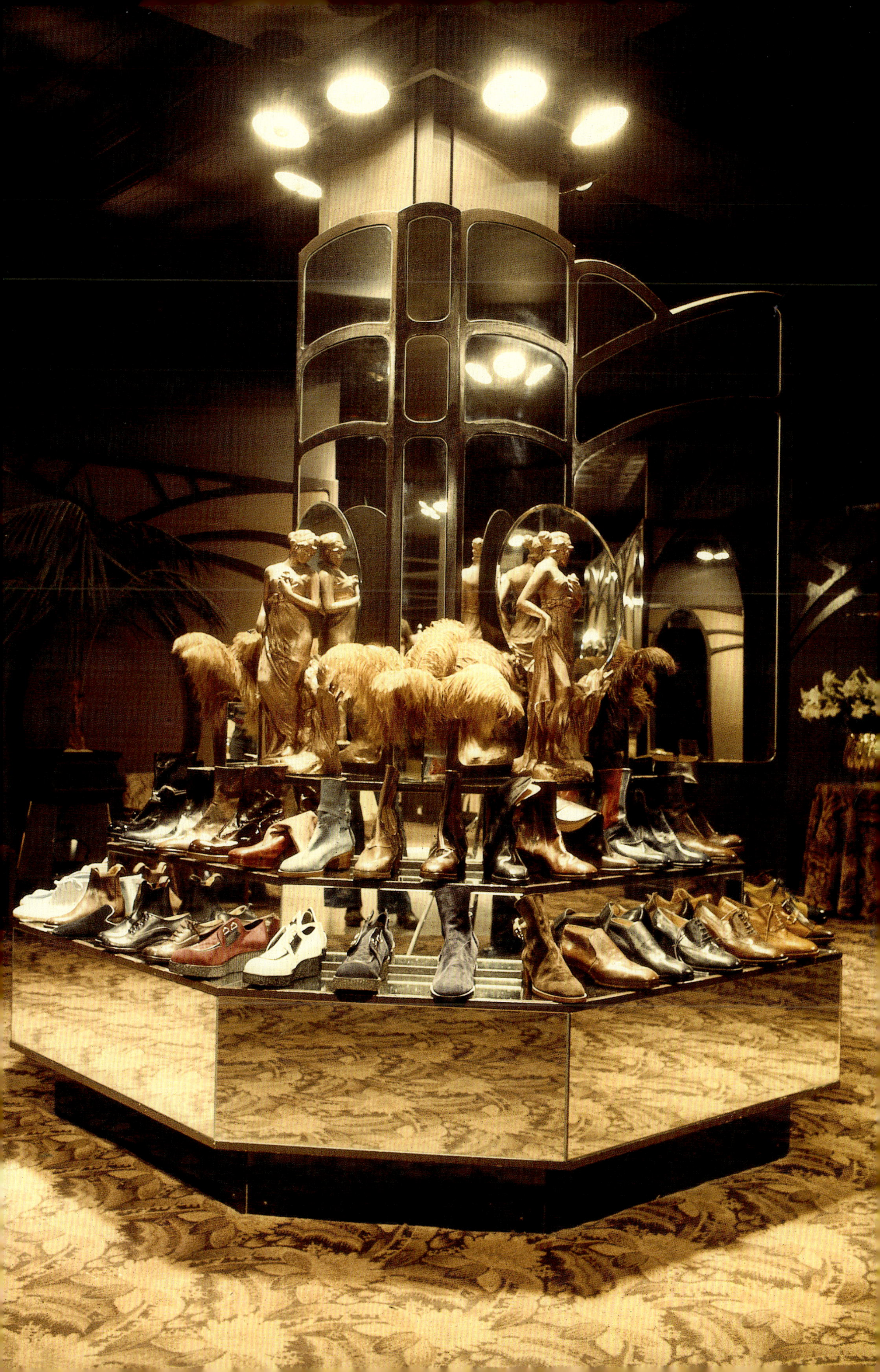

THE BIBA FLOOR

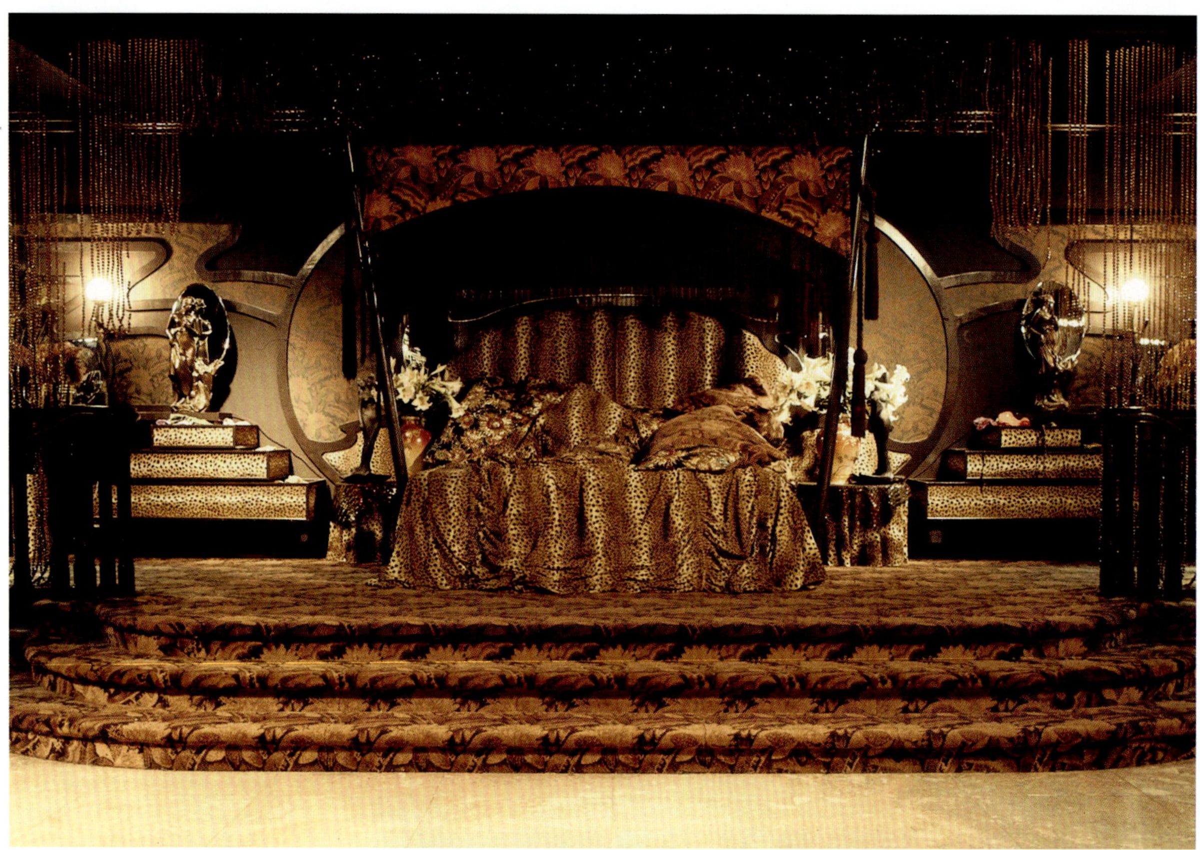

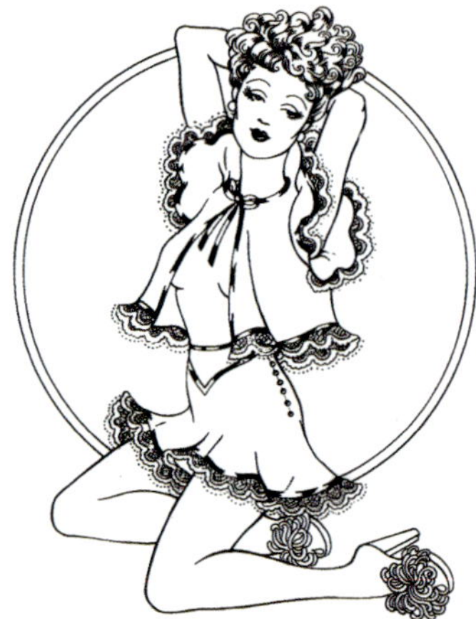

At one end of the first floor was the leopard-skin luxury of the Gallery, an 85-foot wide raised platform on which stood a nouveau bed and wardrobe set. Known as the Sarah Bernhardt area, this was the lingerie department, with bras and knickers, nightdresses and negligees spilling out from the drawers and scattered on the bed.

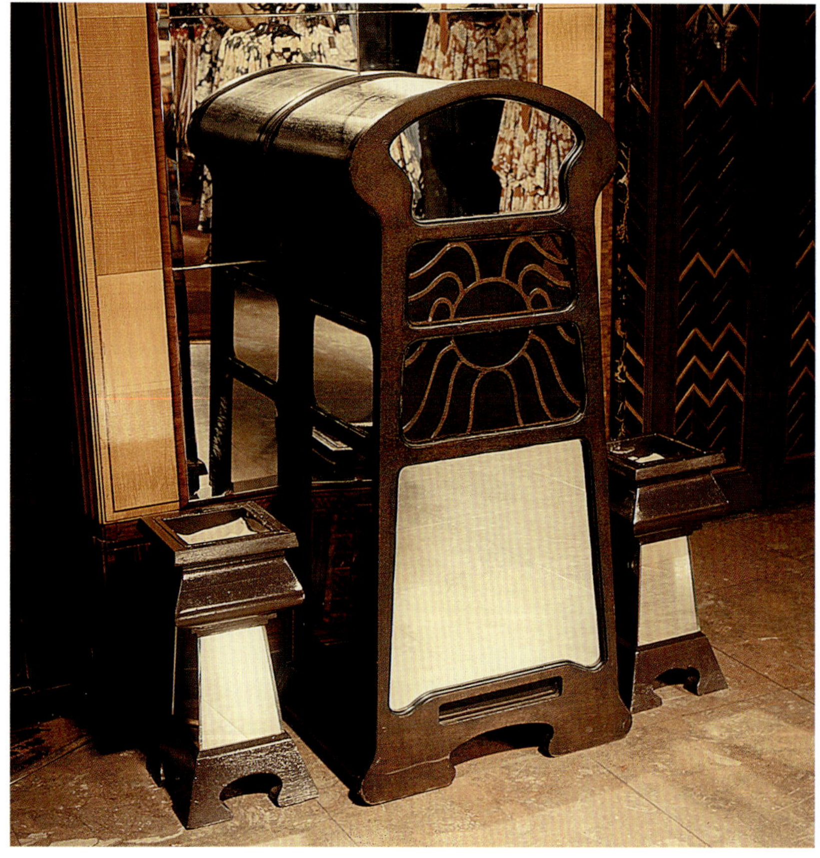

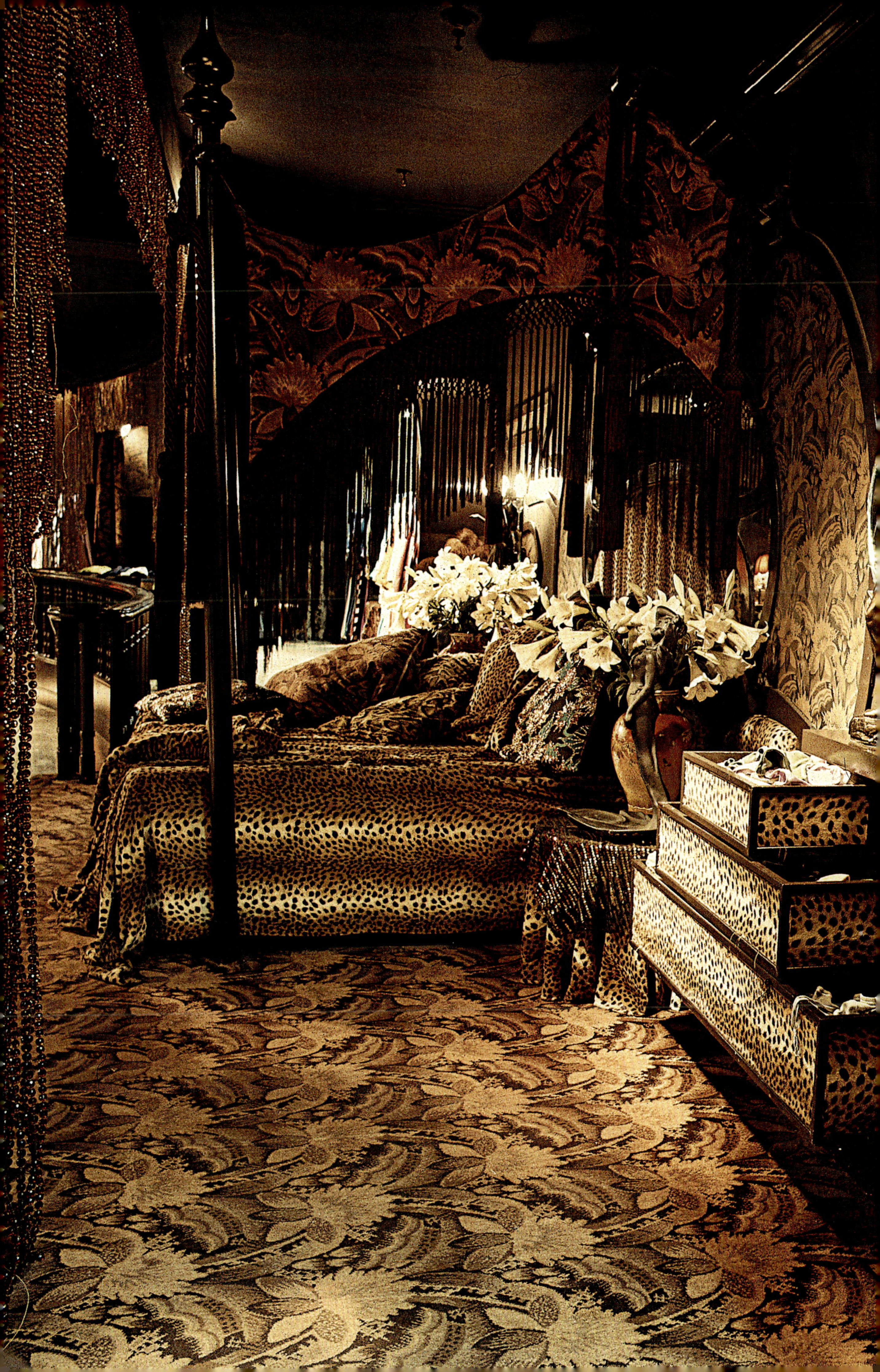

THE BIBA FLOOR

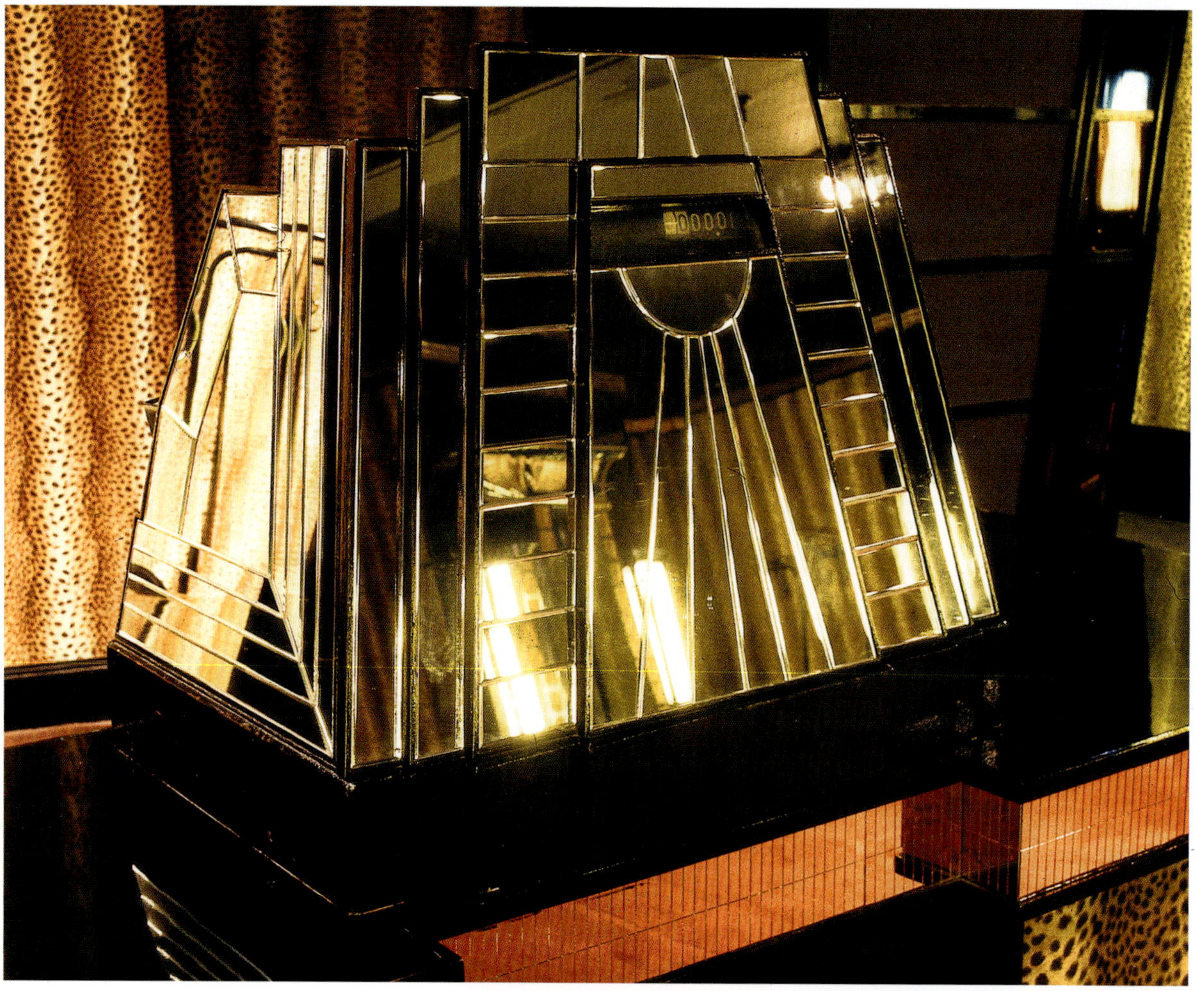

Originally intended in Abingdon Road days as a temporary measure, born of economic necessity, the communal changing room was new to Britain and became associated with Biba, with other stores following suit. For Big Biba the scale was lavish in the extreme, with a huge Egyptian-themed changing room, but the same caution applied as ever: 'Please keep an eye on your valuables, especially your handbag, all the time.'

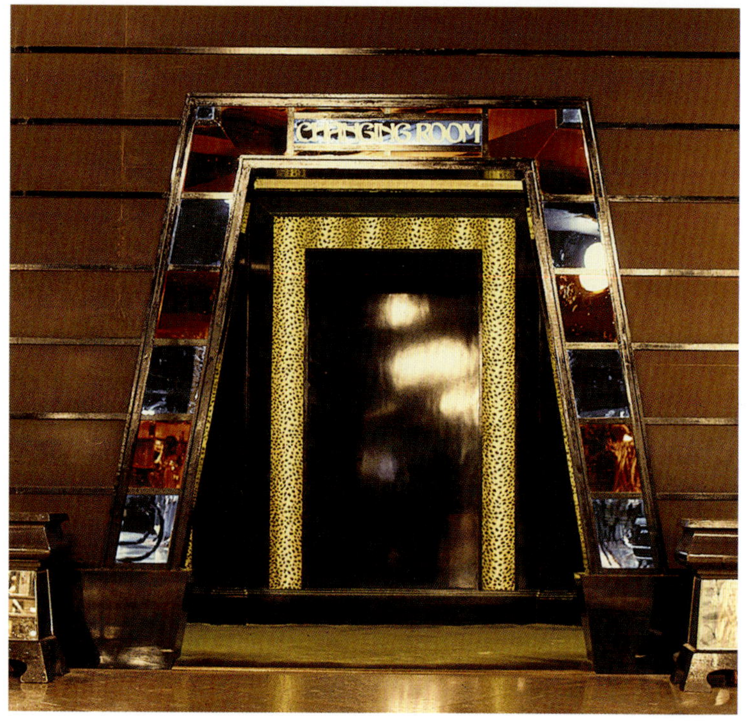

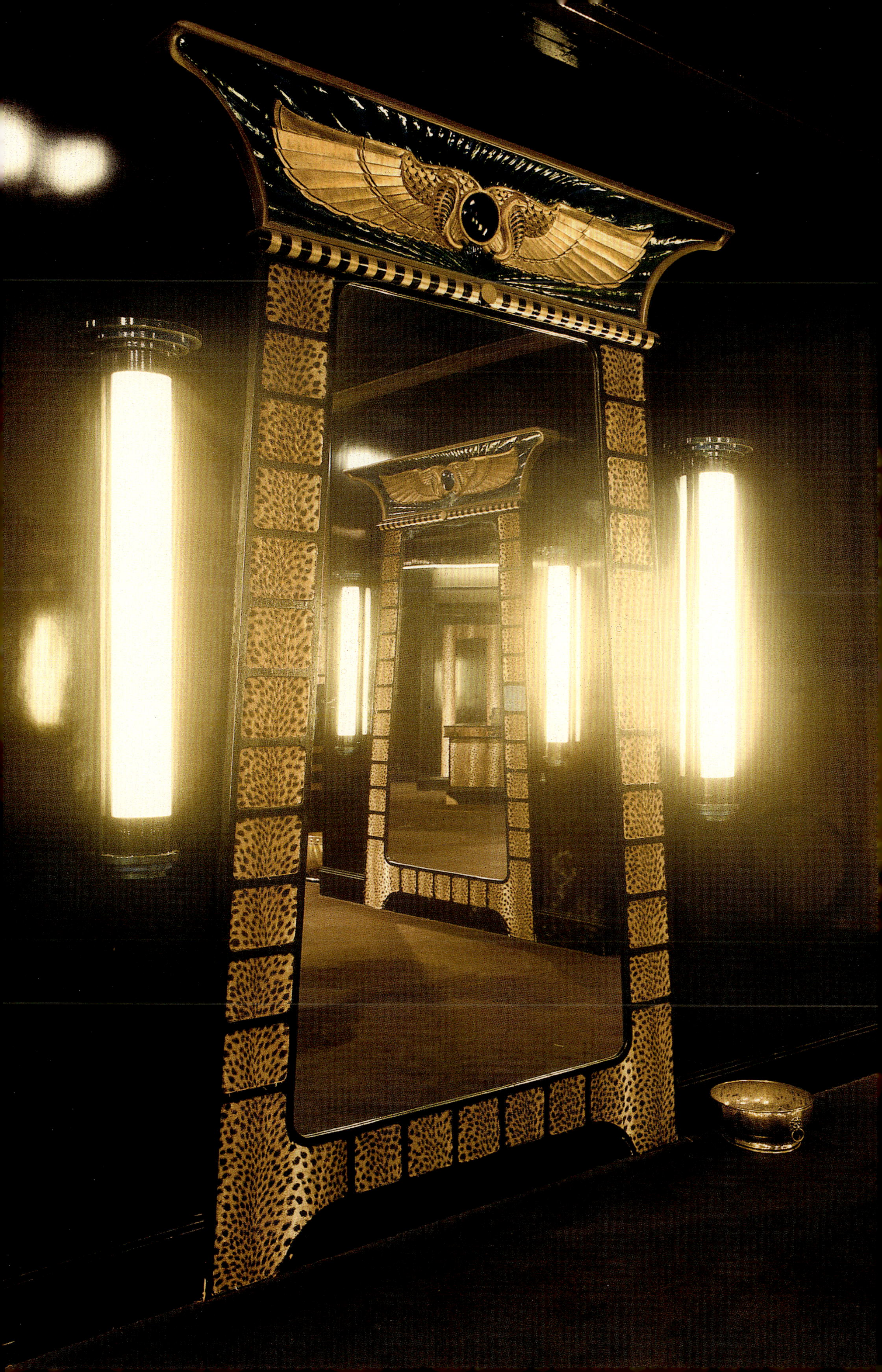

CHILDREN

Children's clothes had been part of Biba's stock since the Church Street shop, appearing shortly after Barbara Hulanicki and Stephen Fitz-Simon's son, Witold, was born.

In Big Biba the range was expanded to allow separate sections for babies (where Biba-coloured nappies could be bought), for children, for early-teenage girls (the Lolita department) and for pregnant women.

On Hulanicki's instructions, the fittings were designed to be fun: 'straight Disneyland,' as she described it. The resulting village was designed by Steven Thomas working with Bernard Spencer, art director at Thames TV.

The units, like those in the Food Hall, were built by Tony Graysmark and Terry Apse of FTV, a company more normally employed constructing film sets.

They included a giant record-player turntable, a Wild West saloon, a castle – complete with moat – which housed the kids' books, and what was claimed to be the biggest radio in London. Also appearing were old favourites including Peter Rabbit and Snoopy, the latter lying in characteristic pose on top of a walk-in kennel.

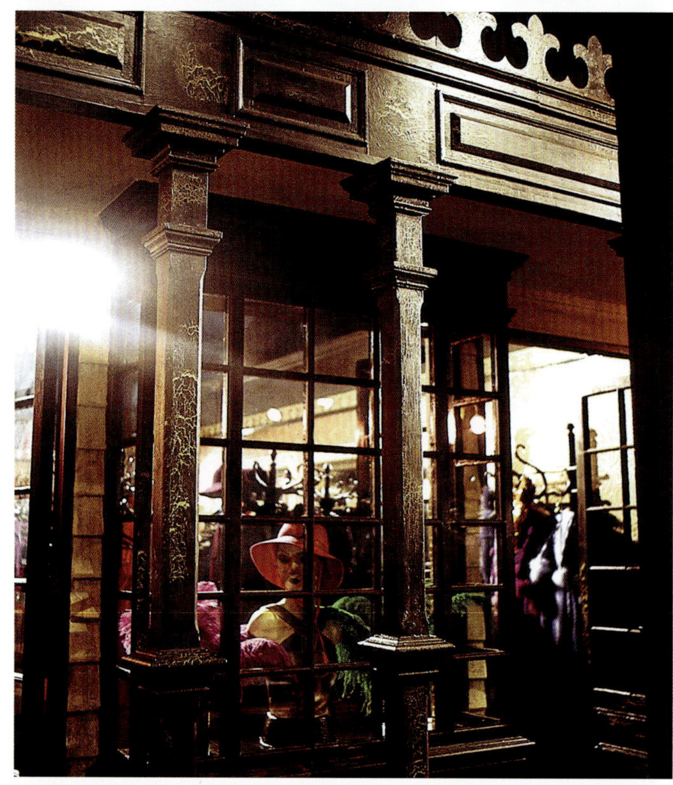

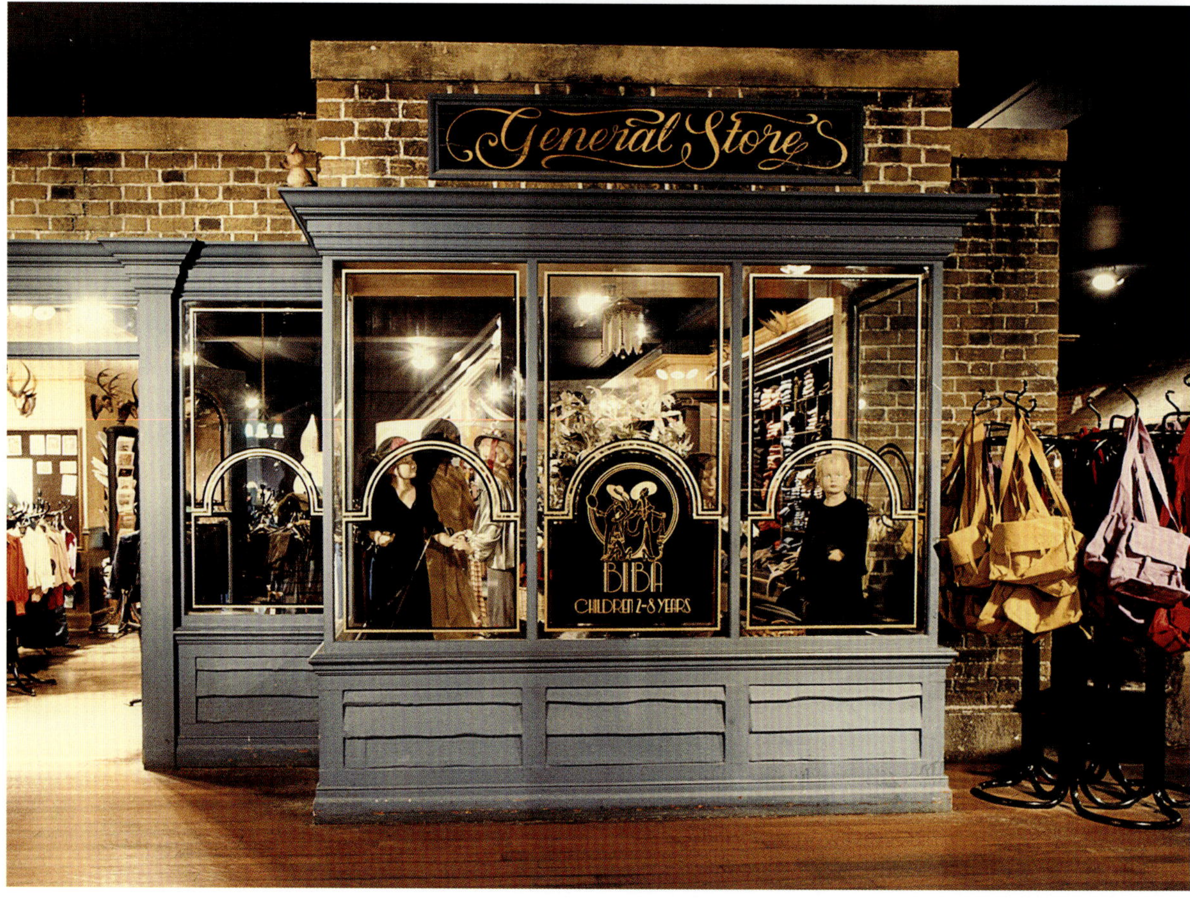

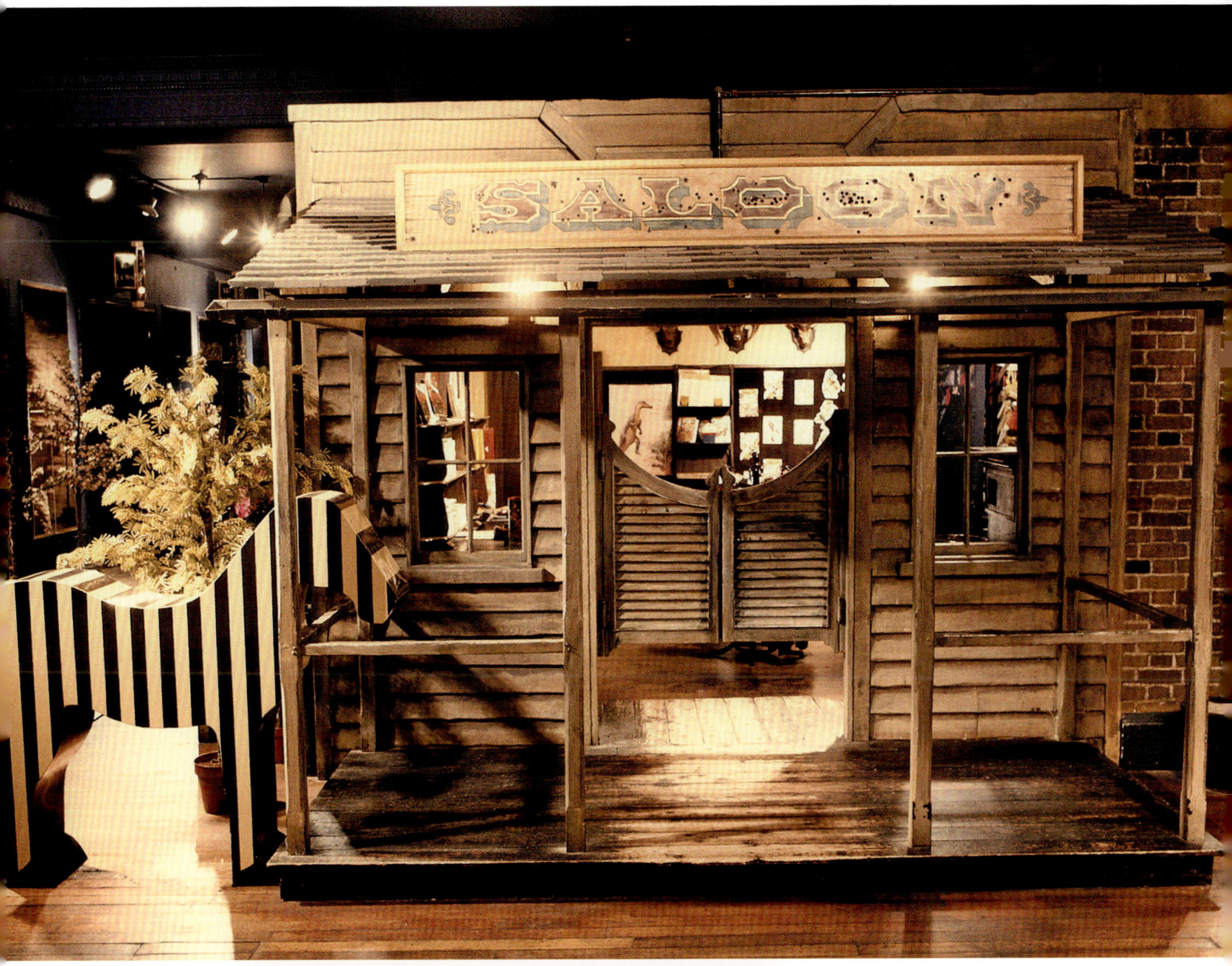

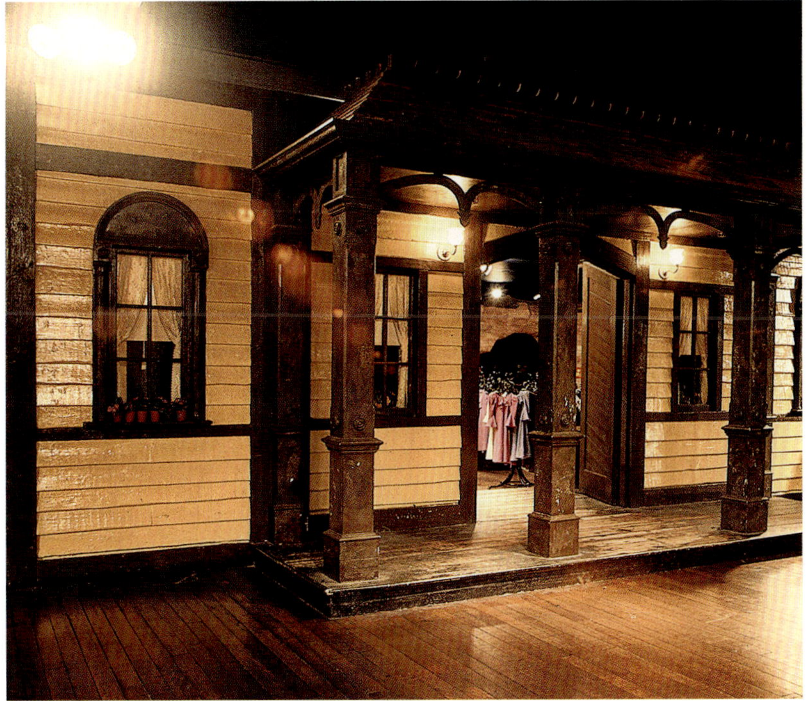

In the '60s Biba had pioneered the concept of shopping as a leisure activity, and the new store brought that to fruition.

For many aficionados Big Biba became a place to spend the whole day, and the children's department simply extended the idea to a younger age-group: there was a café with toadstool seating, while in the castle a story-teller would supply entertainment on a Saturday. A crèche was also provided, done out in the style of *West Side Story*, with scaffolding, oil drums and wire mesh fences.

Also on the second floor was the pregnant mums department, where maternity wear was sold amidst furniture that had been purposely built to an exaggerated scale so that expectant mothers would feel svelte by comparison.

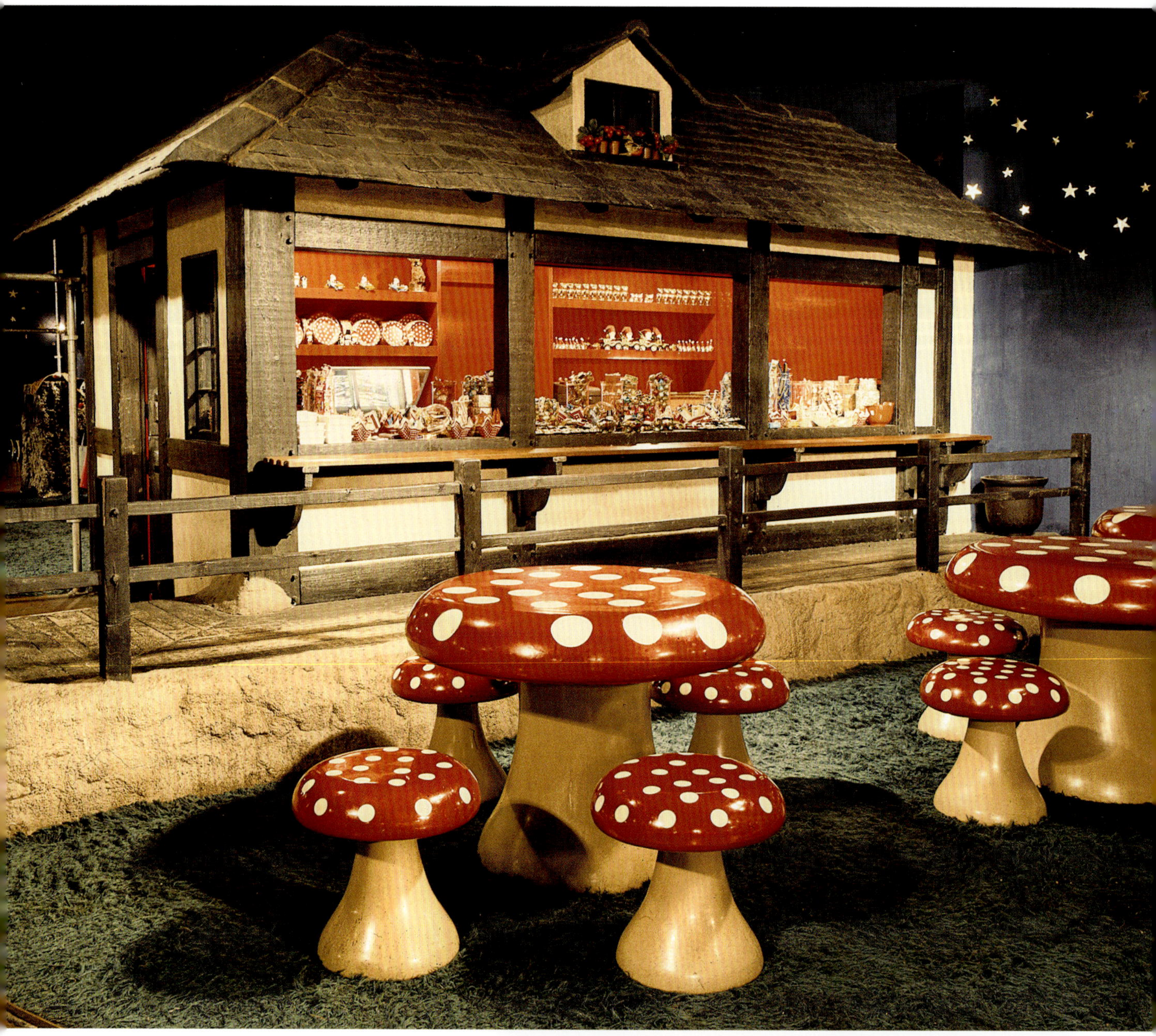

Previous pages: The Lolita department (top left) was a New Orleans-style mini-boutique, somewhat redolent of the Church Street Biba, selling clothes, tights and cosmetics for young teenage girls. The children's department was based around a Wild West theme with a General Stores and Saloon (the latter complete with fake gunshot holes in the sign), with clothes and accessories, everything from bags and books to playing-cards and crayons. Both departments had scaled-down hat-stands.

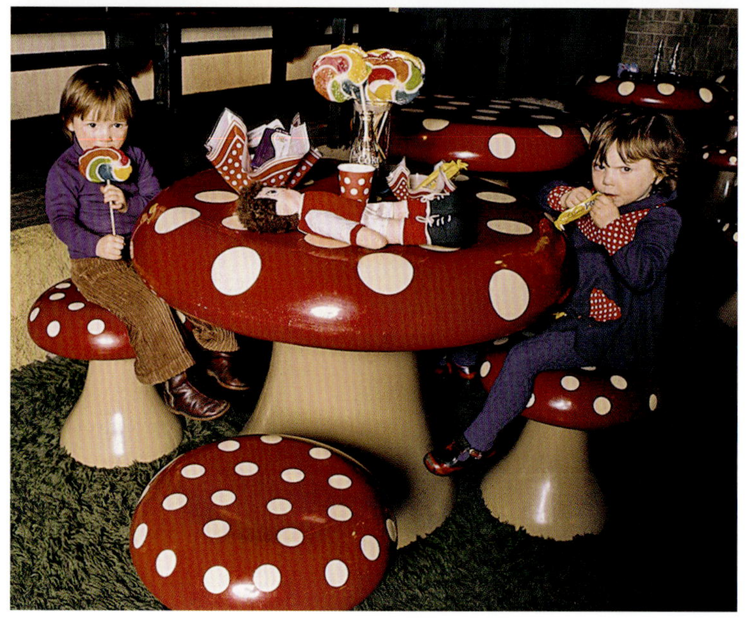

This page: The café on the children's floor was known as the Thatched Cottage, since it was originally proposed to have a thatched roof – in the event, it was built with a slate roof, but the name remained.
Opposite page: The babies' department (top) was a doll's house that comprised a complete department store in miniature. The different areas on this floor had their own logos for (left-to-right) Lolita, kids and pregnant mums. The swing ticket shows the logo for the babies' department, with the children's floor gift voucher.

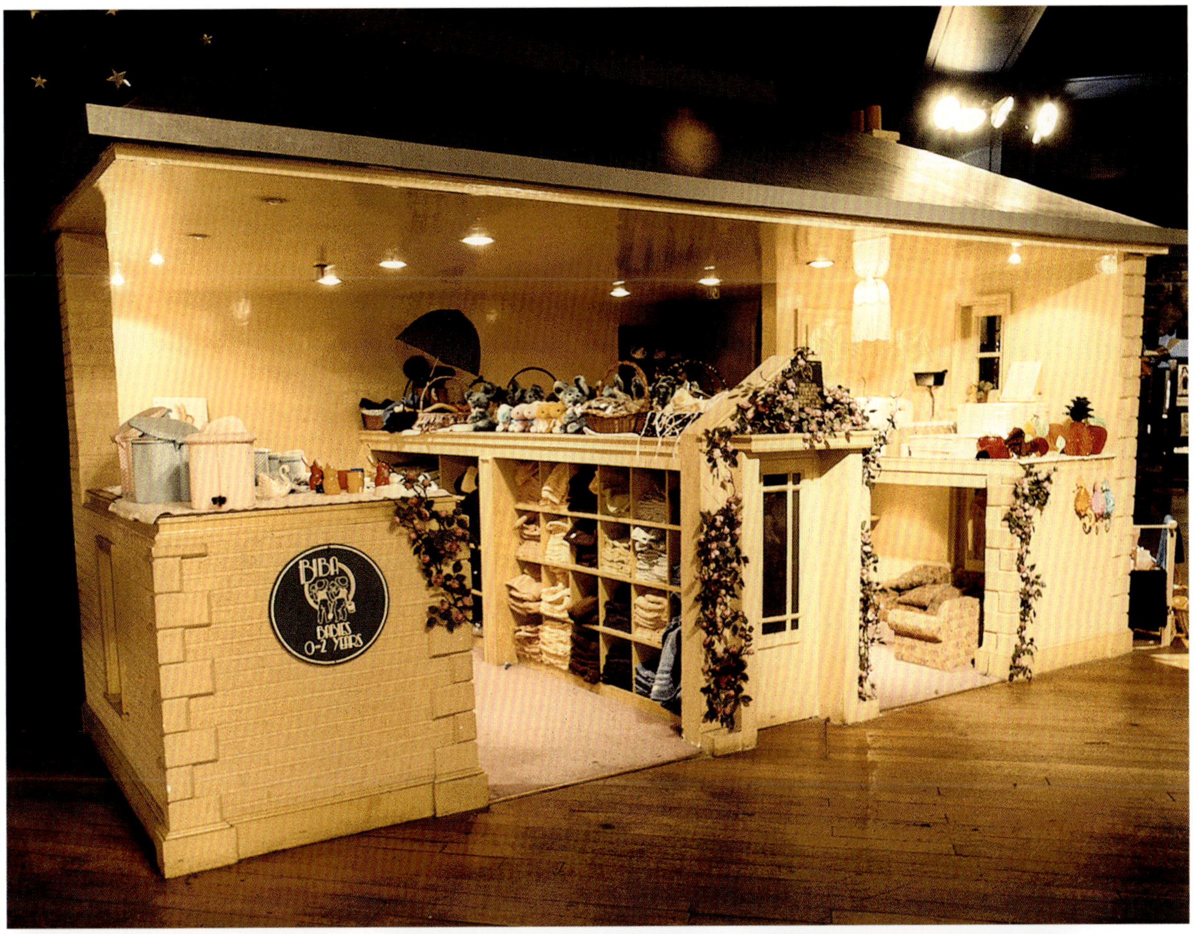

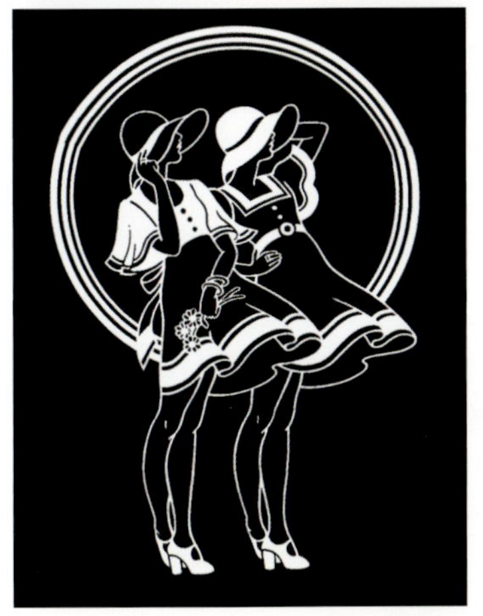

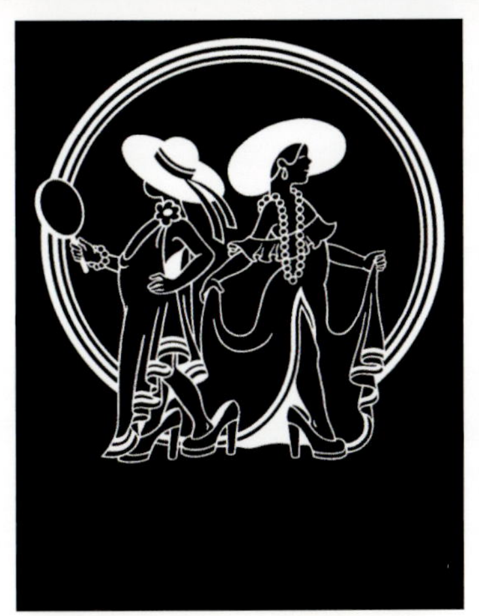

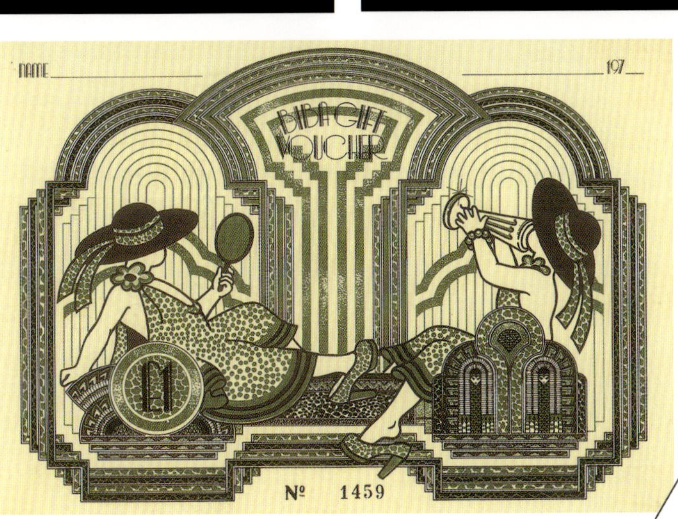
NAME
197
BIBA GIFT VOUCHER
£1
№ 1459

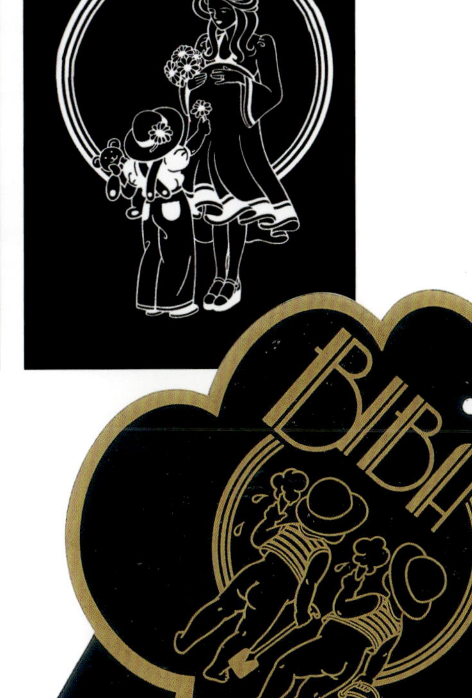
BIBA
NUMBER
PRICE

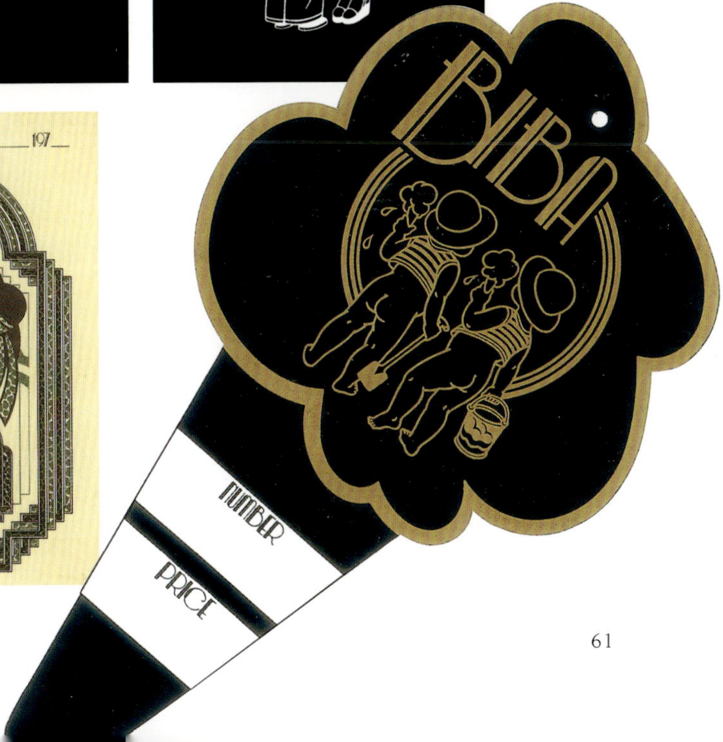

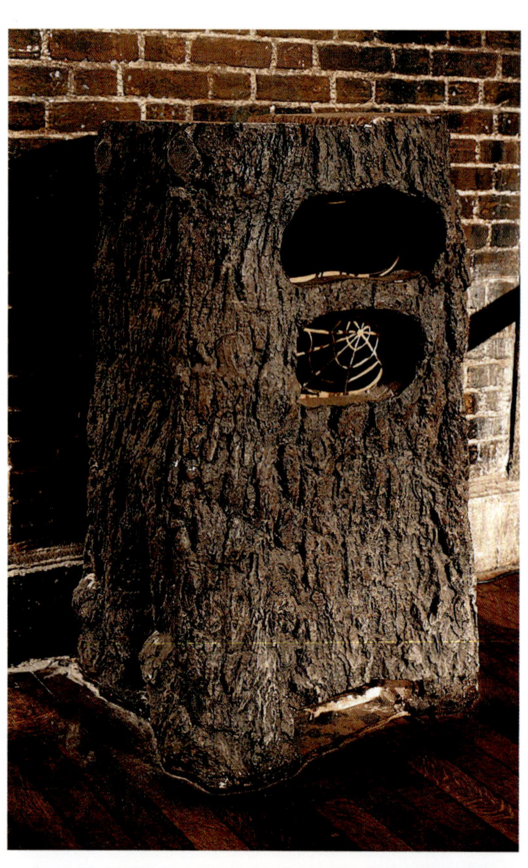

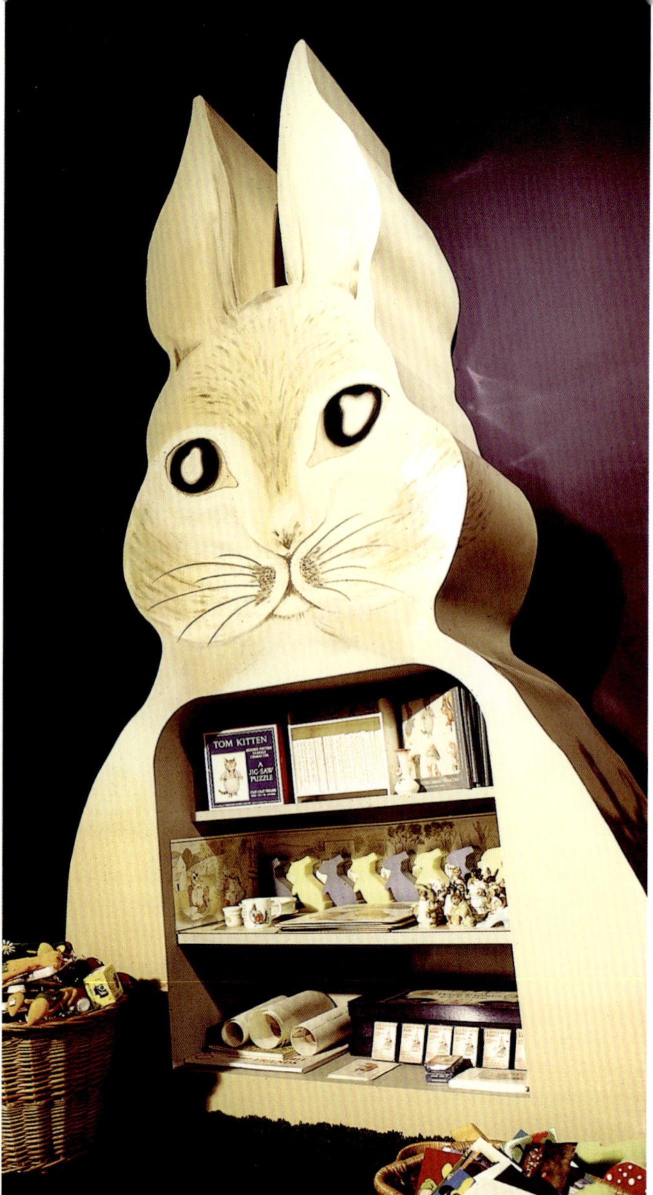
TOM KITTEN
A
JIG-SAW
PUZZLE

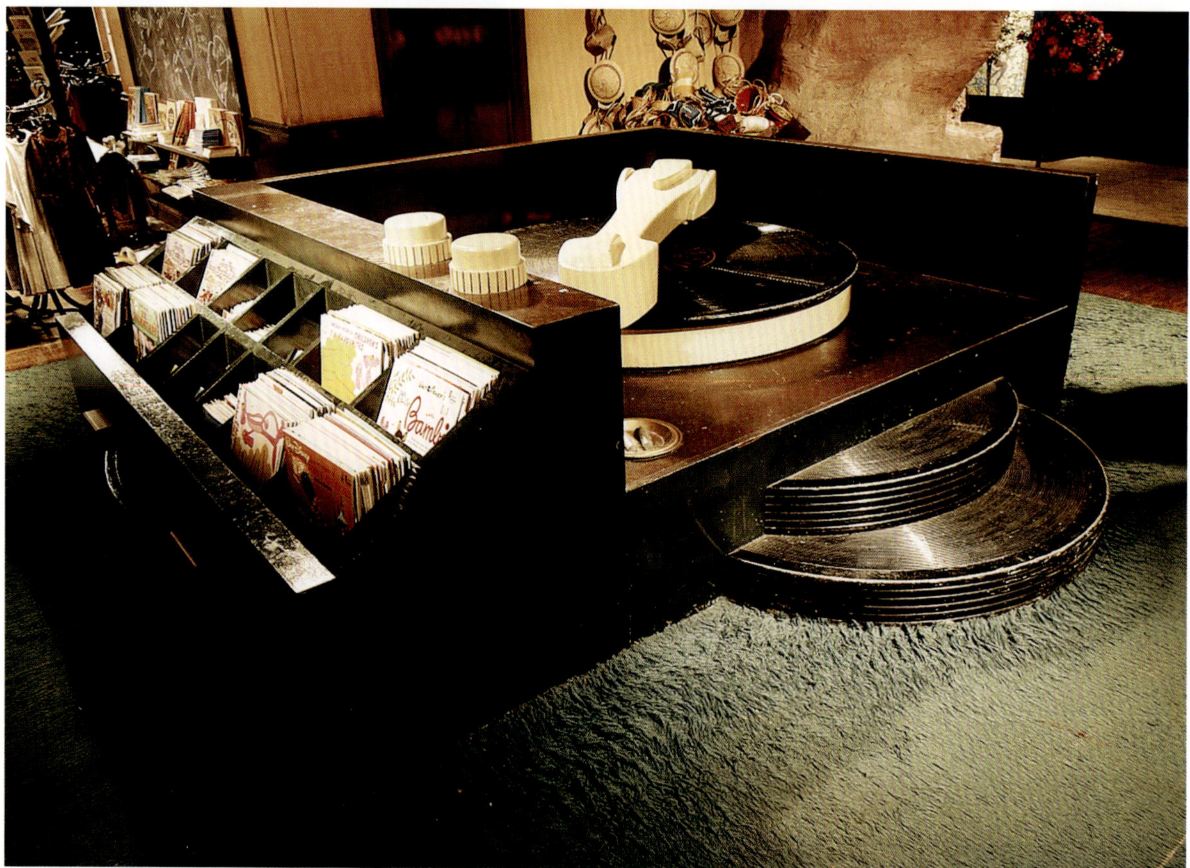
Bambi

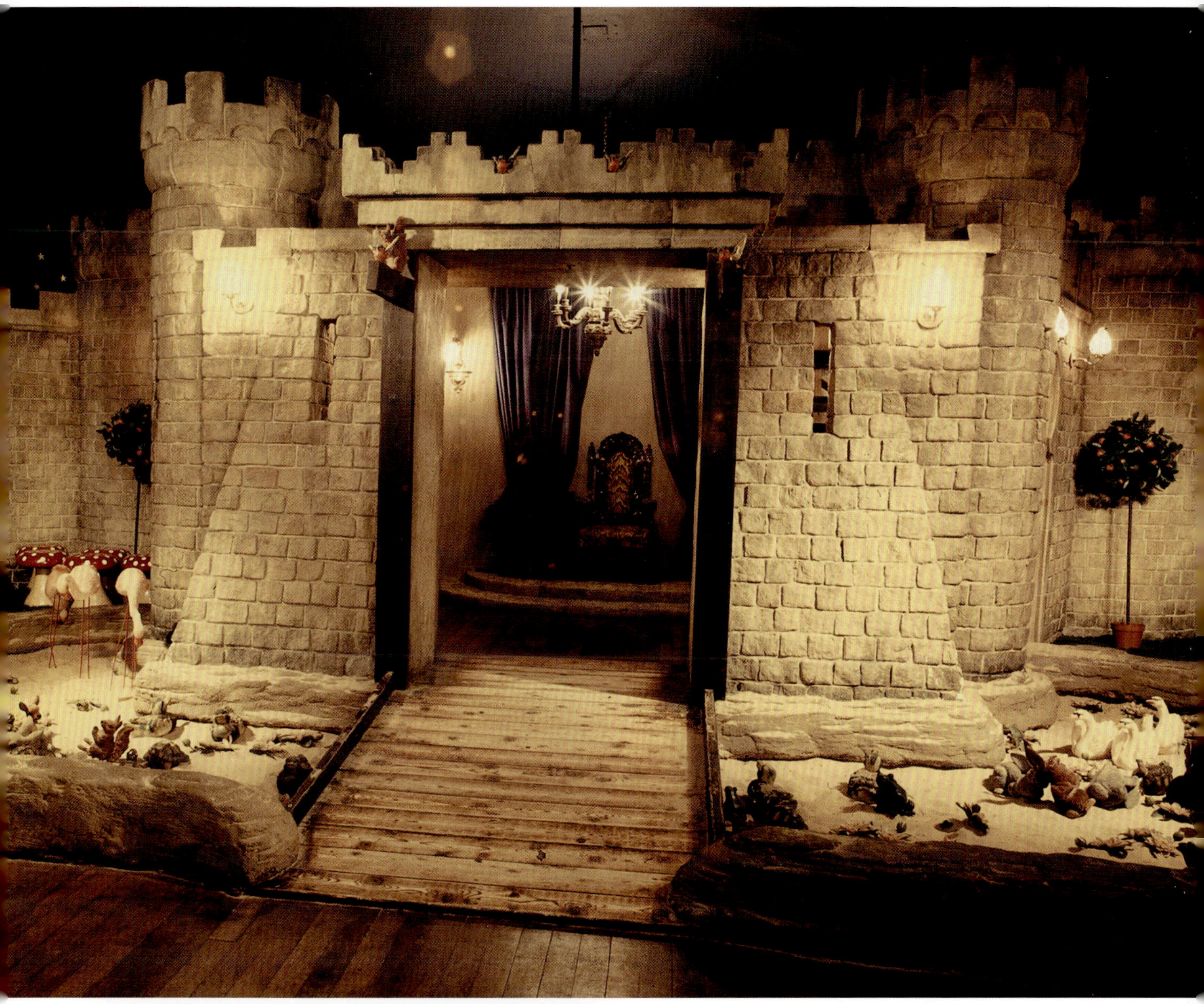

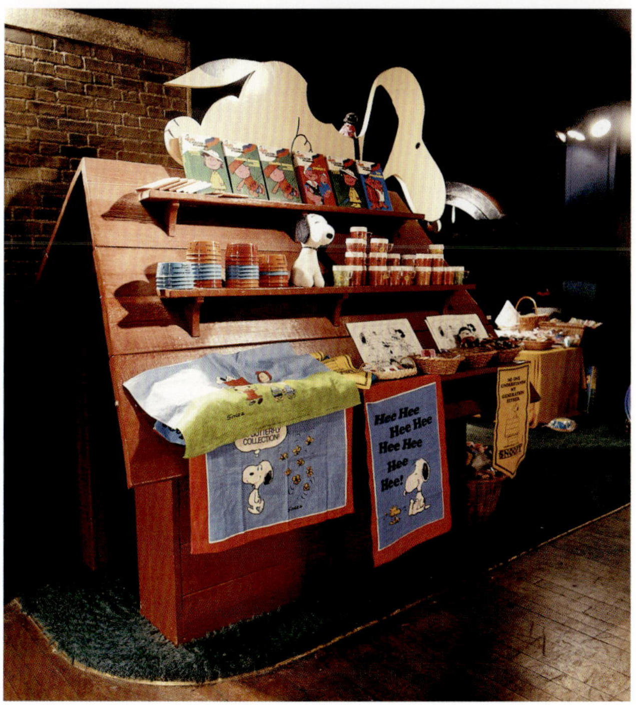

Biba's interest in branding extended to other major brand names, so that the Snoopy kennel (left) and the Peter Rabbit unit (opposite right) sold Peanuts and Beatrix Potter merchandise respectively. The giant turntable (opposite bottom) was a fully functioning roundabout that has lived long in the memories of those who played on it (and survived the experience). The speaker (opposite top left) came with fake spider's web to keep prying hands out, whilst other children played in the castle (above).

MEN'S FLOOR

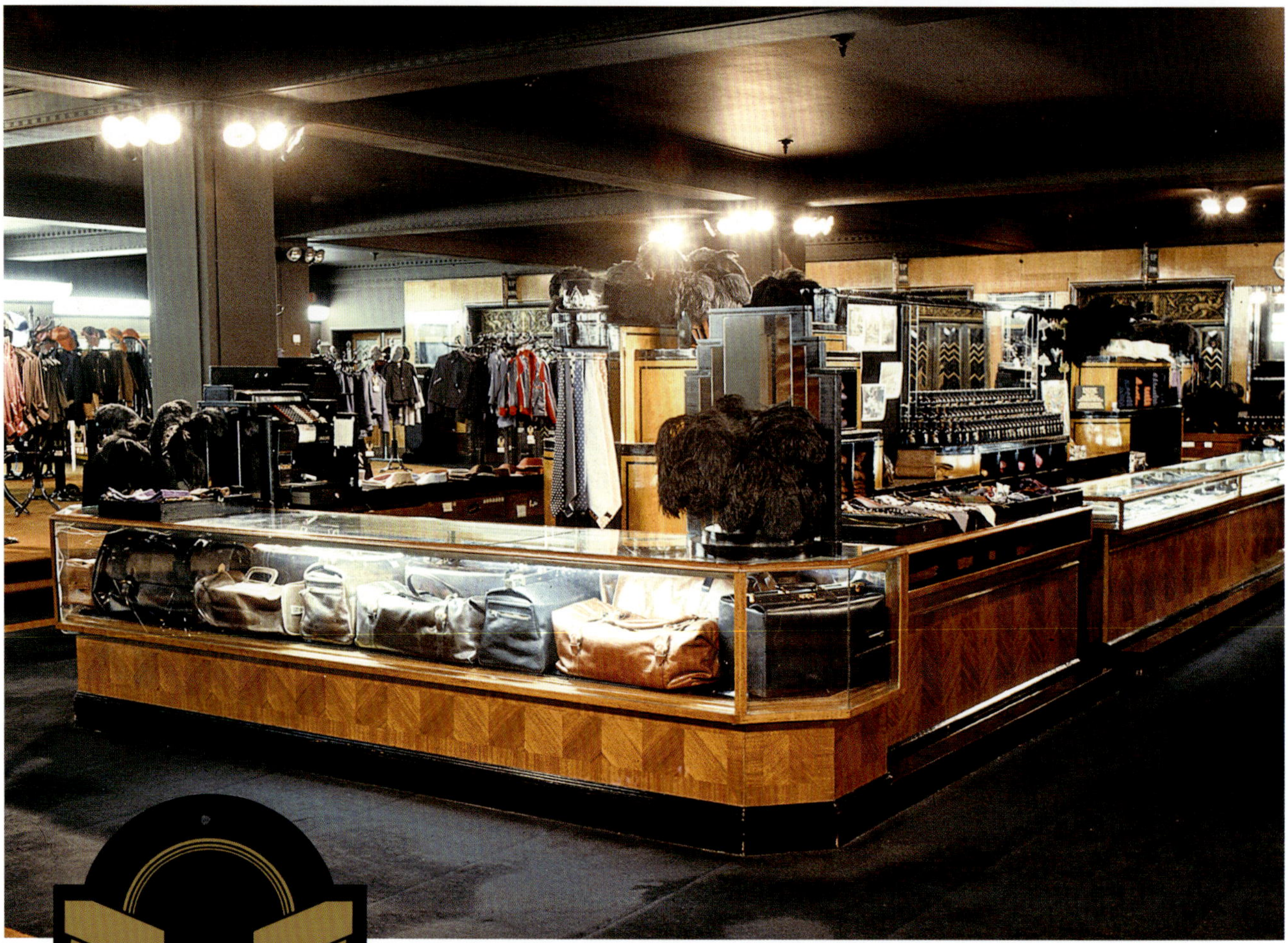

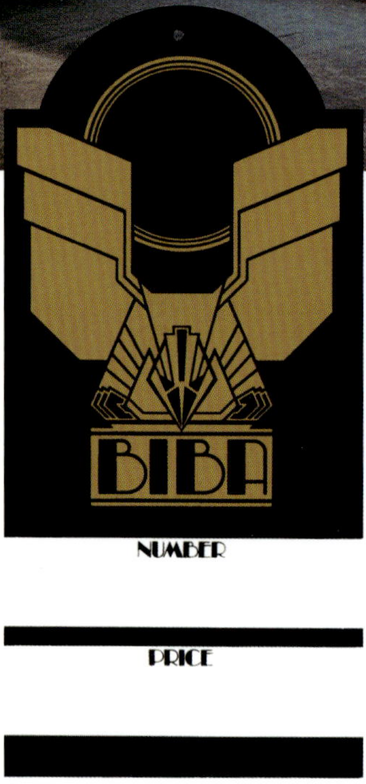

BIBA

NUMBER

PRICE

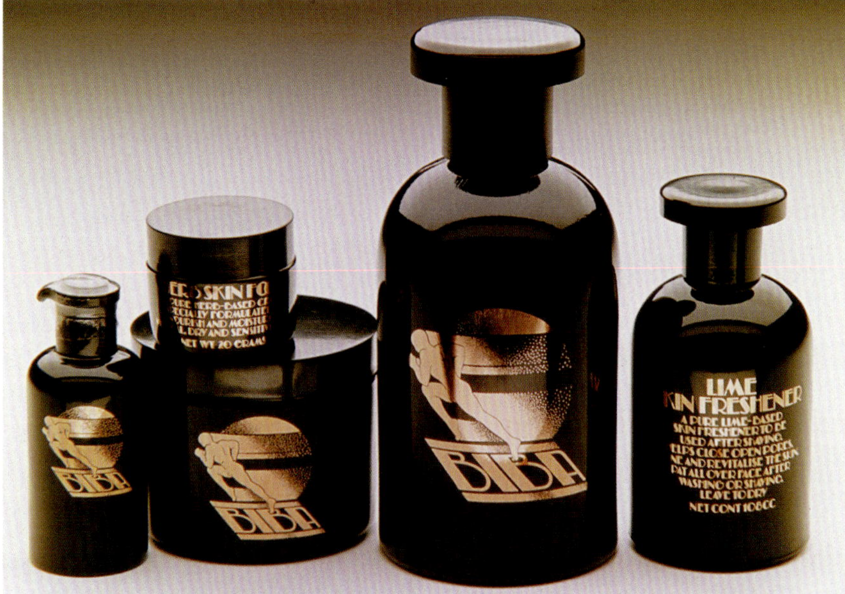

The central counter on the third floor (top), a series of black marble plinths with walnut-veneered display units and bronze fittings, was retained from Derry & Toms. The plan of the floor inspired the eagle logo for the men's and boys' department (left). *Above:* Items from the men's health cosmetics range.

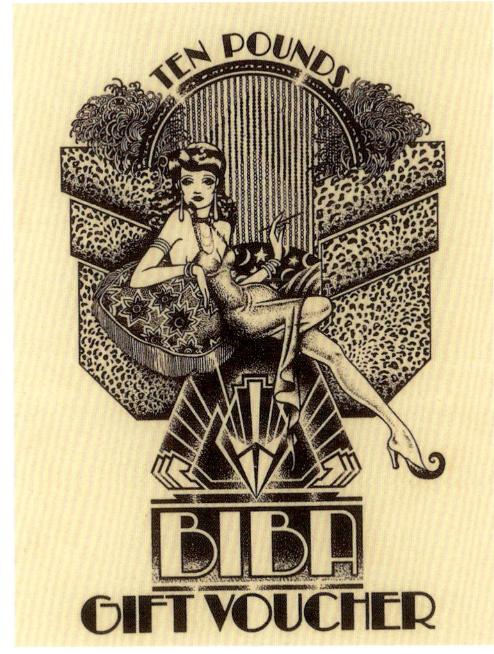

'We have consciously opened up our market and gone up the age bracket,' commented Fitz-Simon on Big Biba and nowhere was it more apparent than here. The men's clothes, like much of the store itself, drew inspiration from the '30s while bringing the influences up to date for the '70s.

Traditional suits and shirts came in mostly conservative colours – black, coffee, deep plum – and, typically of Biba, though not perhaps of most men, there were undergarments in matching colours. And even when the checks got loud they were still presented on a double-breasted suit. There were influences too from the '40s and '50s.

The clothes were displayed in wardrobes arranged around the edges, classic old-style wardrobes that were even more aspirational than the clothes themselves, of a kind that cried out for a Jeeves to assist a gentleman to dress. Pyjamas, luggage and accessories – up to and including monocles and Stetson hats – were also for sale.

Again, as in the children's department, there were diversions, here centred on the sports area of the floor. 'It is clearly intended to be a place where people can relax while they shop,' said the *Sunday Telegraph*. 'With this end in view, darts and indoor bowls are provided, for use either by bored male shopping companions or undecided customers.'

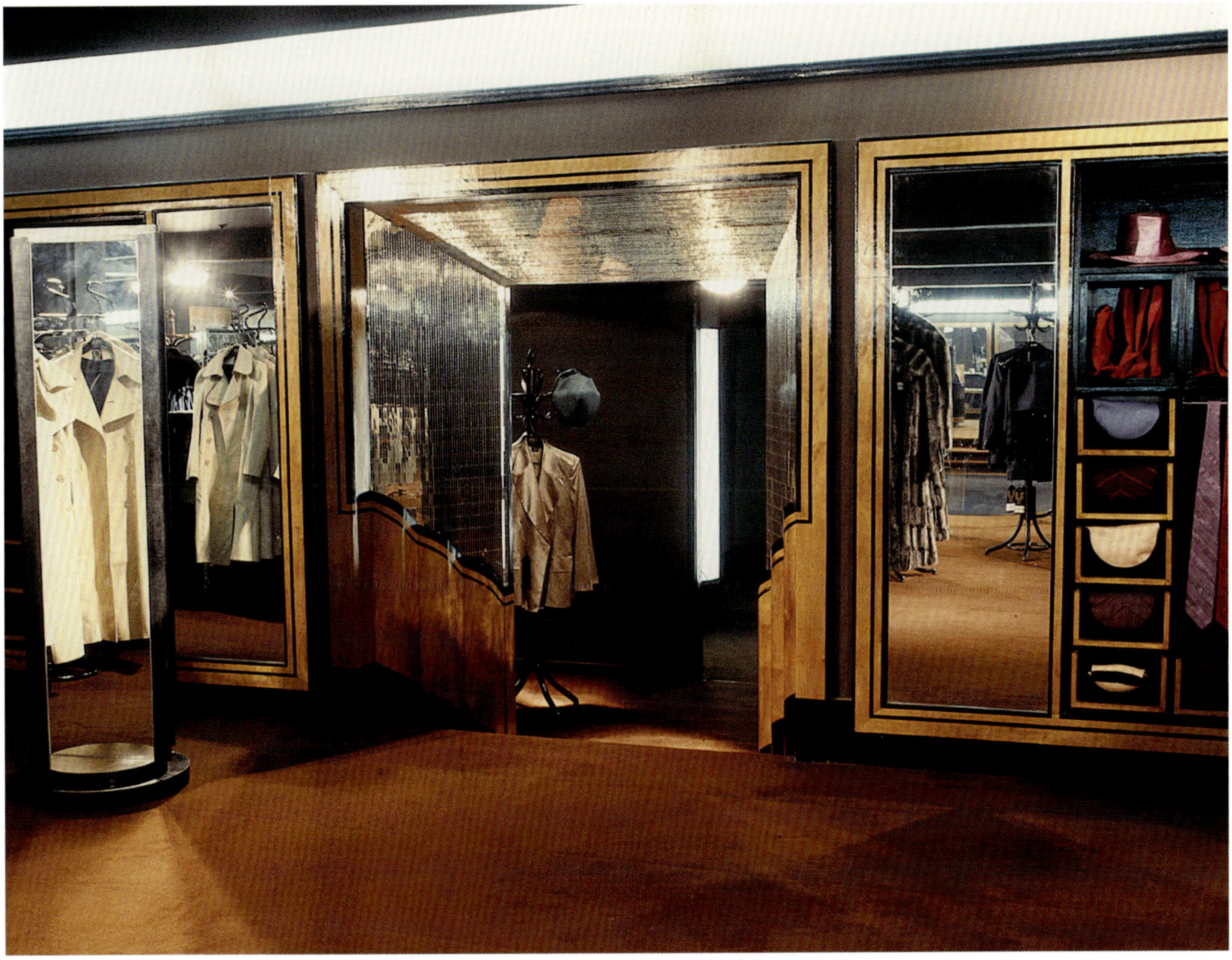

MEN'S FLOOR

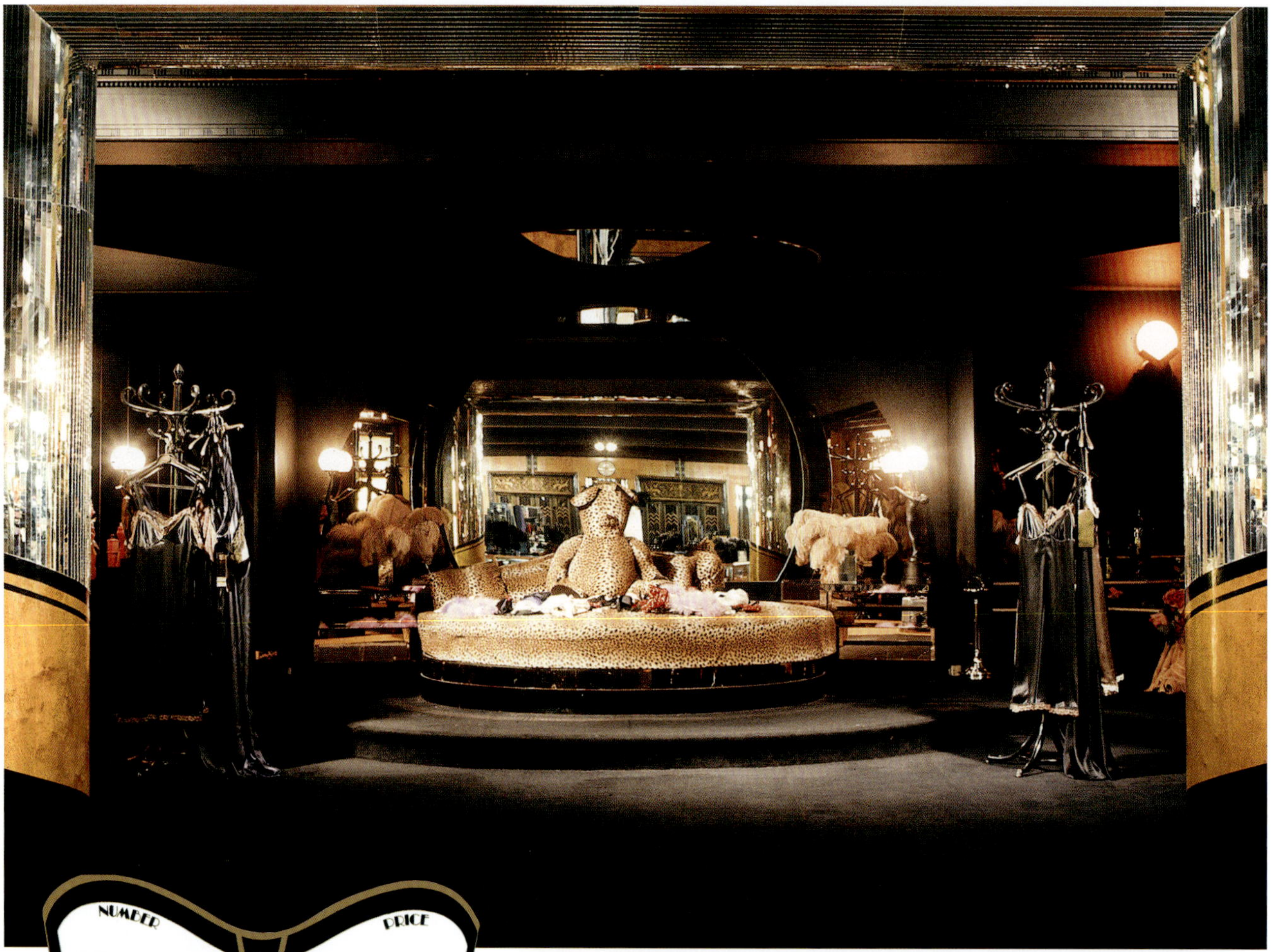

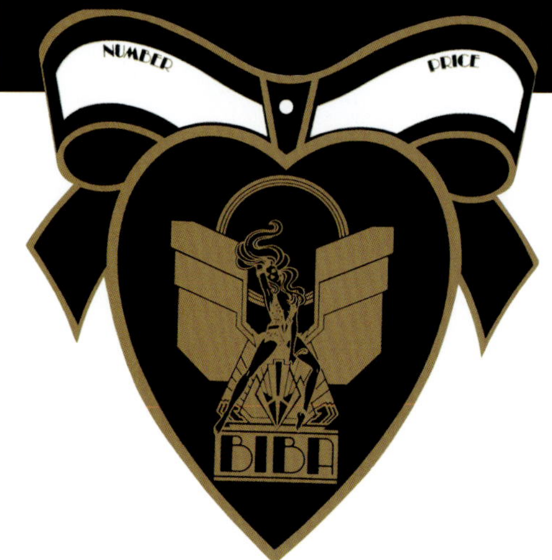

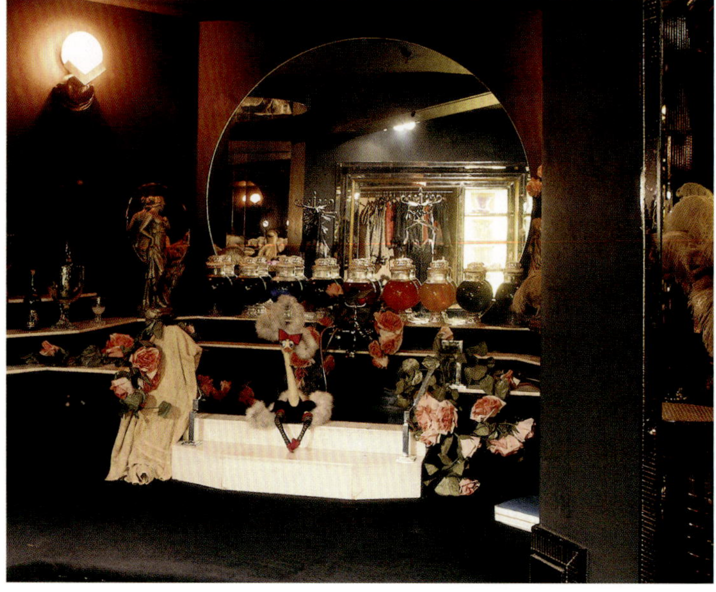

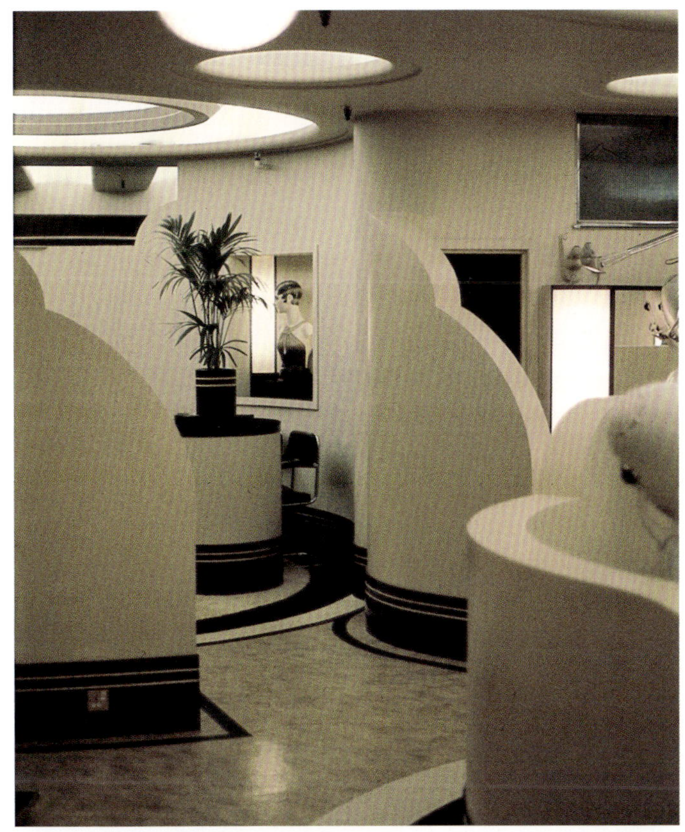

In the centre of the floor was the Mistress Room with a huge bed covered in satin sheets and a kitsch pink marble bath. The intention was to sell 'long satin gloves, naughty negligees, edible underwear and other pieces of ersatz erotica', though most visitors settled for a pack of playing cards adorned with 1950s-style cheesecake pin-ups.

A later addition to the third floor was the beauty parlour, which opened in early-1974. Designed by Tim Whitmore in full-on deco liner style, and run by Regis (a soi-disant visagiste) it was, like the Food Hall, ahead of its time, offering natural beauty products and therapies as well as sun beds and massages.

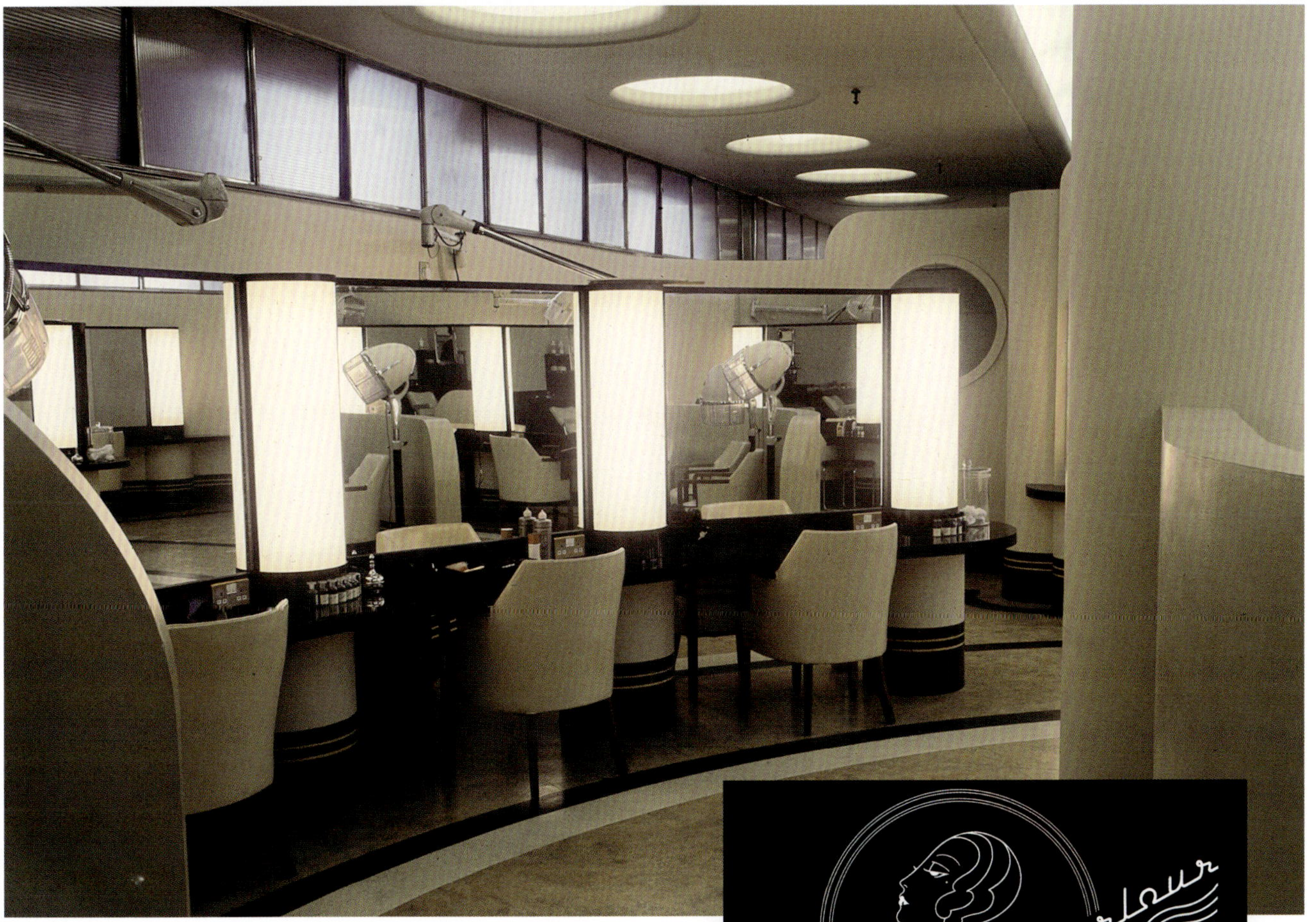

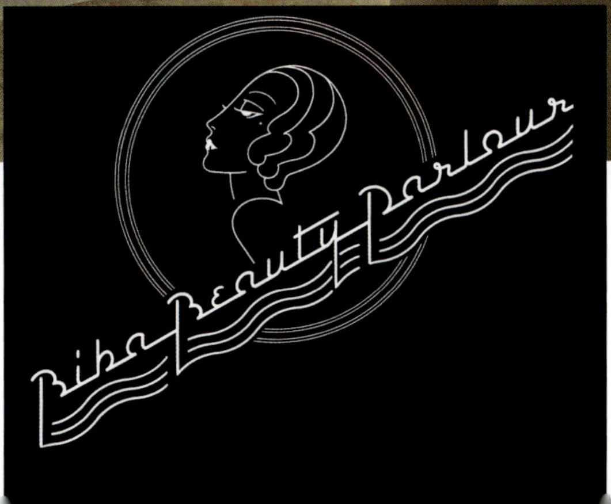

Biba Beauty Parlour

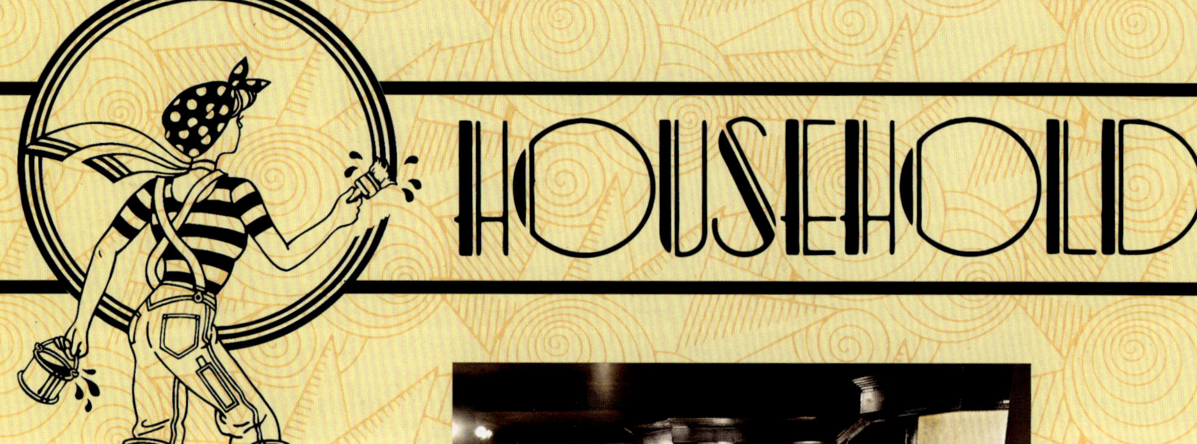

HOUSEHOLD

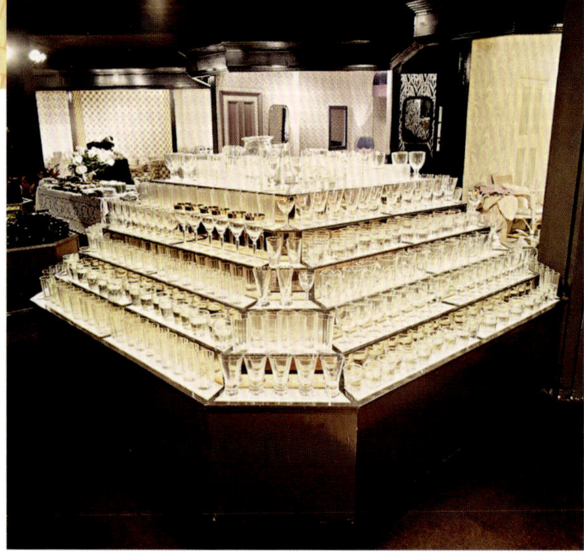

The spread of Biba into lifestyle goods had begun in the previous store, but was massively expanded in the new premises. Everything from wallpaper and paint, through kitchen products and tableware to lampshades and light bulbs – all were now available in the familiar colours and adorned with the Biba logo.

All that was missing were electrical goods, and then only because of the difficulties of sourcing appropriate pieces: 'To get one black fridge, we would have had to have bought 25,000,' regretted Fitz-Simon. Even by the standards of Big Biba, that was an excess too far.

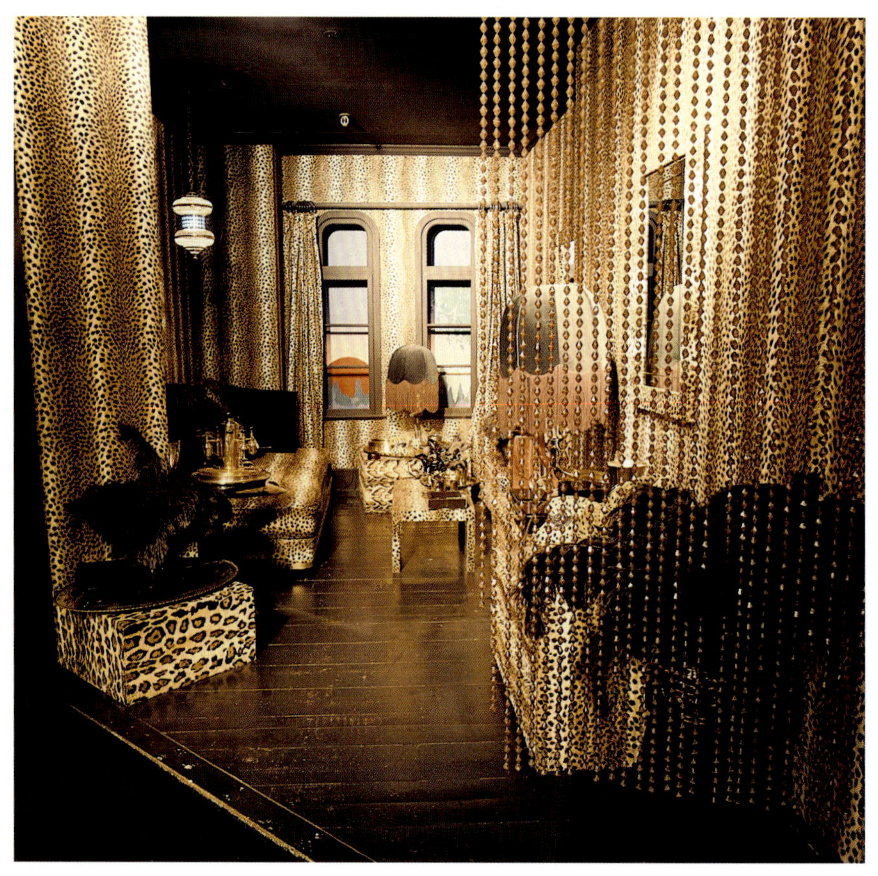

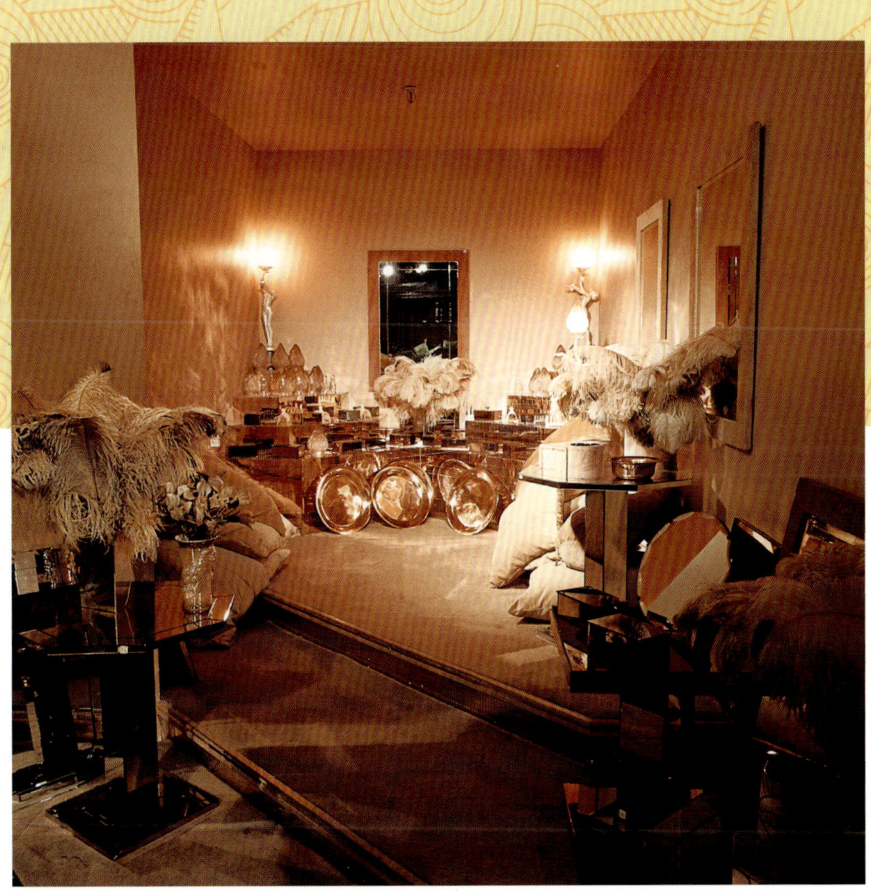

'Biba isn't so much a shop, it's a way of life,' had said the *Daily Mirror* of a previous incarnation. Now, ten years on from the launch of the Postal Boutique, and much of the core Biba market was grown up. Girls who had once taken their pocket-money or their first wage-packet to Abingdon Road or Church Street, seeking to buy admission to the adult world, had now left home and were renting their first flats.

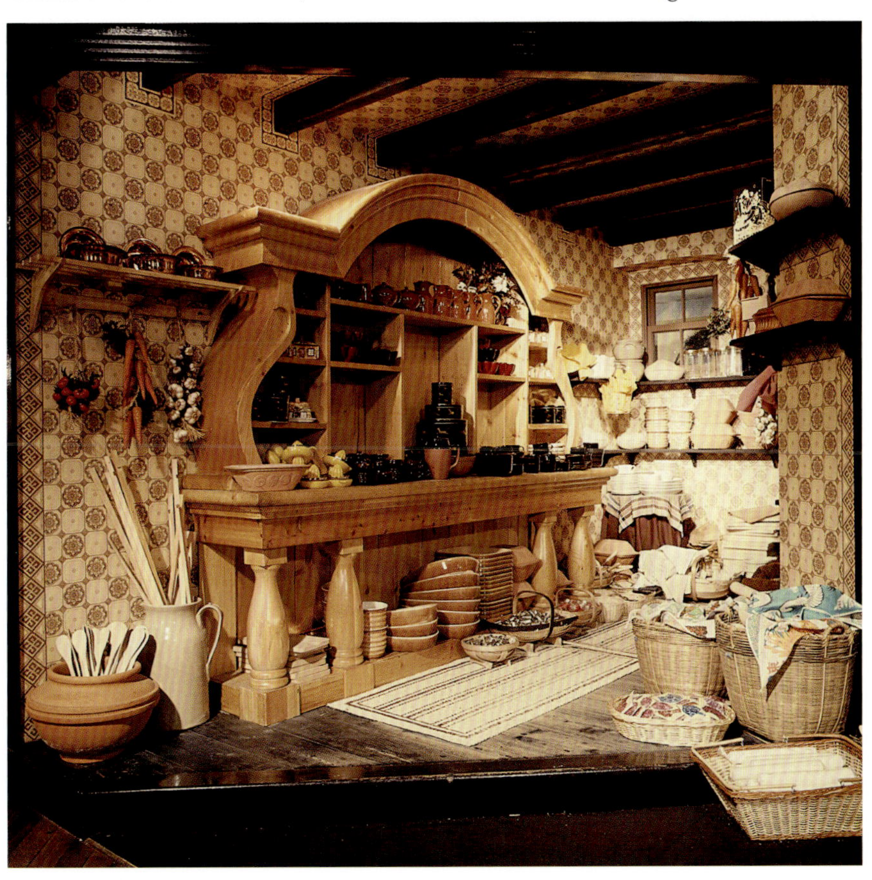

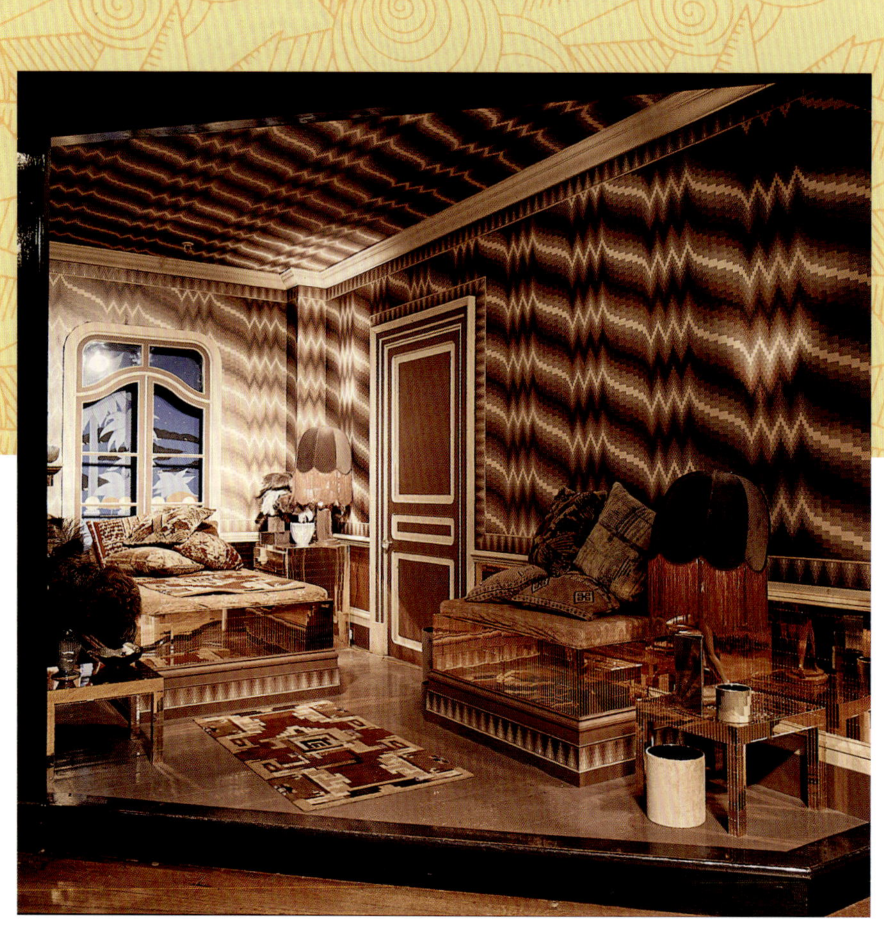

To help them theme these new premises, the household department centred on twenty-four room sets, all decorated and stocked with Biba products, showing how even the clumsiest bedsit conversion in Earl's Court could be transformed into the hippest place on Earth. 'This is where houses start becoming homes,' trumpeted the advertising copy.

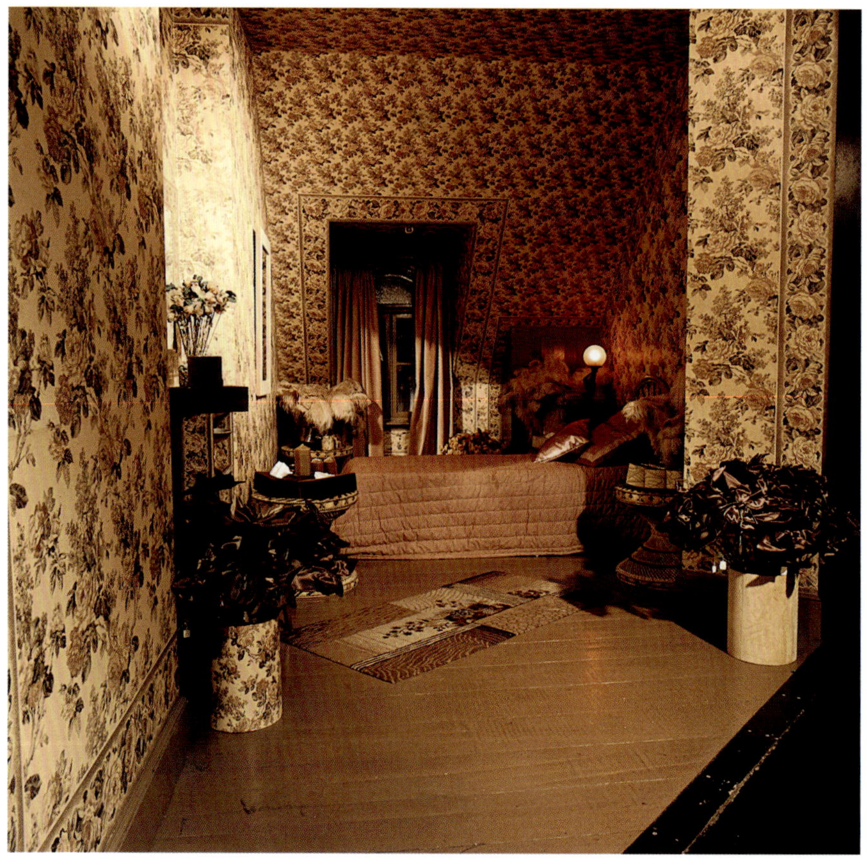

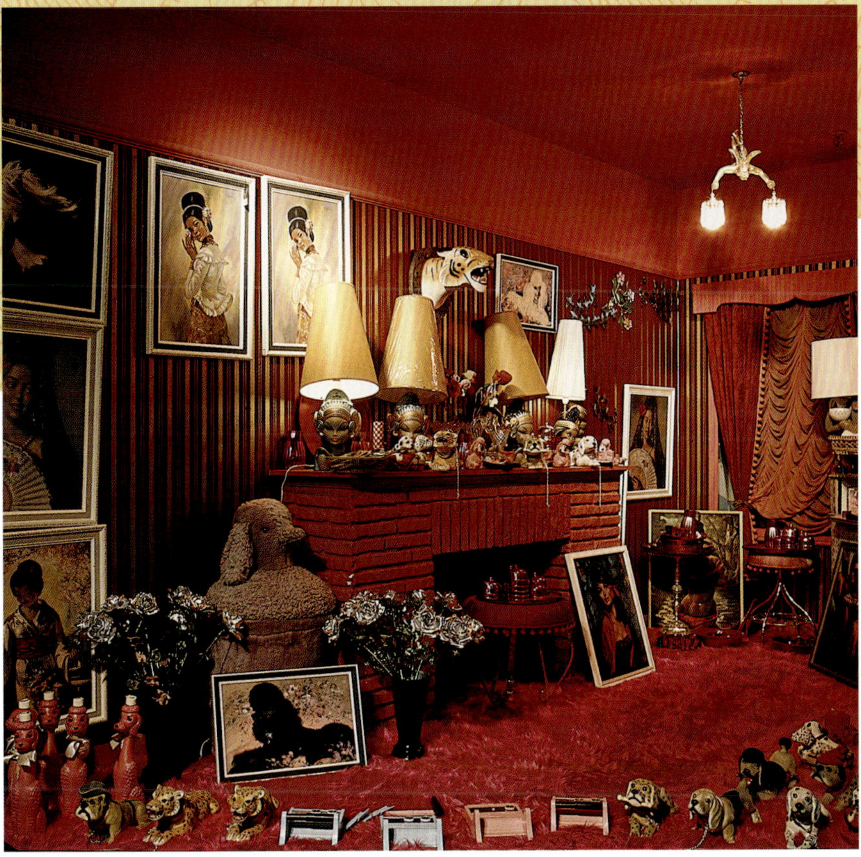

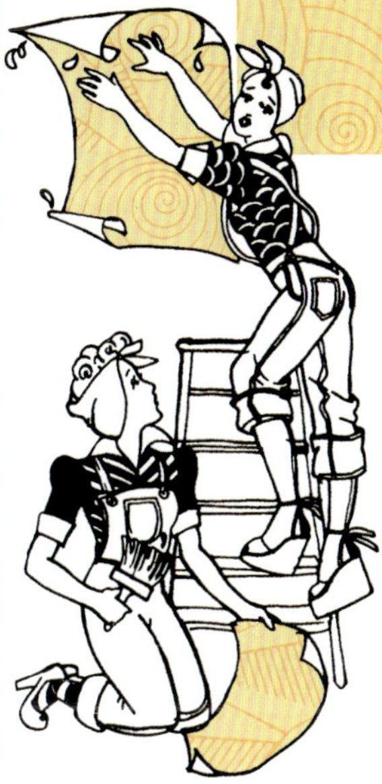

The contents of the Kitsch roomset were itemized by Bevis Hiller in the *Sunday Times*: 'frilled plastic boxes, ashtrays like miniature loos, school of Tretchikoff paintings, nude plastic babes rising from plastic roses, urinating cupids who perform when you warm a glass with your hand, and framed poems apostrophising granny.' Or, as the *New Yorker* put it, 'Mae West's broom closet.'

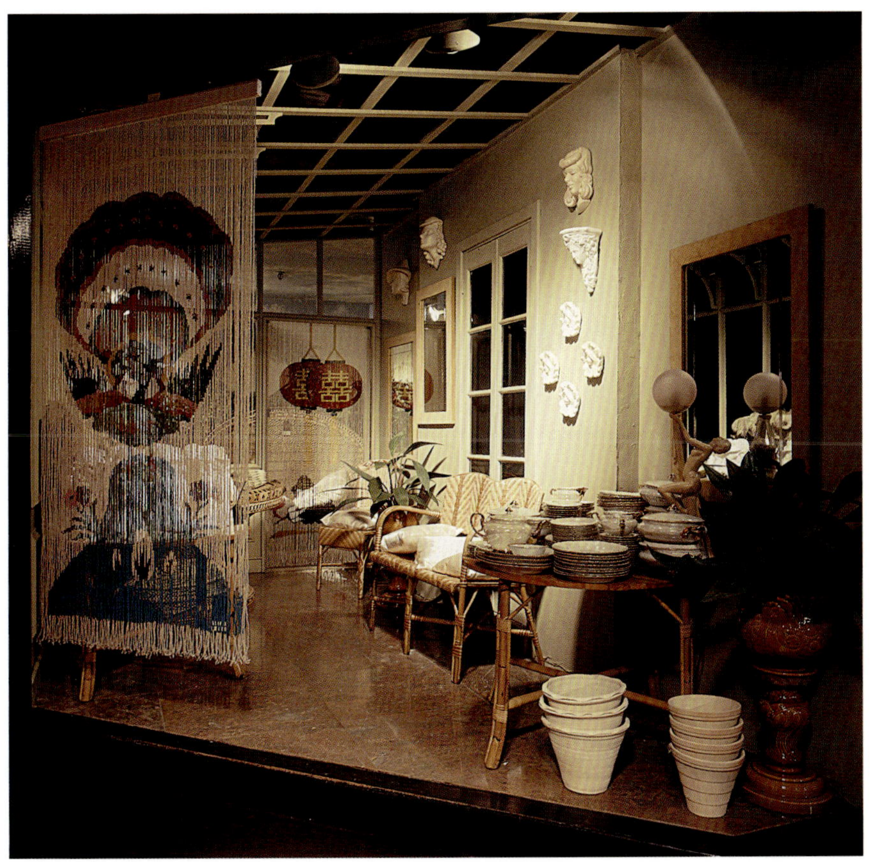

THE RAINBOW R

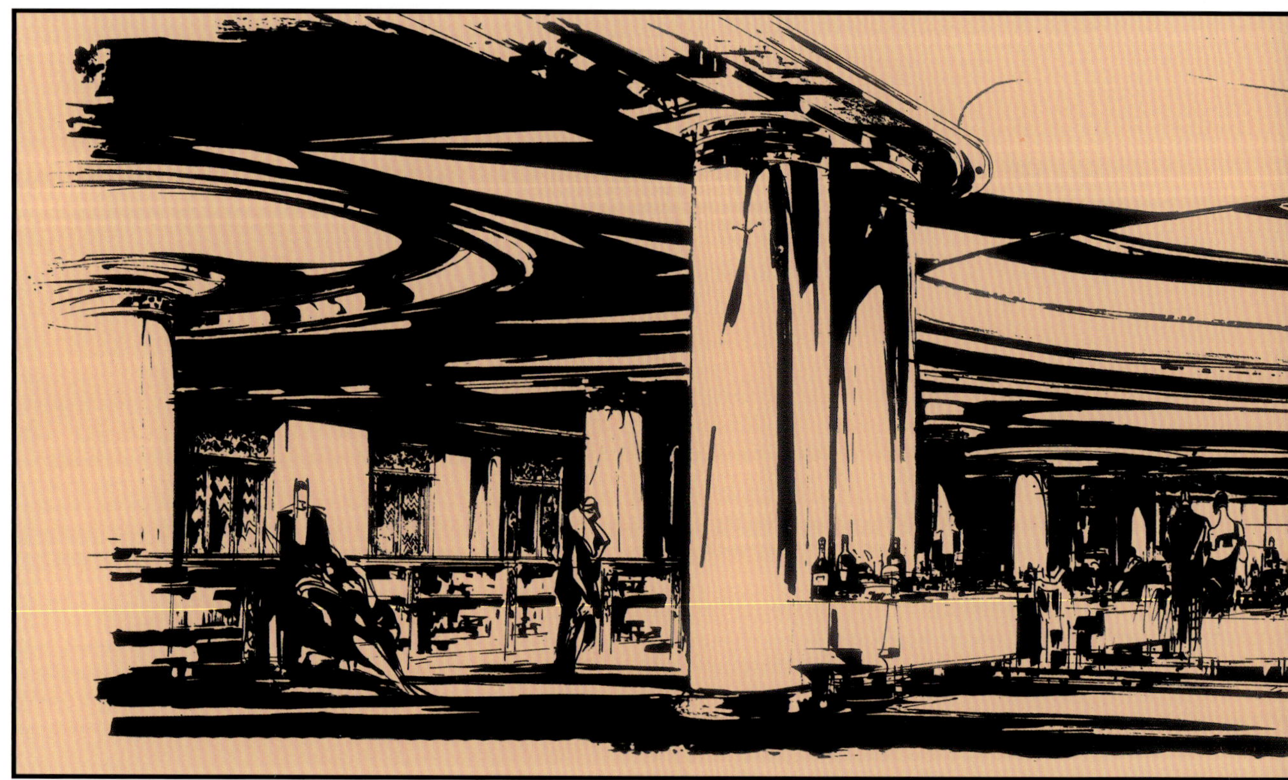

The Rainbow Room, designed by Marcel Hennequet, was acclaimed as an art deco classic immediately it was opened in 1933: 'The ceiling seems to float overhead as though one were inside a balloon,' enthused the architectural press, and four decades later the *New Yorker* said it was 'in a class with such masterpieces as the Chrysler Building and Radio City Music Hall.'.

The task for Biba was not to change but to restore the room to its original grandeur. The most expensive item in the building contract, it required the sympathetic addition of new facilities (a modern kitchen, for example), as well as the removal of all later elements, to recreate one of the splendours of 1930s London. And at the end of it all, the critics sighed with relief that it had been 'preserved intact'. 'Perhaps,' reflected the thankless designers, 'they all "remember" it as it should have been.'

Primarily a working restaurant, the Rainbow Room offered traditional British cuisine with a smattering of foreign dishes and with an adventurous health food and vegetarian counter, because 'there is more to healthy eating than a limp lettuce leaf, some tinned fruit salad and stale dandelion coffee.' In keeping with the longstanding Biba theme of non-intrusive staff, there was a strict rule that no tipping was expected or allowed.

But the Rainbow Room really made its name with the series of gigs that it staged. The New York Dolls played one of the first, an incendiary event that inspired what would become the punk generation, and were followed by the likes of Bill Haley, Cockney Rebel, the Ronettes and Ian Dury's first band, Kilburn & the High Roads. Regrettably Iggy Pop's two scheduled dates in 1974 were cancelled, but right at the end, in the last month of the store's existence, the swing revivalists Manhattan Transfer – the band who were born for Biba – performed there.

Here too was staged a private party for Liberace and members of his British fan-club, for which a cake in the shape of his piano was designed by Steven Thomas – it looked impressive, but required so much structural support that it couldn't be cut. After the store closed, the venue saw the filming of the promotional film for Bryan Ferry's single 'Let's Stick Together'.

Also on the fifth floor was an exhibition space that was used for a Marilyn Monroe photographic retrospective and for the launch of the book *Rock Dreams*, a collaboration between writer Nik Cohn and Belgian artist, Guy Peellaert. It was at the latter show that David Bowie met Peellaert and commissioned him to paint the cover of his next album, *Diamond Dogs* (thus annoying Mick Jagger, who had intended the artist to do the new Rolling Stones sleeve). 'Biba itself,' wrote Bowie, 'seemed to me an excellent place to show off the pictures as it also has an up-to-the-minute appearance combined with a lovely, nostalgic feel of the Thirties.'

An alternative view came from Dennis Potter, who described Biba as a 'tat palace in Kensington High Street which has timed its Thirties decor to such perfection that it only wants a pavement band of the unemployed outside.'

STAURANT

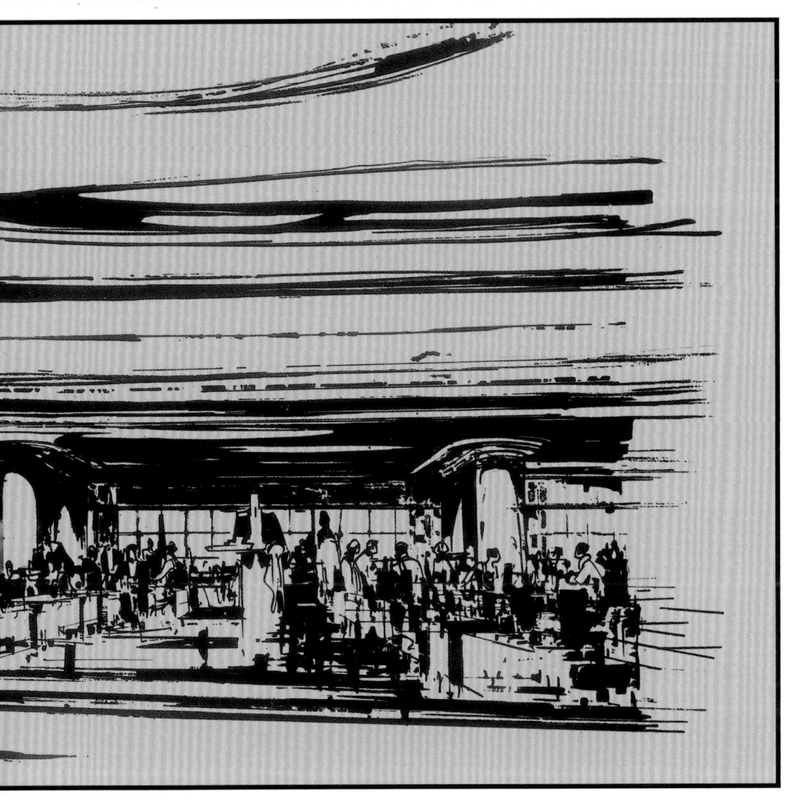

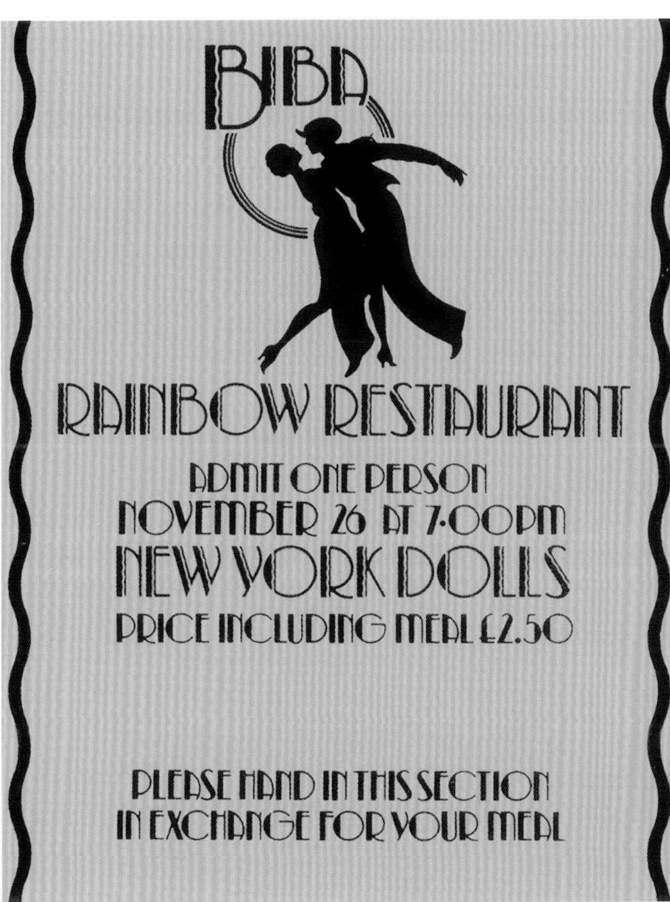

RAINBOW ROOM

MENU

STARTERS

Fish Sausage
Fish Tart
Mackerel Pate
Crudite and dressing
Smothered Ham
Herb Frittata
Briani with Yoghourt
Fish Soup
Chinese Noodles

MAIN COURSES

Boiled Beef and Carrots
Roast Beef
Roast Lamb
Roast Pork and Crackling
Turkey and Walnut Pie
Saudekraut and Kassleribben
Ham and Pease pudding
Chicken and Cherries
Fishsnacks
Fish stew with Saffron Rice

PUDDINGS

Biba Rainbow Cake
Pouffs Pudding
Ginger syllabub
Hindi dessert
Strawberry Mousse
Yoghourt, nuts and raisins
Spotted Dick
Sorbets

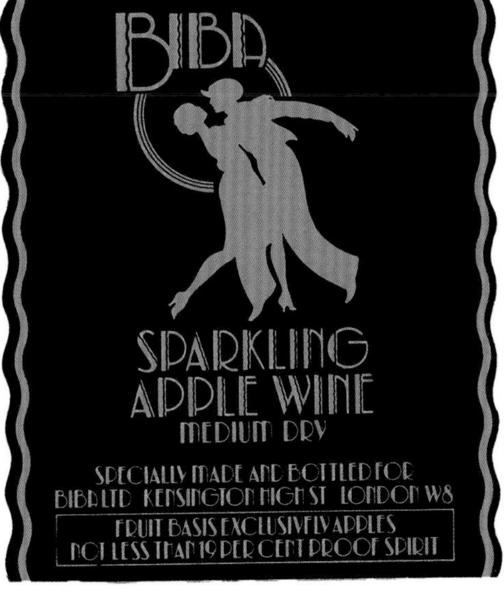

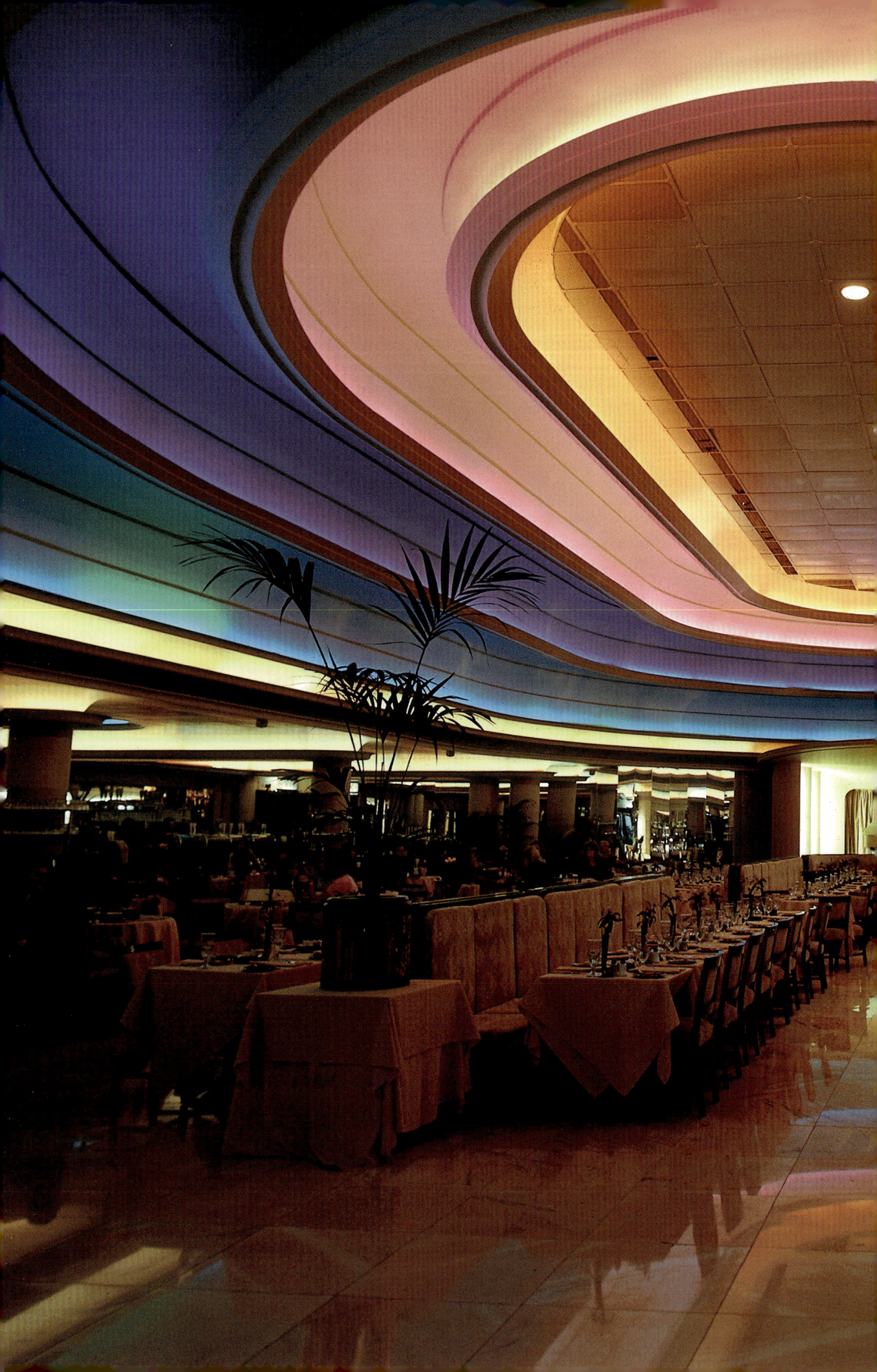

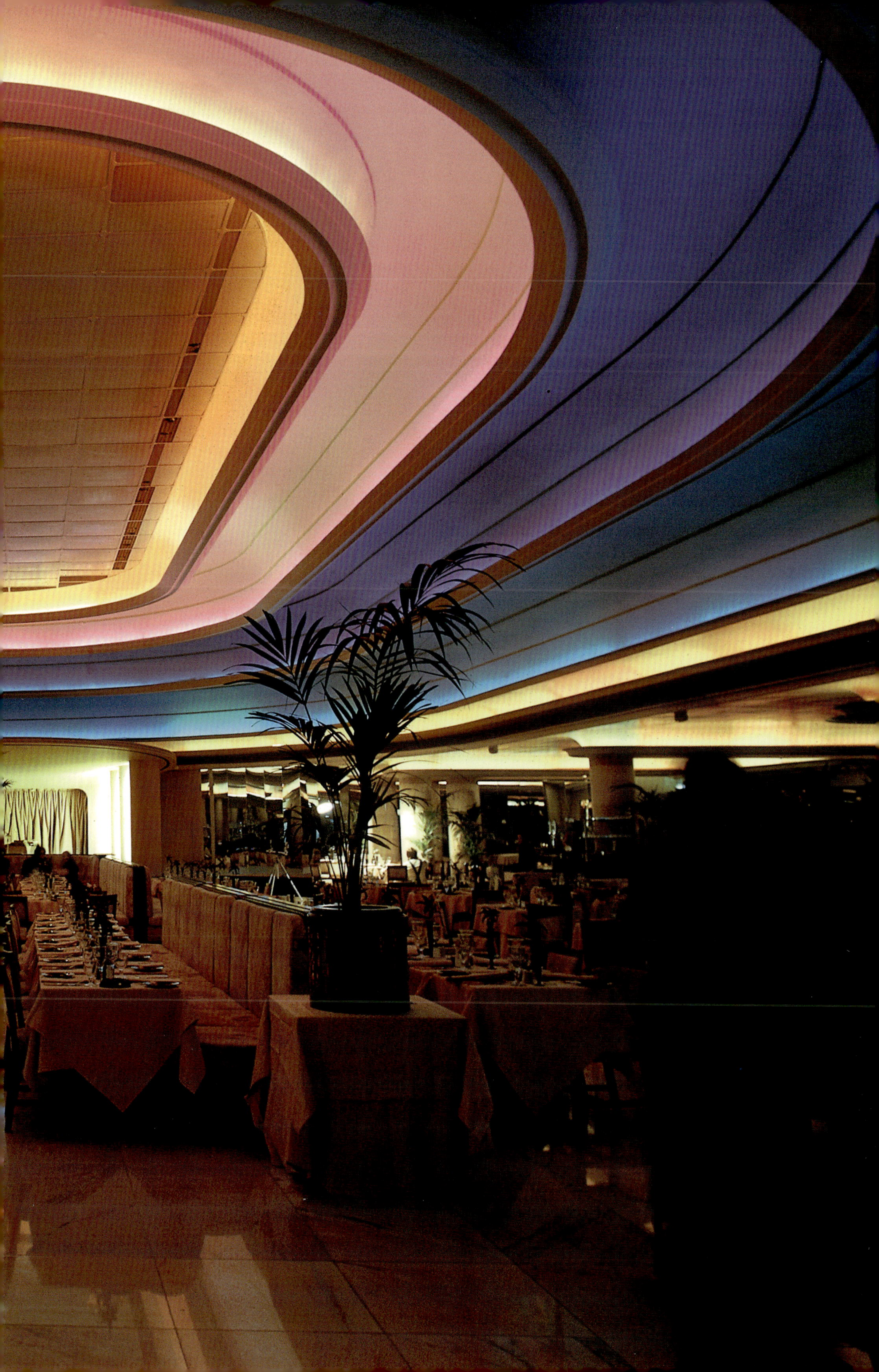

THE ROOF GARDEN

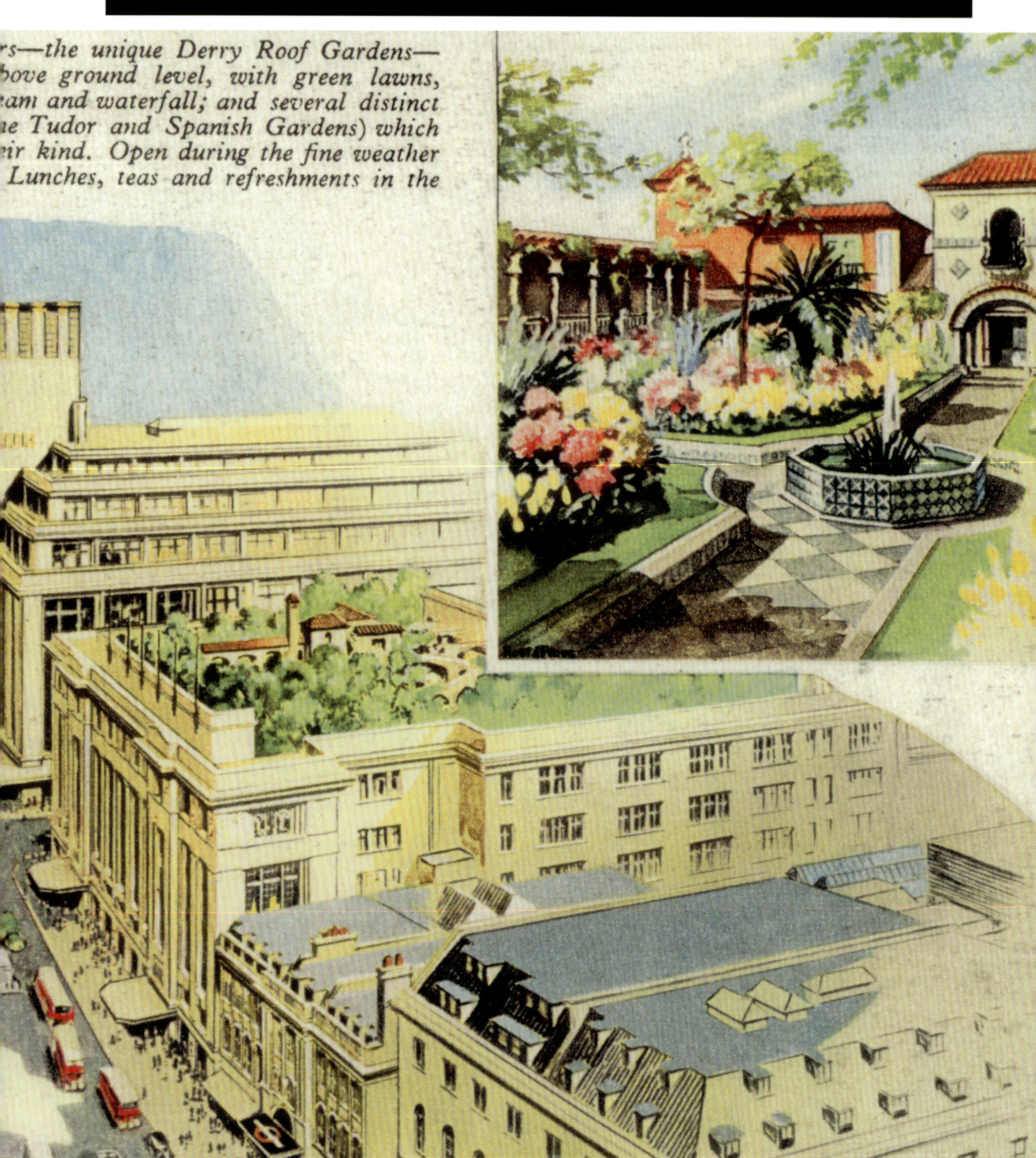

Designed by Ralph Hancock in 1936-38, and opened by Queen Mary, the acre and a half of gardens, some 30 metres above street level, became one of the most celebrated features of Derry & Toms. Above, part of the 1951 advertising campaign, taken from the 'Festival of Britain' launch brochure.

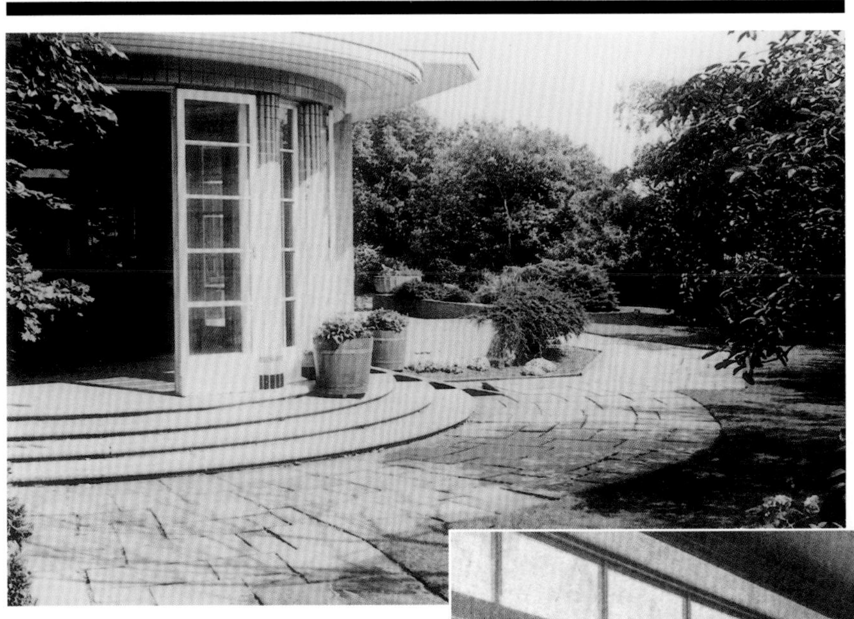

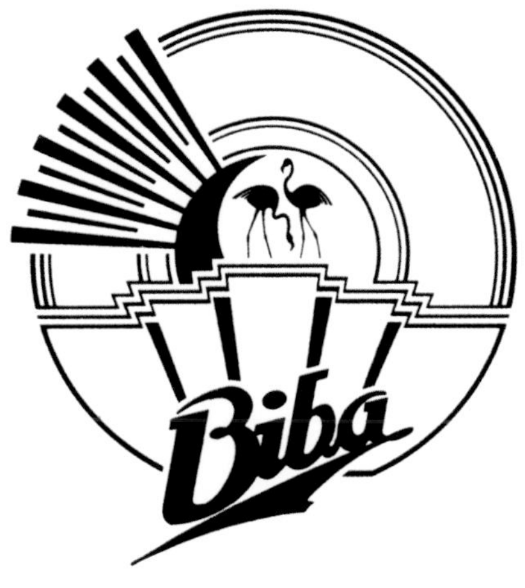

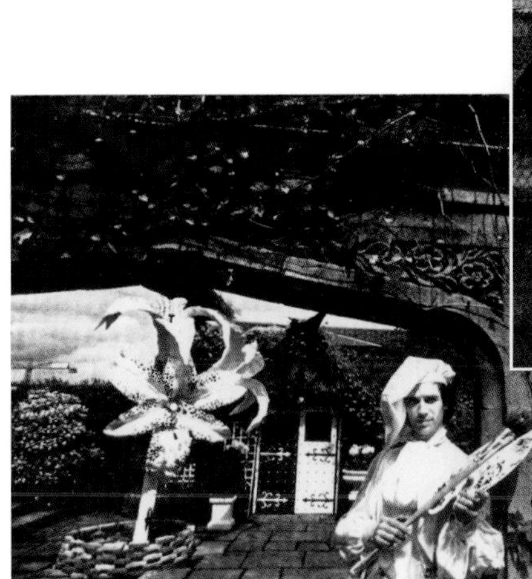

In May 1974 the roof gardens were re-opened with one of the great parties of the decade. 'It was like walking into a film set of rather jolly moral depravity,' wrote Sandy Fawkes in the *Daily Express*, neatly summing up the Biba experience.

Little had changed in the gardens, save for the addition of Andrew Logan's extraordinary 15-foot high horticultural sculptures ('I think of this as the Sistine Chapel of Kensington,' he commented). The division of space into an English woodland garden, a Tudor garden and a Spanish garden remained, and the flamingos that had become identified with the place returned in force, alongside ducks, doves, and penguins, though the penguins failed to settle and soon took their leave.

The pavilion meanwhile was re-opened as the Roof Garden Restaurant. Decorated in beige and fawn, and furnished with wicker and cane chairs and tables, it served lunch, dinner and – most importantly – tea, offering cucumber sandwiches, scones and cream cakes for one pound. It had, said Molly Parkin, 'a sort of gracious living, Somerset Maugham, champagne and caviar style.'

EPILOGUE

For five years Biba had been an independent company. Then in 1969 a new company was formed and the majority of the shares in Biba Ltd were sold to Dorothy Perkins, which in turn became a wholly owned subsidiary of the property firm British Land in August 1973, just a month before the opening of Big Biba.

The timing couldn't have been worse. The oil crisis, the rise in world commodity prices, the miners' strike and the three-day week combined to produce a property slump that reduced British Land's shares to just 10% of their value within a matter of months. Big Biba, which always had been expected to make a loss in its first trading period as it bedded in, found itself under heavy pressure from its parent company, increasingly desperate to show a quick profit.

The need for the elegant escapism of Big Biba was never greater, but behind the scenes the financial strain was starting to tell. By July 1974 relations between Barbara Hulanicki and Stephen Fitz-Simon on the one hand and the management of British Land and Dorothy Perkins on the other had reached terminal collapse, and in October, after barely a year of operations, the founders of Biba were informed that 'you will cease to be involved in the day-to-day management of the store and of the cosmetics business.'

The store staggered on, but it was living on borrowed time. In March 1975 the third and fourth floors were closed down. The ambitious plans to add a cinema on the fifth floor and a tennis court on the roof (doubling as an ice rink in winter) were clearly long since lost.

In August the last rites were read, and in September 1975 the most beautiful store in the world finally expired. With it died the last vestiges of the '60s dream that the revolution would be stylised.

'The birds in High Street Ken seemed to've grown longer legs since I was there last,' noted Brian Freeborn's anti-hero, Harry Grant, in the classic crime novel *Ten Days, Mr Cain?* as he returned to London in 1976. 'But Biba had gone quiet.'

And life returned to a slightly duller normality.

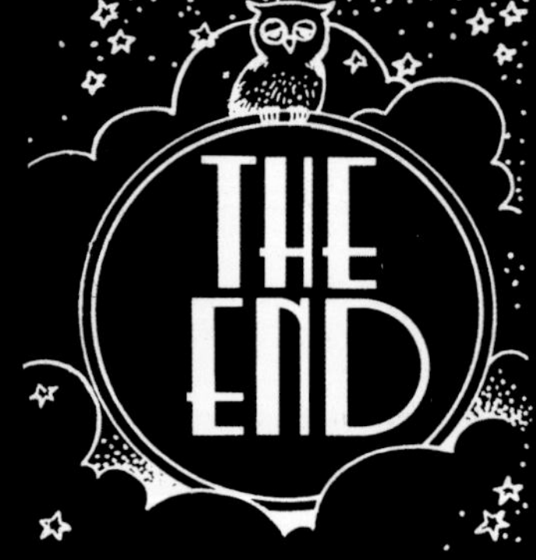

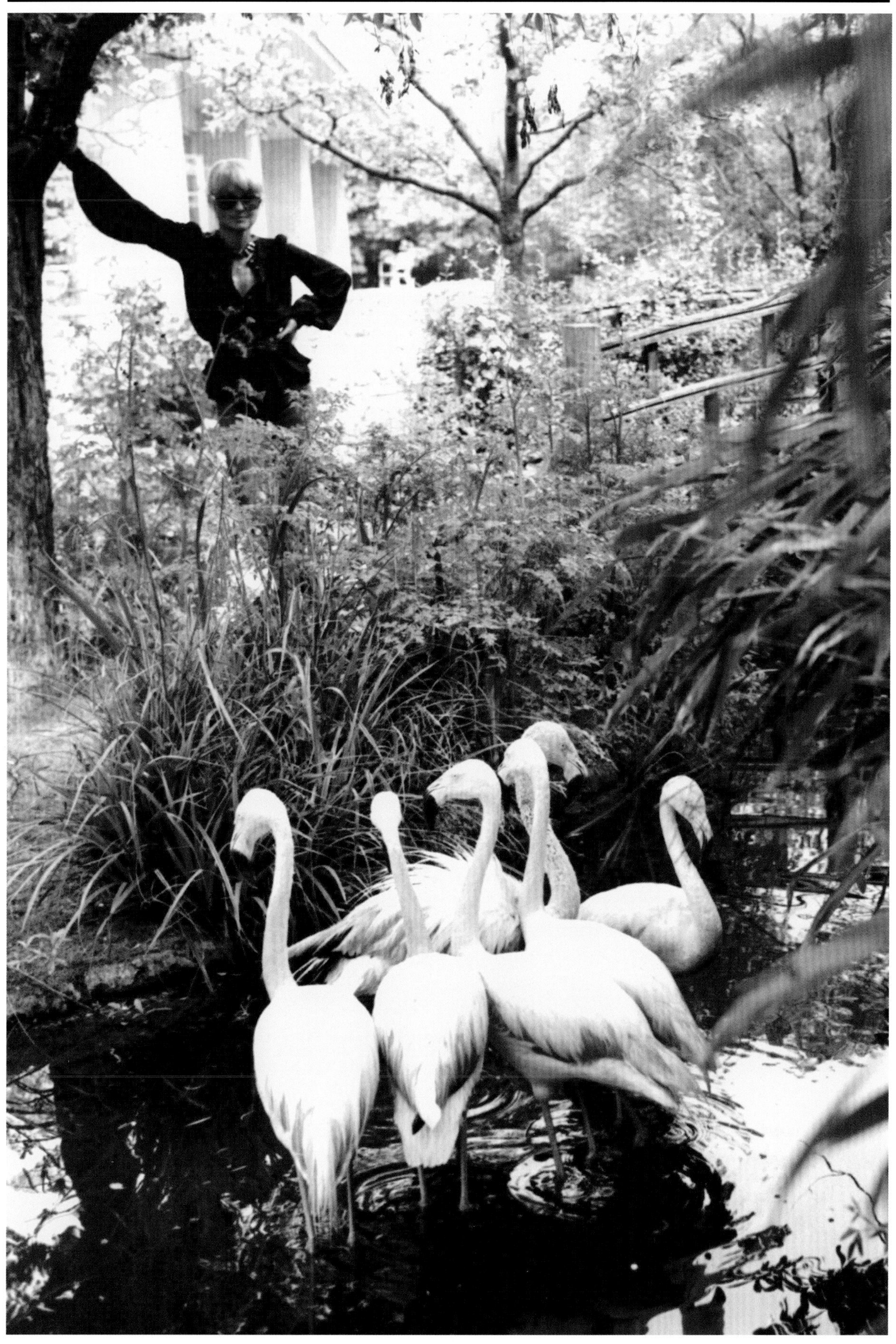

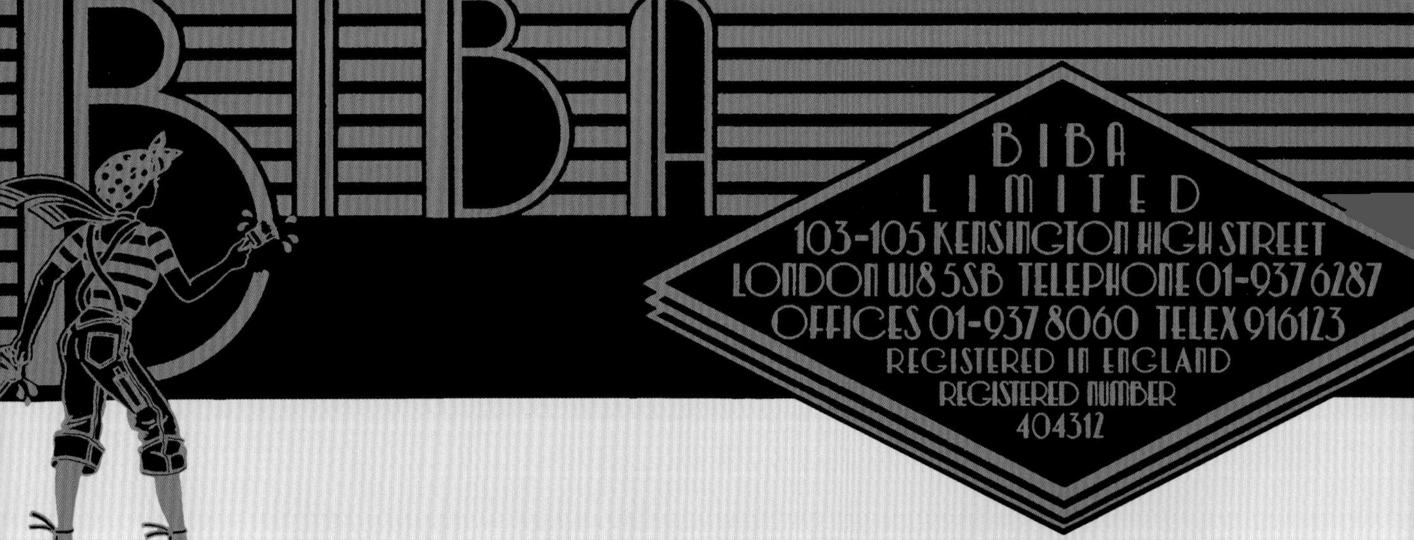

APPENDIX

BIG BIBA OPENING DAY NEWSPAPER

10 SEPTEMBER 1973

THE FOLLOWING PAGES REPRODUCE THE NEWSPAPER HANDED OUT TO CUSTOMERS ON THE OPENING DAY OF BIG BIBA. THE TOTAL PRINT RUN COMPRISED 300,000 COPIES ON NEWSPRINT AND A LIMITED EDITION OF 1000 ON CREAM CARTRIDGE PAPER.

ART DIRECTION: STEVEN THOMAS

GRAPHIC DESIGN AND TYPOGRAPHY:
CHRIS ANGELL AND MICK PARTLETT

ILLUSTRATION: KASIA CHARKO

ALL OF WHITMORE-THOMAS DESIGN ASSOCIATES

PHOTOGRAPHY:
BARBARA HULANICKI AND ROLPH GOBITS

TEXT: DAVID SMITH

Produced by Stephen Fitz-Simon and David Smith

I L FARMER / CHAIRMAN
S C FITZ-SIMON / MANAGING DIRECTOR
B S FITZ-SIMON DAVID ROXBURGH R D COLLARD

BIBA

SEE CENTRE PAGES AND PLAY **LIFTS & STAIRCASES** PLUS **FREE POSTER**

WELCOME TO THE NEW BIBA

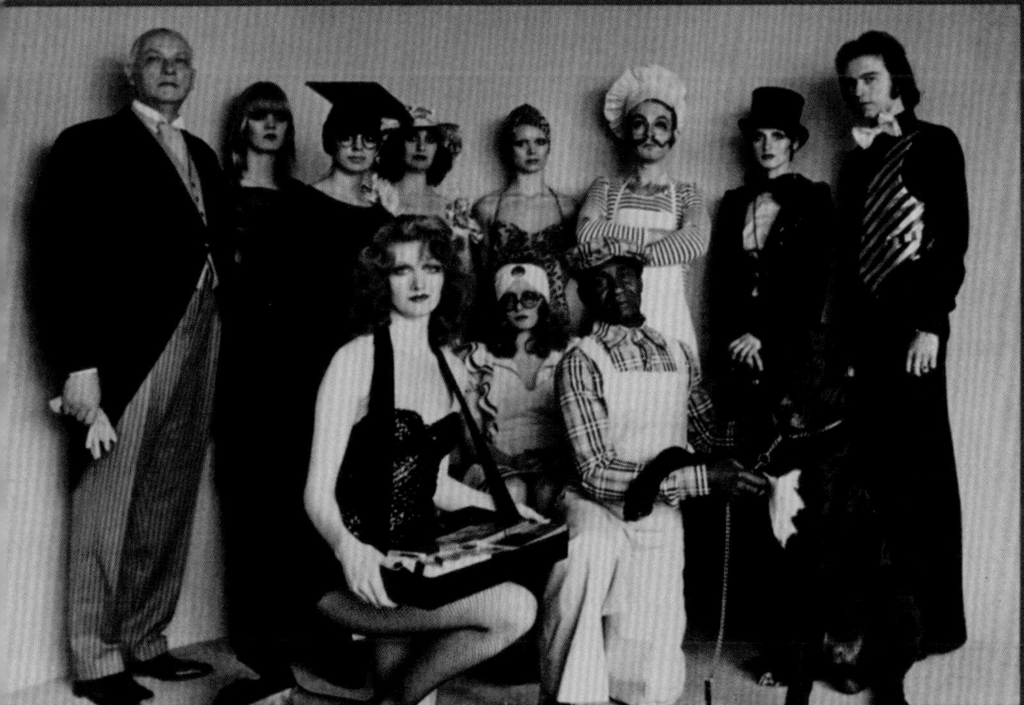

The waiter, the doorman and the upstairs maid . . . you'll see them all at Biba, each in a special uniform.

FIFTH FLOOR
See pages 14 and 15
The Rainbow Restaurant
to eat, drink, meet friends, dance and be happy in.

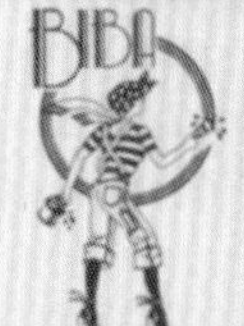

FOURTH FLOOR
See page 13
Household
Furniture, room-sets, china and glass, kitchenware, paint, fabric and wallpaper.

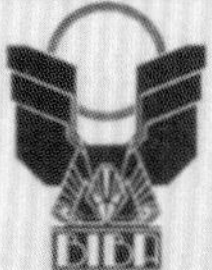

THIRD FLOOR
See pages 11 and 12
Men Only
Only the Mistress Room separates the men from the boys.

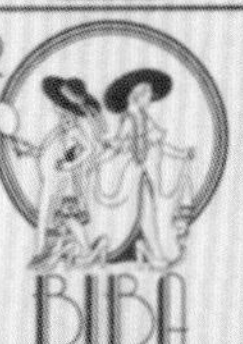

SECOND FLOOR
See page 6
Children
Everything for babies, children, 'Lolitas' and pregnant Mums.

FIRST FLOOR
See pages 4 and 5
The Biba Floor
Clothes, and more clothes, and colour-matched accessories.

GROUND FLOOR
See pages 2 and 3
Accessories
Accessories of all kinds; shoes, hats, tights and underwear, sweaters, jewellery, cosmetics, leather, books and newspapers, stationery, sounds, Casbahand Men's Sweaters.

BELOW STAIRS
See back page
Food
Everything to eat and drink – take-home meals.

rom the moment you step inside Biba for the first time, we want ›u to know your way around and feel at home. This tells you ›w the store is laid out, and about some of the departments at are new to Biba.

ıe index on the right shows ıat is on each floor, and on ıich page that department is entioned. There is a pull-out ›ster on the centre spread, and ı the reverse, a 'snakes and dders' game that also tells you ıite a lot about the store.

LIFT SERVICE

The lifts serve each floor, and ere is an escalator to the first ›or. The best way to see every-ing is to use the stairs—they e a happening in themselves, ıd the music is very uplifting. Welcome to Biba. We hope at you will enjoy it here.

Mary is a little lamb,
She's kind from head to toe.
And anything that Mary's asked –
Well, Mary's sure to know!

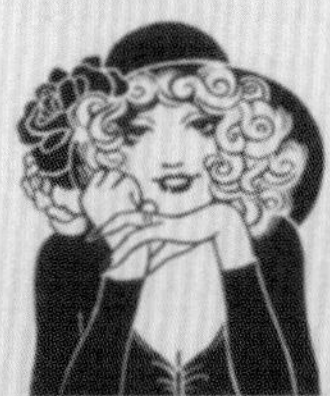

You'll find Mary sitting in the information booth by the lifts on the ground floor, so if you can't find what you're looking for, just ask Mary. And if you're on the first floor, well – there's another Mary there, too.

Opening hours: Biba is open from 9.30 to 8.00 from Monday to Friday, and from 9.30 to 5.30 on Saturdays. The Rainbow Restaurant is open from 9.30 to 2.30 am from Monday to Saturday, and from 10.00 to 12.00 pm on Sundays. (Outside the store's opening hours, the Rainbow Restaurant is reached by the entrance in Derry Street, and a direct lift service to the 5th floor.)

Loos: On the 5th floor. There are loos for children only on the 2nd floor.

Telephones: public call-boxes are on the ground floor, by the escalators and on the 5th floor.

Public transport: Underground to Kensington High Street (Circle and District lines), or buses 73, 9, 28, 31, 52 (Church Street), 33, 27 or 49.

Cheques: acceptable only when supported by a recognised banker's card.

Parking: you must be joking! (However, there is parking space for evening visitors to the Rainbow Room in the loading-bay off Derry Street. Please do **not** park in Kensington Square.)

Deliveries: sorry – only for large pieces of furniture, and then only in the London area.

The Roof Garden will not be open until next Spring. Meanwhile, the flamingos are alive and well and staying with friends.

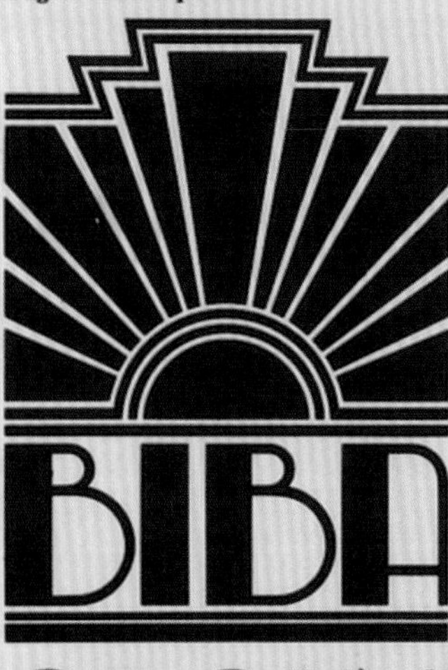

GROUND FLOOR

If you think at first glance that the ground floor sells just about everything, you'd be almost right. But remember – there are six more floors!

A lot of the stock here is things you come in for when you're in a hurry. A pair of tights. A lipstick. Today's paper. A bunch of flowers. That sort of thing.

But you could also stay longer, choosing some new shoes, or browsing in the bookshop, or listening to the new LPs.

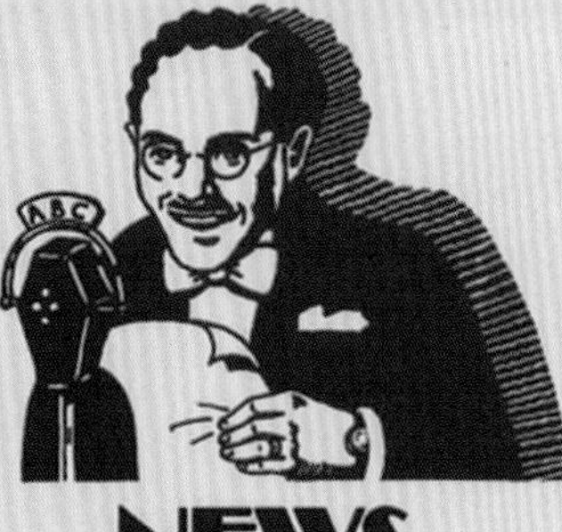

NEWS

Apart from your usual British dailies and magazines, there is a multi-national array of foreign newspapers and periodicals.

COSMETICS

Here's the whole paintbox, in lipsticks, mascaras, nail varnishes and powder. Scents and colognes, too, and cosmetic accessories, from emery-boards to silk-tasselled scent-sprays.

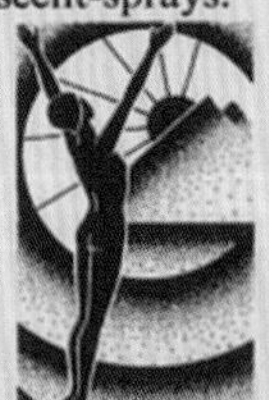

HEALTH RANGE

You will also find our new Health Range – cosmetics and skin preparations specially formulated for the tender loving care of faces and bodies.

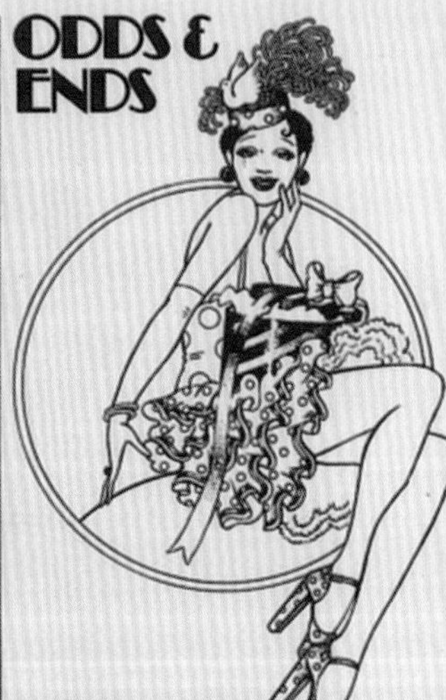

ODDS & ENDS

Full of scarves, hats, hatpins and thoroughly modern millinery; and some that's not so modern, such as veiling by the yard.

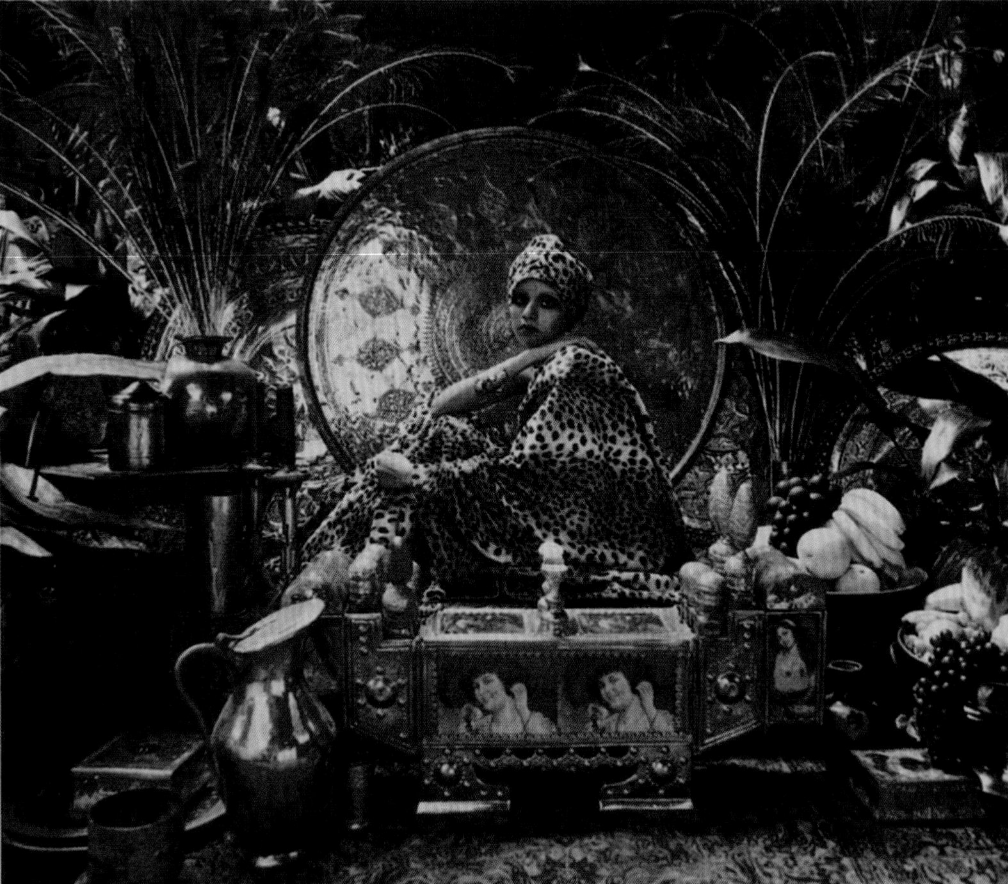

TIGHTS AND UNDERWEAR

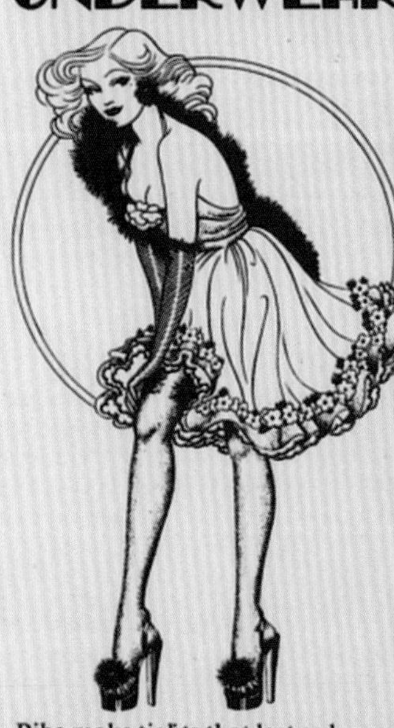

Biba make tights that last as long as possible, but you still go through them. Never mind, there are plenty more, in 24 colours yet this winter. As for underwear, there are pants and bras, and bra and pants sets, that don't cost a bomb. If you want to spend more, go up to the gallery Room on the first floor.

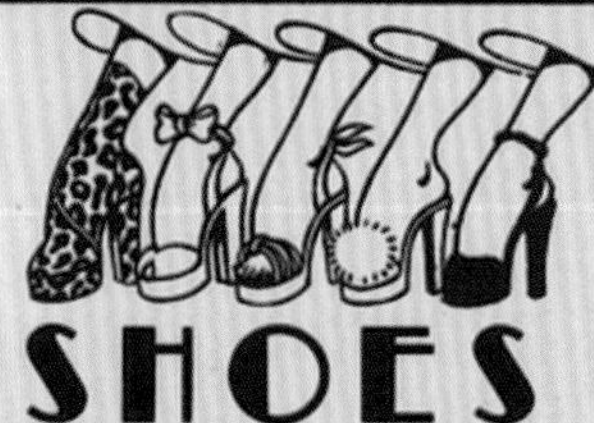

SHOES

Not to mention boots, slippers, espadrilles, sneakers, evening shoes and gumboots. You'll find them all in the middle of the ground floor, so just direct your feet.

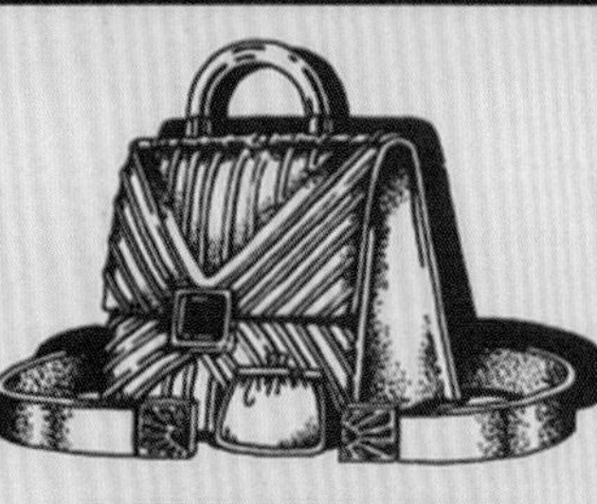

LEATHER

Bags and suitcases and holdalls, in leather or canvas, for globetrotting or weekending. Smaller things too, such as notecases and chequebook covers, evening bags and purses, belts and watchstraps.

SOUNDS

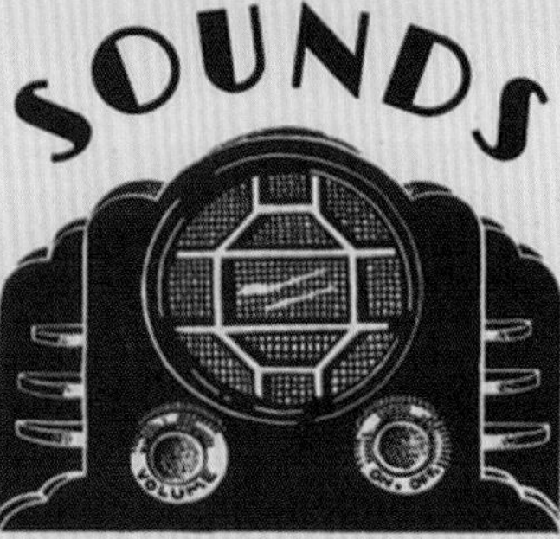

Biba, as your ears will have told you by now, is wired for sound. Those you like (and others too) can be bought at the 'Sounds' counter – records, tapes, cartridges or cassettes.

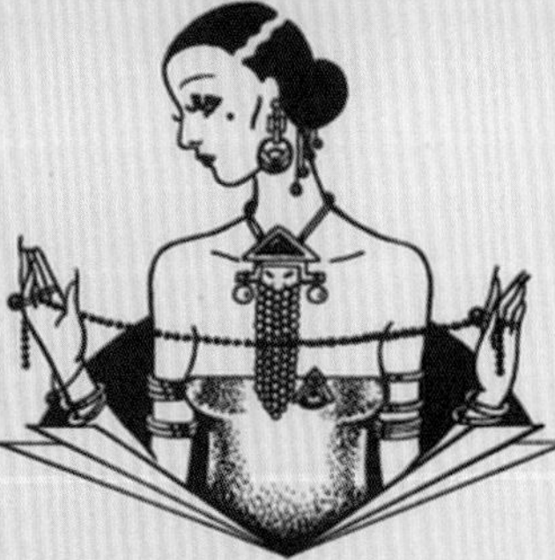

JEWELLERY

If all that glitters here is not real gold, it's probably silver or tortoiseshell. Bracelets, necklaces, barbaric chokers, earrings. And watches too.

SWEATERS FOR MEN

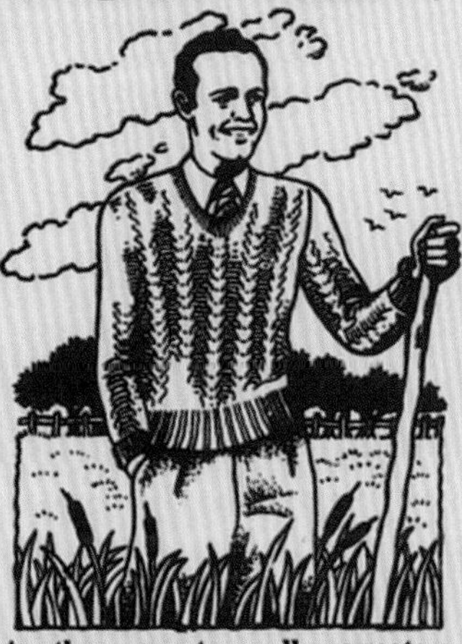

Another counter sells sweaters, cardigans and T-shirts for men.

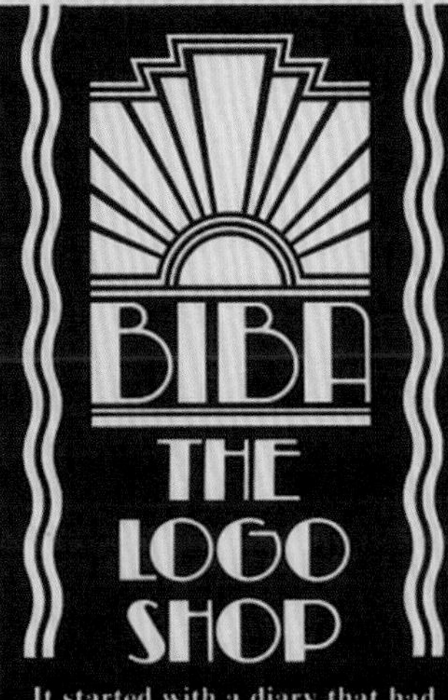

THE LOGO SHOP

It started with a diary that had the Biba logo design on it. Now there are Biba posters, playing cards, greeting cards, balloons, chocolates, matches, ashtrays . . . all sorts of things.
And if you want to gift-wrap anything in the store, you can take home black tissue paper and black satin ribbon.

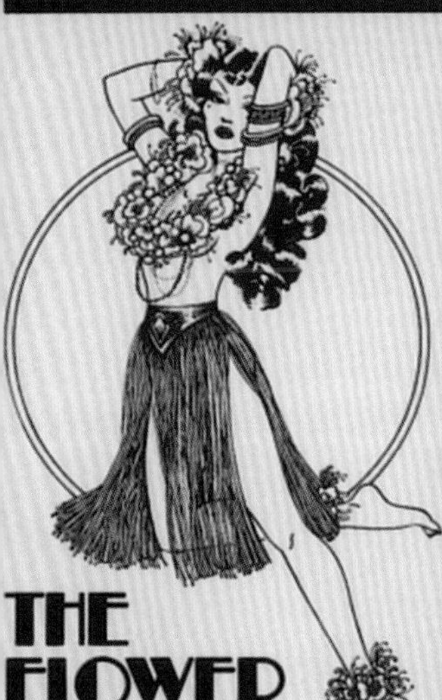

THE FLOWER SHOP

As many flowers as we can find that are fresh and beautiful. And a few honest fakes – artificial flowers, palms and grass.

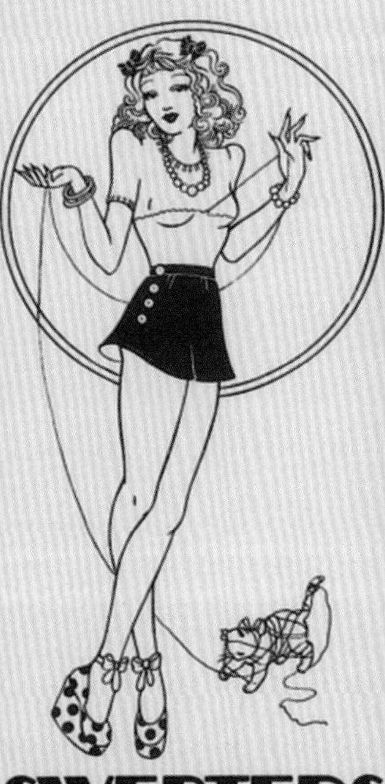

SWEATERS

A whole counter devoted to sweaters, cardigans, evening tops and T-shirts, all in 24 special Biba colours.

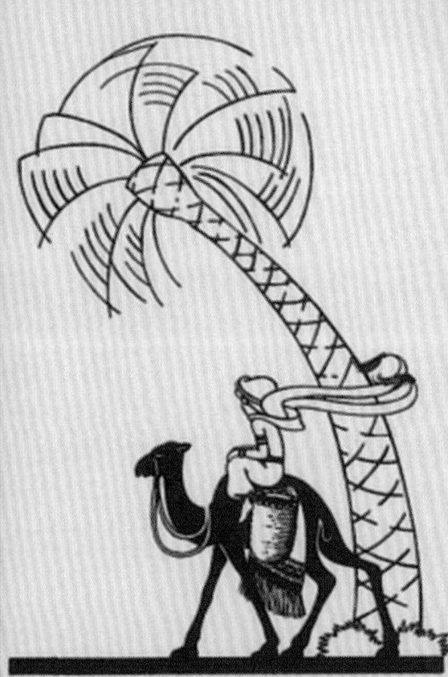

THE CASBAH

Turkey . . . Tunisia . . . India . . . Morocco . . . China . . . Biba really shopped around. The result is a bazaar-ful of mysterious goodies. Apart from the exotic clothes, there are slippers and fezzes and mantillas . . . cushions and bolsters, rugs and mats . . . jewellery, lanterns, knives and pistols . . . toys and clean postcards . . . henna for your hair and kohl for your eyes.
So come to the Casbah. It's worth the trip, for the incense alone.

THE BOOK SHOP

The most interesting new publications, with a strong emphasis on art books, and some books imported by Biba which you might otherwise miss. Browsing is encouraged. (If you buy a book and want to keep it, get some of the 'ex libris' stickers from the stationery counter.)

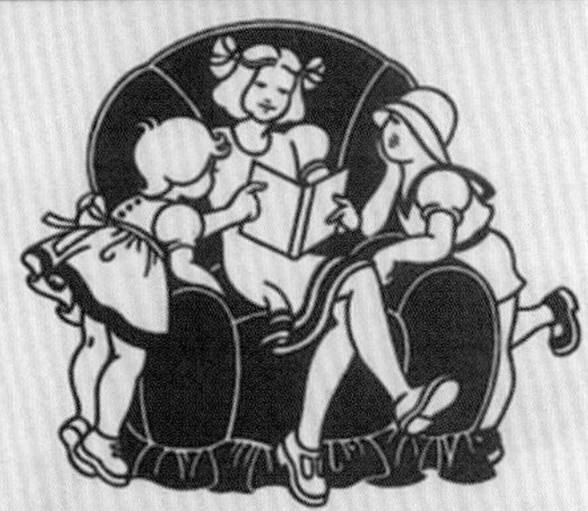

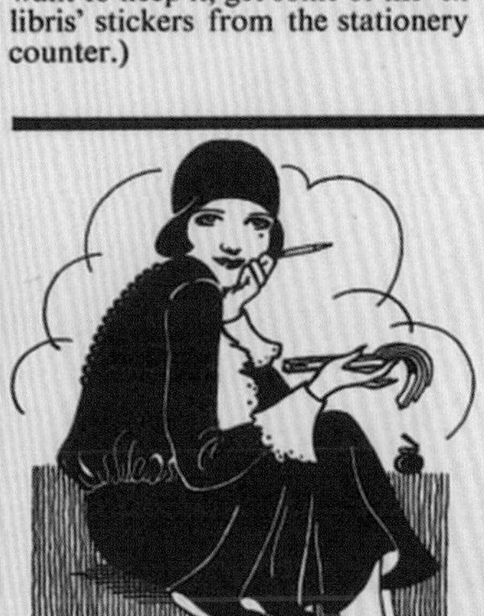

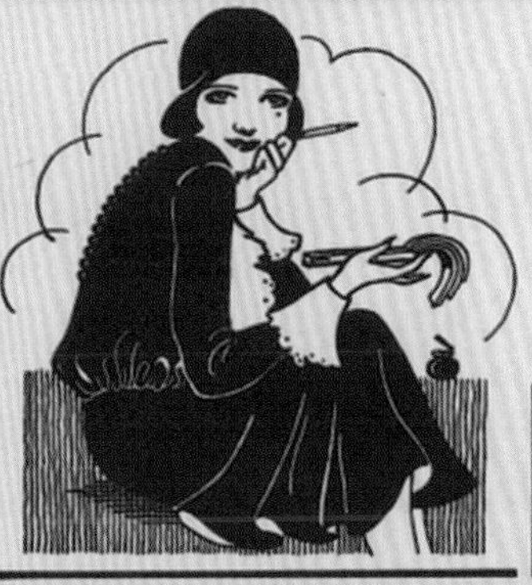

STATIONERY

Everything you need to keep in touch and stay organised, from a typewriter to a paperclip. Tidy-minded people like our fabric-covered range: files, record boxes, pencil tubs and even a small chest-of-drawers.

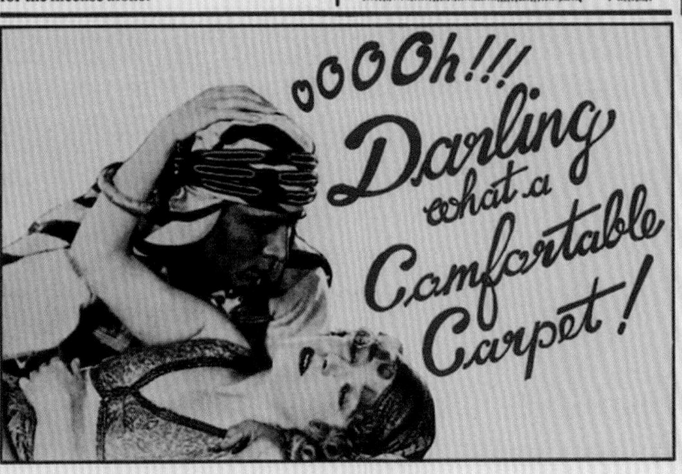

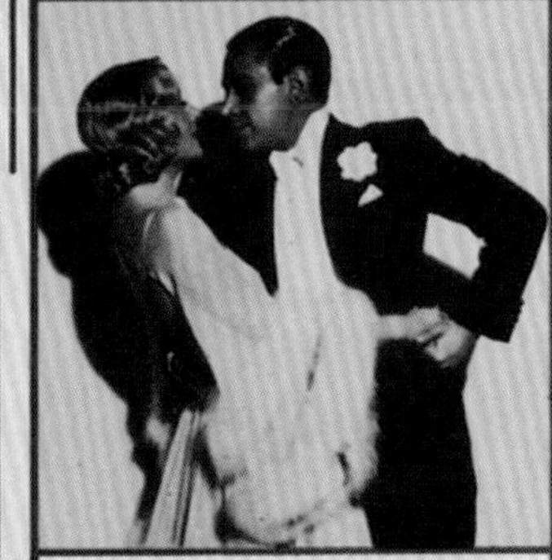

THE RAINBOW RESTAURANT

ONE OF THE NICEST PLACES TO EAT IN LONDON,
BIG MENU, LITTLE BILLS,
NO TIPS.

THE BIBA FLOOR

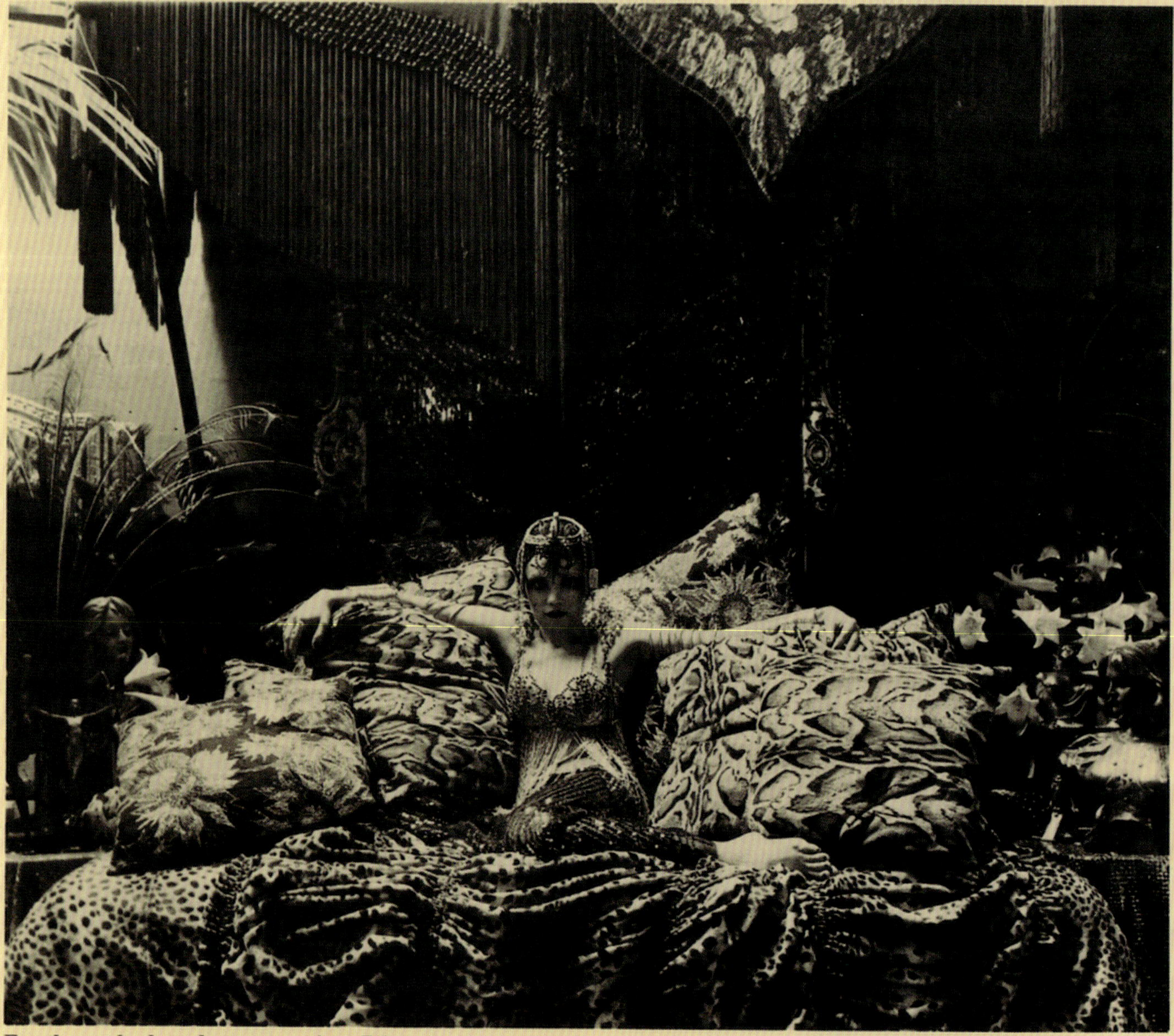

For those who have been to previous Bibas this floor will be vaguely familiar, this is where the clothes are, with units selling matching accessories dotted between the hat stands. The clothes here will change more frequently than anything in the store (except the food, flowers and newspapers) each day new things arrive.

One more thing: you won't hear that deathly phrase "Can I help you, Modom?" Almost everything is on the clothes-stands, so go ahead and browse.

All of the clothes can be colour-matched to different accessories – shoes, sweaters, cardigans, T-shirts, tights, bags, hats and flowers.

All these colour-matching accessories can be found on the different counters.

If you're aiming for a total make-over, you can also buy a selection of Biba cosmetics up here, although the largest stock is on the ground floor.

When you've found what you want, you'll find the cash-tills just inside the changing-room doors. (A word of warning: the changing-rooms are open plan. Please keep an eye on your valuables, especially your handbag, all the time.)

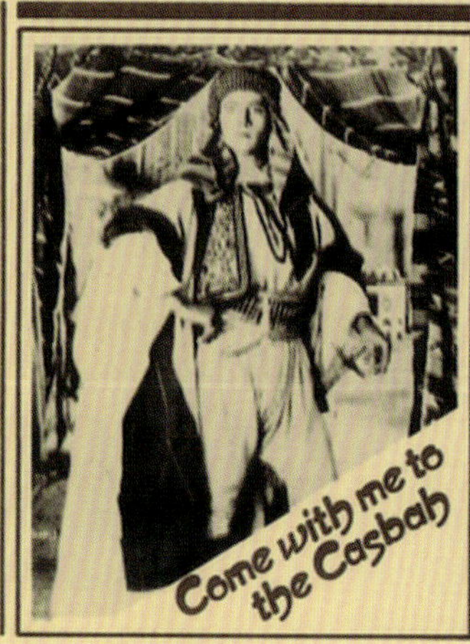

CATS EYES

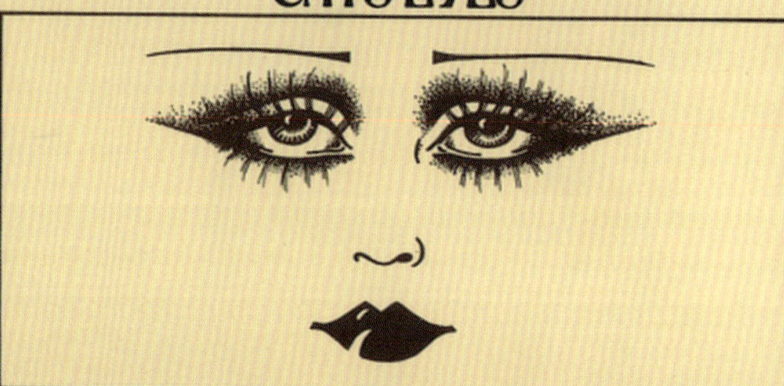

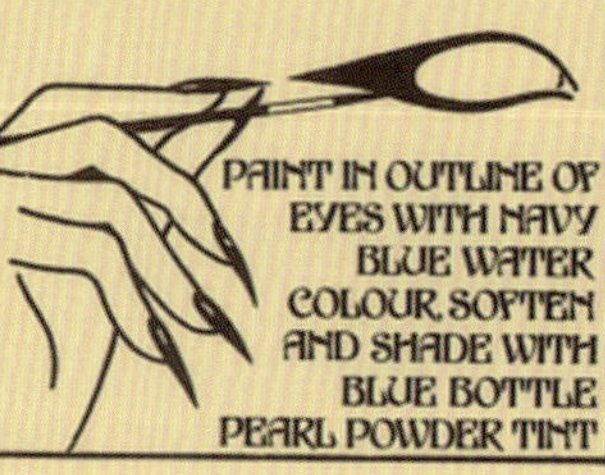

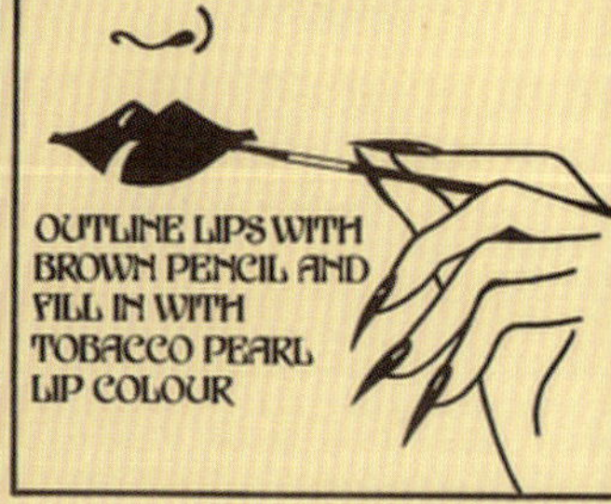

THE GALLERY

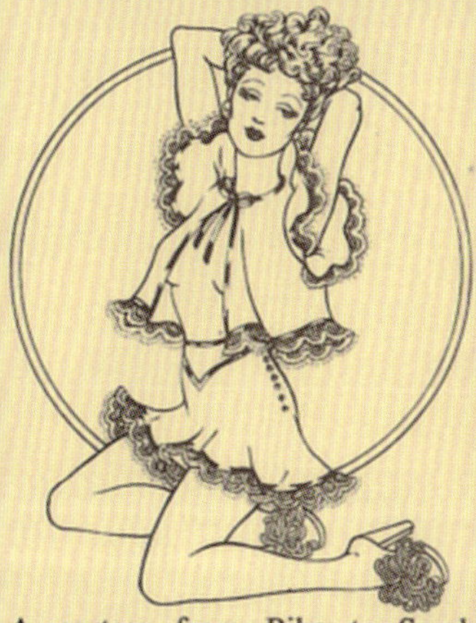

A curtesy from Biba to Sarah Bernhardt: the kind of very feminine clothes she might enjoy if she had lived in London now, instead of Paris then.

Negligees
Petticoats
Nightdresses
Dressing Gowns
Bras and Pants
Headbands

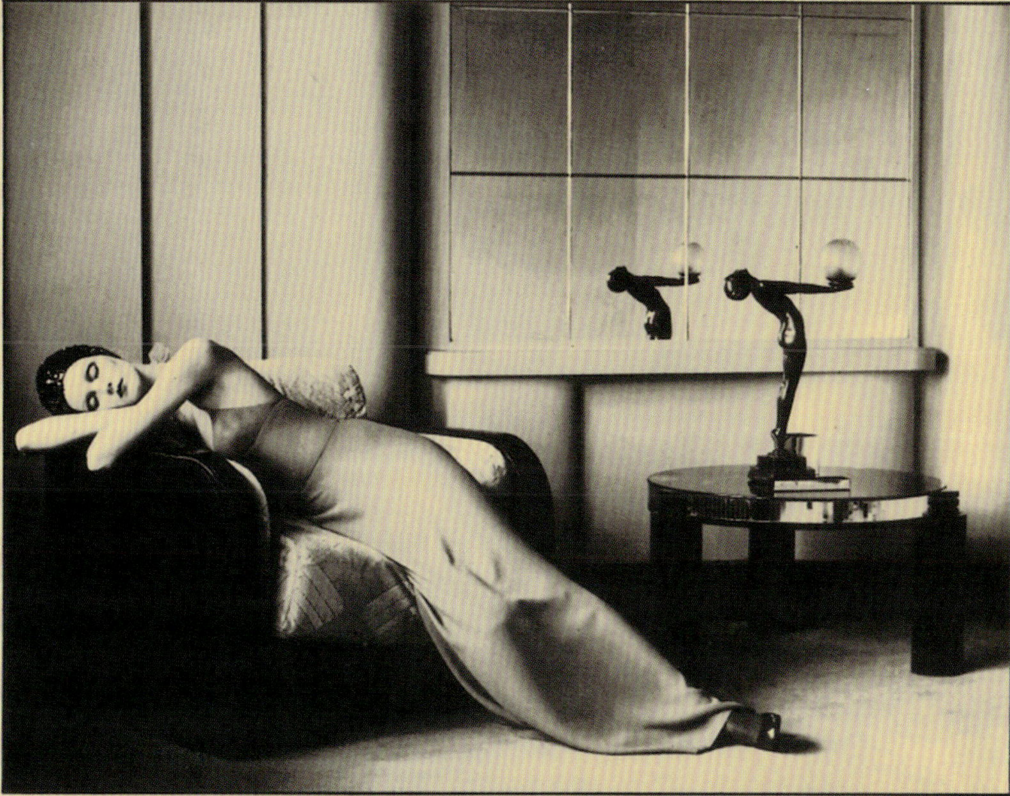

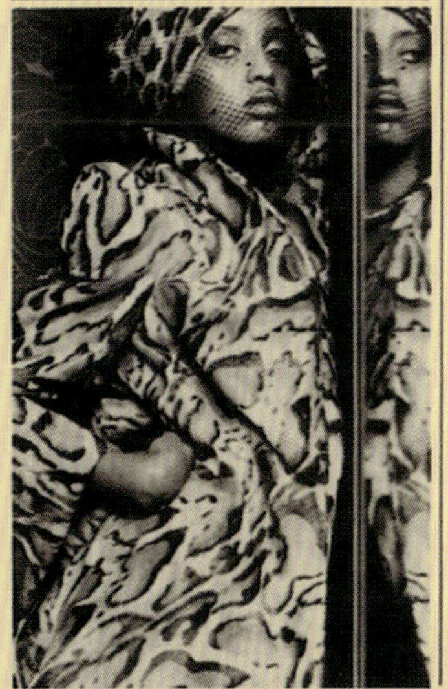

WINTER COLOURS 1973

ELECTRIC BLUE
RED CAMELIA PINK
ORCHID CREAM
JADE CYCLAMEN
AMETHYST ARMY
MIDNIGHT COPPER
BROWN PETROL
RAINBOW PINK
BLACK TOBACCO
NAVY SAND
DARK FLANNEL
PALE FLANNEL
PLUM CAMEL
THIN DENIM
THICK DENIM

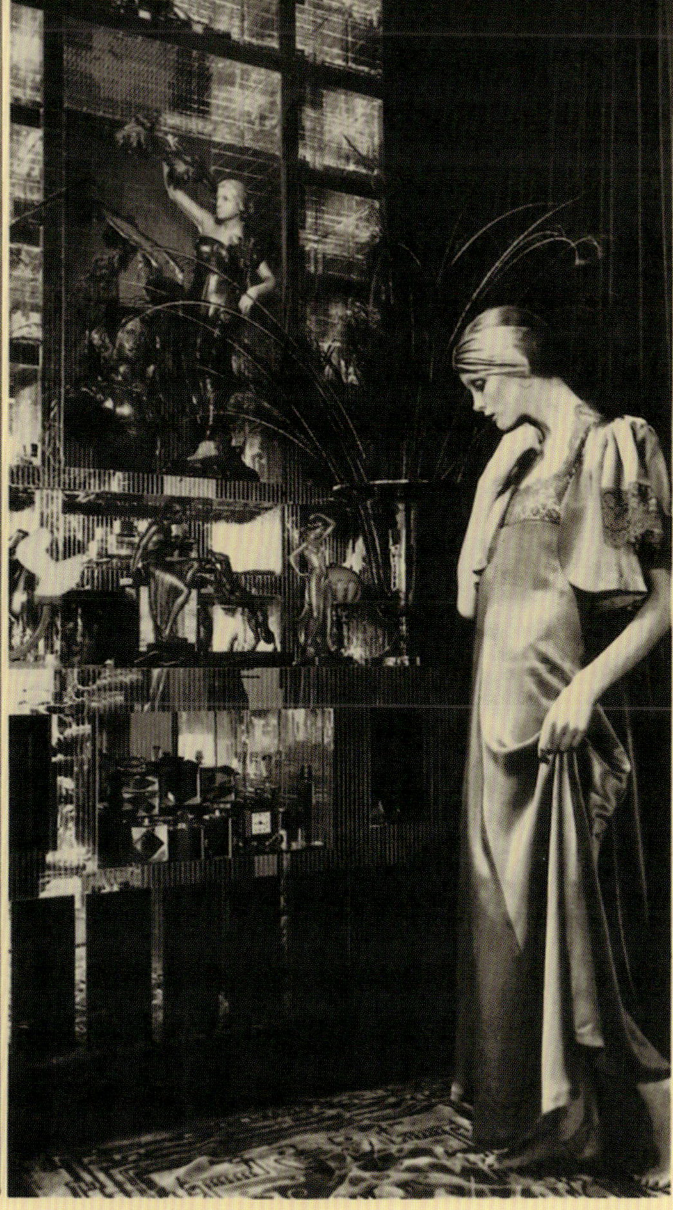

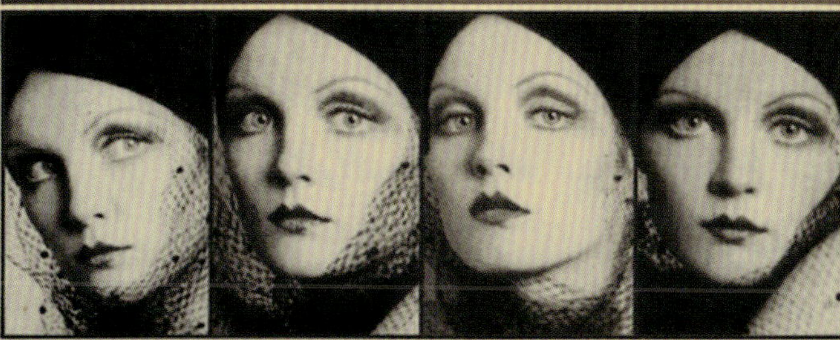

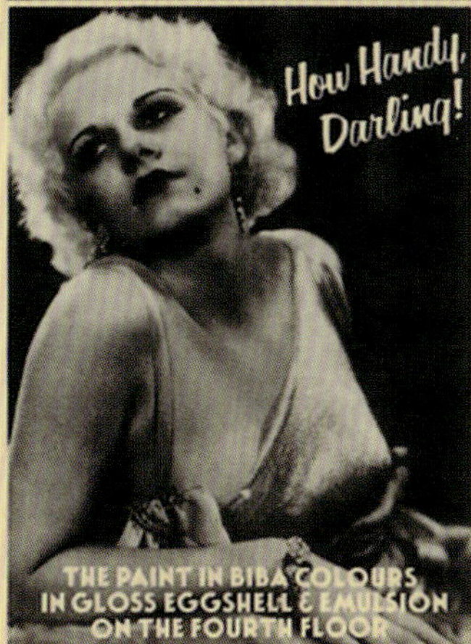

THE PAINT IN BIBA COLOURS IN GLOSS EGGSHELL & EMULSION ON THE FOURTH FLOOR

BIBA BODYMUSCLE OIL

FOR BORN SAND KICKERS
MENS DEPT THIRD FLOOR

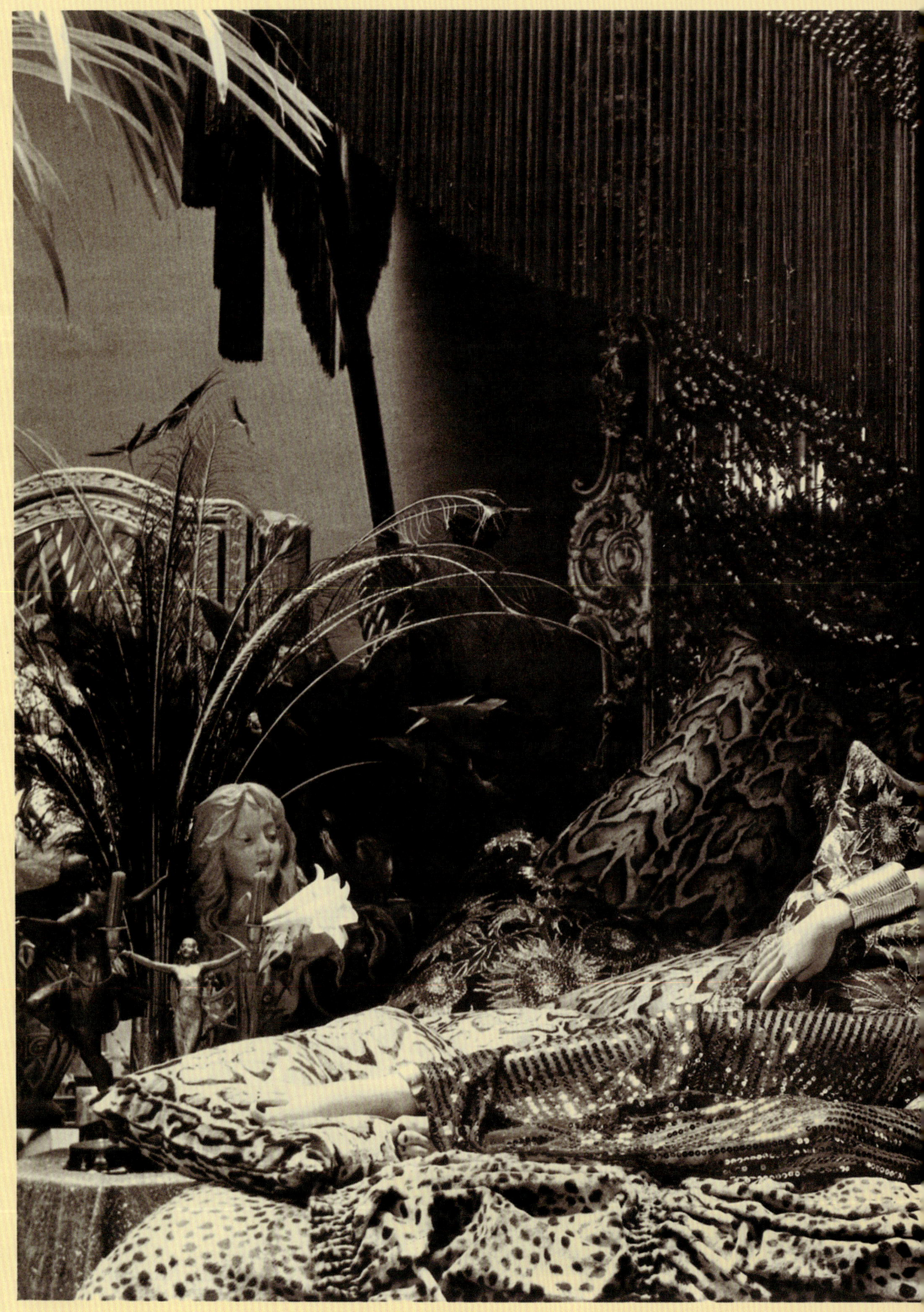

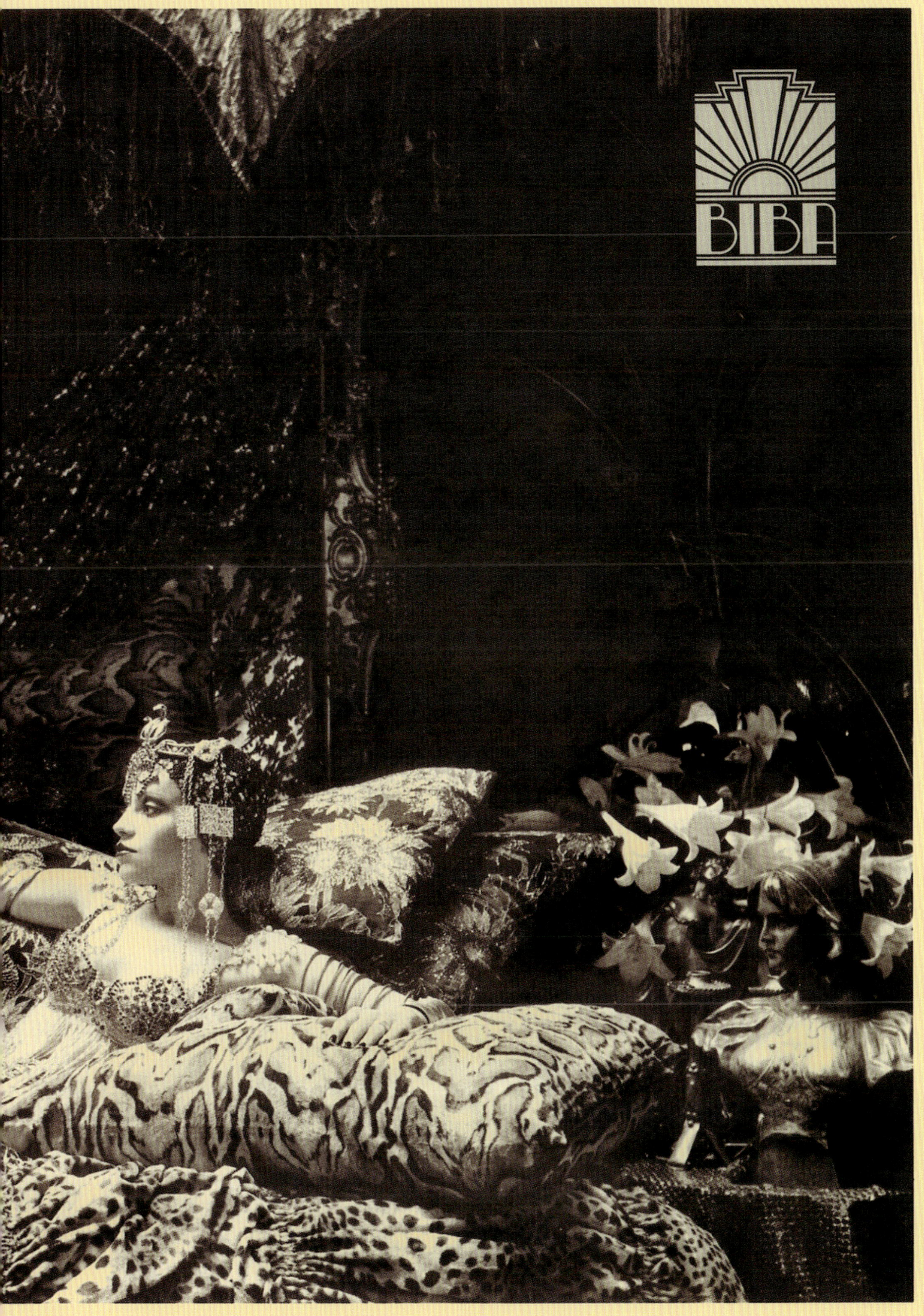
BIBA

PLAY 'LIFTS AND

ALL YOU NEED IS A DICE. PLAY IT LIKE SNAKE

FIFTH FLOOR THE RAINBOW ROOM

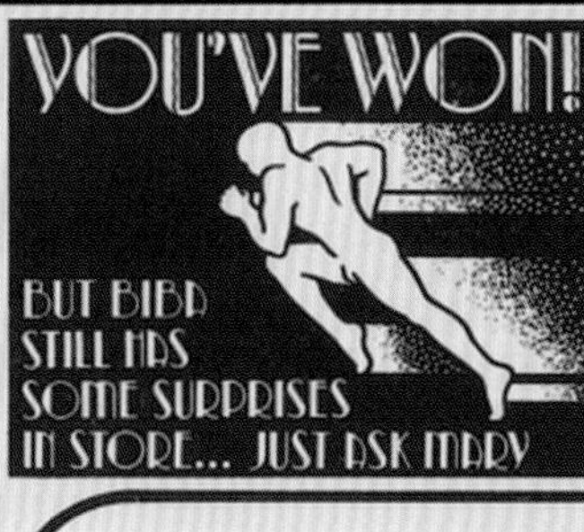

YOU'VE WON!

BUT BIBA STILL HAS SOME SURPRISES IN STORE... JUST ASK MARY

YOU CAN HAVE A QUICK LUNCH OR A LEISURELY DINNER, A CUP OF HOT COFFEE OR A COLD MILKSHAKE, A STEAK OR A SIMPLE SALAD, AT ALMOST ANY HOUR OF THE DAY.

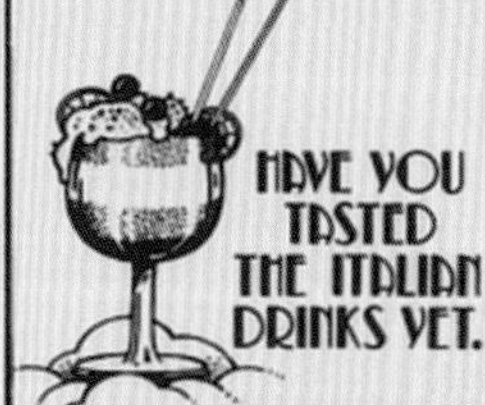

HAVE YOU TASTED THE ITALIAN DRINKS YET.

YOU MISTAKE YOUR AUNT FO MAE WEST. SHE IS SO FLATTER SHE ASKS YOU TO HELP HER C A NEW LAMPSHADE, MATCHING A WASTE-PAPER E THREE BA AND

FOURTH FLOOR HOUSEHOLD

ALL THOSE PLASTER DUCKS IN THE KITCH SHOP HAVE MADE YOU FEEL HUNGRY, YOU'D BETTER GO UP TO THE RAINBOW ROOM AND HAVE LUNCH. DUCK PATE?

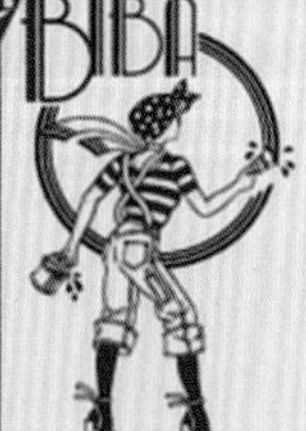

BIBA KNOWS A FEW TRADE SECRETS: ABOUT PAINT AND BRUSHES AND LADDERS AND SCREWS AND NAILS AND WALLPAPER. SSSH!

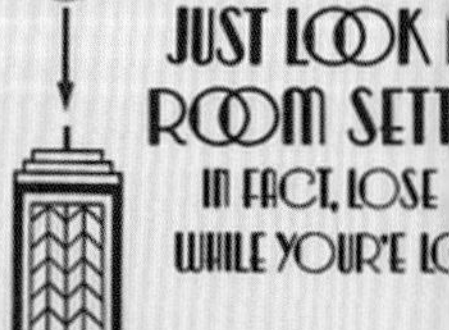

JUST LOOK ROOM SET IN FACT, LOSE WHILE YOU'RE L

THIRD FLOOR MENS & BOYS CLOTHES

YOU LOOK SO DISHY IN YOUR NEW BOW-TIE, YOU'D BETTER GO DOWNSTAIRS AND BUY YOURSELF A NEW ADDRESS BOOK IN THE LOGO SHOP. YOU'RE GOING TO NEED IT.

SNOOPY WINS, THE DOG. STAY ON THIS SQUARE - LOSE ONE TURN.

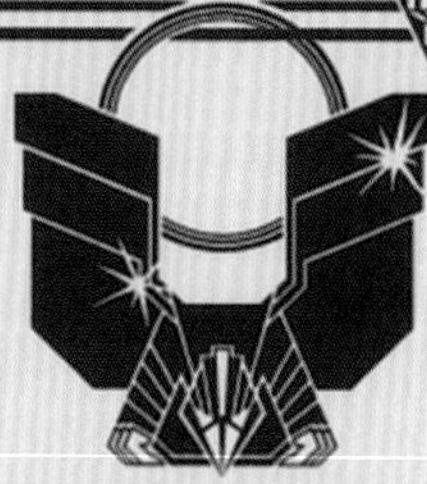

YOU HAVE JUST CRACKED THE SAFE IN THE MISTRESS ROOM. RUN UPSTAIRS WITH THE DIAMONDS!

SECOND FLOOR CHILDRENS WEAR

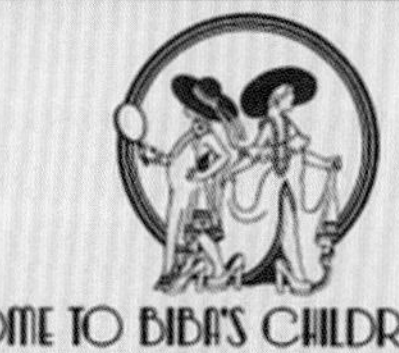

WELCOME TO BIBA'S CHILDRENS FLOOR IF YOU'RE UNDER 16 HAVE AN EXTRA THROW. IF YOU'RE OVER 16 LOSE A TURN.

HAVING A BABY WAS NEVER MORE FUN... SMOCKS, DRESSES, TROUSERS FOR FUTURE MUMS.

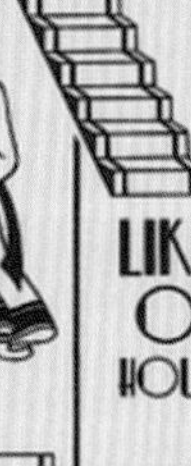

SNOOPY ASKS IF YOU FEEL LIKE A GAME OF BOWLS. HOW CAN YOU REFUSE?

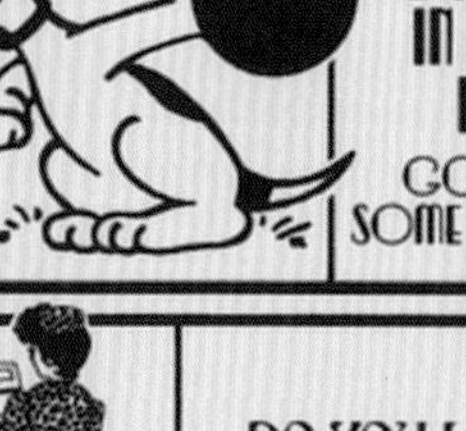

DIV IN Y NI GO SOME S

FIRST FLOOR CLOTHES & ACCESSORIES

A FOREST FULL OF COAT HANGERS... LOADED WITH ALL THE BIBA CLOTHES.

SUCH A PRETTY HAT... FOR SUCH A PRETTY FACE.

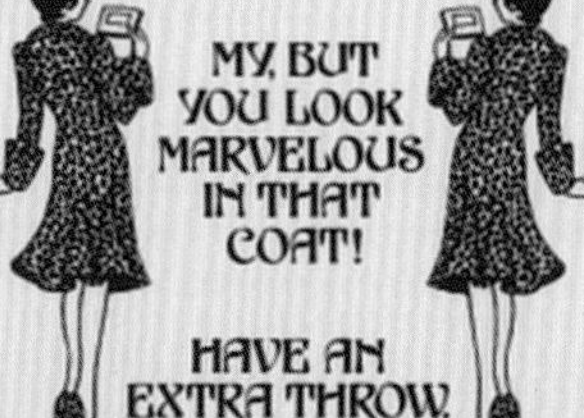

MY, BUT YOU LOOK MARVELOUS IN THAT COAT!

HAVE AN EXTRA THROW.

DO YOU LO IN BLUE SAT BROWN? IT'S TO DECIDE. LOSE A TUR TRY THE

GROUND FLOOR ACCESSORIES

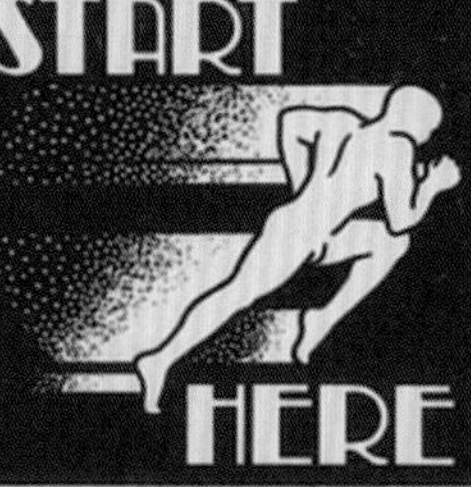

START HERE

BIBA

THE LOGO SHOP. IF YOU LIKE THINGS WITH BIBA'S NAME ON THEM, GO AND SEE OUR FOOD STORE.

AT THE NEWS-STALL, YOU READ THAT AN OLD FRIEND HAS JUST HAD A BABY. GO UPSTAIRS AND BUY A CHRISTENING ROBE.

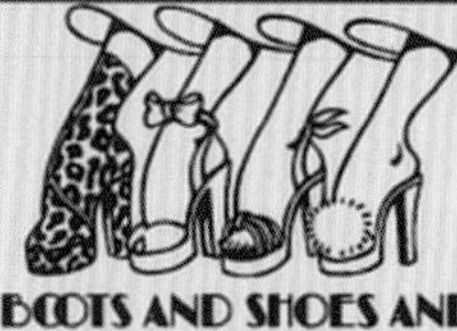

BOOTS AND SHOES AND SANDALS AND SLIPPERS.. HELP STAMP OUT BARE FEET.

YOU D PR BREA GO DOWNS AN BISC

BELOW STAIRS FOOD HALL

NOW YOU'RE DOWN HERE MAKE A SHOPPING LIST:

Fish
Fruit
Vegetables
Dairy Produce
Meat
Tinned Foods
Health Foods
Bacon
Wine
Soap Powder
Delicatessen
There I think that's everything

COME ON-YOU CAN'T SPEND ALL DAY DROOLING OVER THE FOOD DOWN HERE. COME UP TO THE FIRST FLOOR.

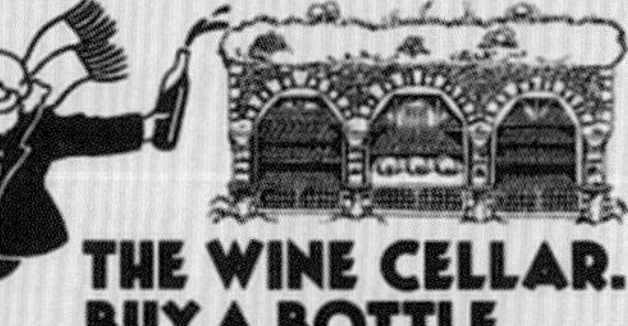

THE WINE CELLAR. BUY A BOTTLE AND LOSE A TURN.

OR SOME CAKES. FRUIT OR CHEESE OR A BUN.

...IRCASES' AT BIBA

...RS, DOWN IN THE LIFTS UP THE STAIRCASES.

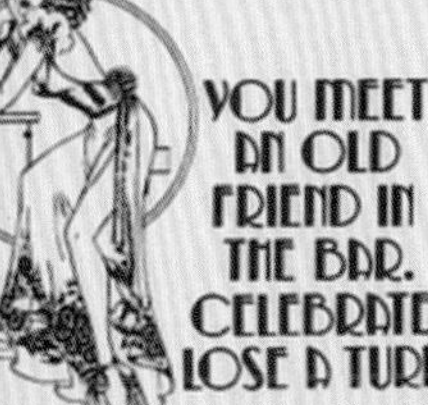

YOU MEET AN OLD FRIEND IN THE BAR. CELEBRATE. LOSE A TURN.

COME TO THE CABARET, OLD CHUM..

WE HAVE SOME VERY FAMOUS STARS IN THIS PARTICULAR HEAVEN.

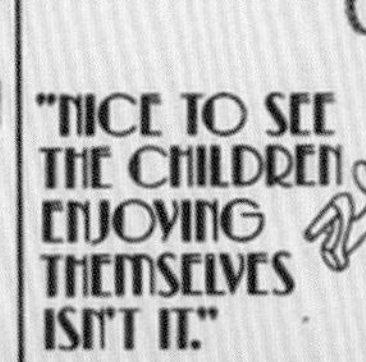

"NICE TO SEE THE CHILDREN ENJOYING THEMSELVES ISN'T IT."

"I CAN'T HEAR YOU FOR THE SOUND OF POTATO CRISPS."

THIS IS THE RAINBOW ROOM. A BIT LIKE BEING ON THE QUEEN MARY.

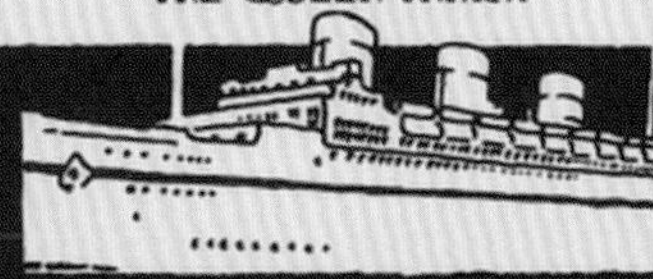

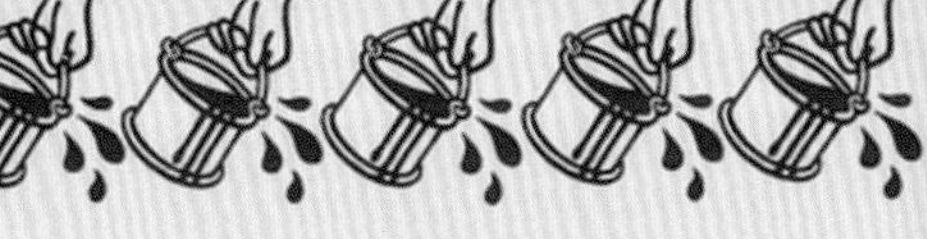

BIBAS NEW PAINT COLOURS ARE SO WEIRD, YOU OFFER TO REPAINT SNOOPY'S KENNEL.

AS YOU ARE ASTOUNDINGLY RICH, YOU ORDER 365 PLACE SETTINGS OF GILT CUTLERY. YOU WON'T HAVE ANY WASHING-UP TO DO FOR A YEAR.

(THIS IS A SPECIAL ORDER, SO LOSE A TURN)

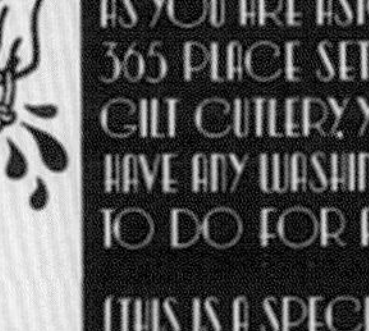

YOU DECIDE ON A NEW WALLPAPER FOR YOUR BEDROOM.

COME DOWN TO THE GALLERY AND SEE HOW PRETTY IT LOOKS, HUNG.

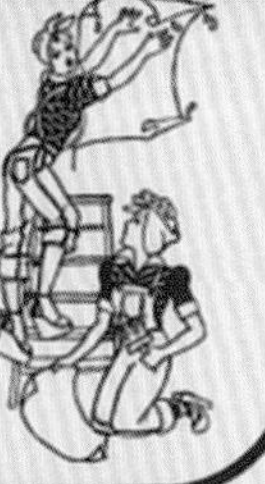

...OLD FLAME
...DS YOU
...KING AT THE
...WELLERY IN
... MISTRESS ROOM.

HAND IN HAND, YOU GO DOWN AND BUY A DOZEN LILIES OF THE VALLEY IN THE FLOWER SHOP.

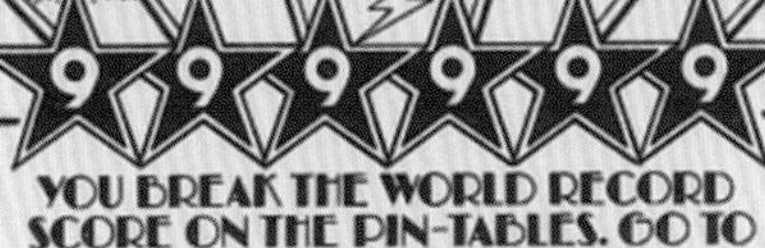

YOU BREAK THE WORLD RECORD SCORE ON THE PIN-TABLES. GO TO THE RAINBOW ROOM FOR A CHAMPAGNE CELEBRATION. THE PRESS ARE WAITING.

YOU'RE PUTTING ON YOUR TOP HAT, PUTTING ON YOUR WHITE TIE, PICKING UP YOUR CANE.

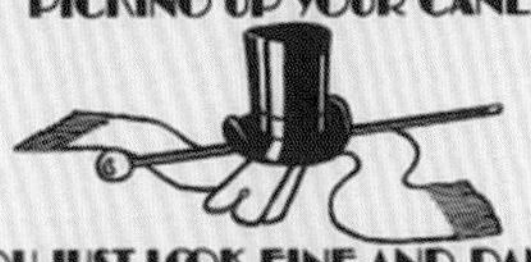

YOU JUST LOOK FINE AND DANDY. SO TAKE AN EXTRA TURN.

...K
...ELY
...ITA
...S.
...PICK
... MATCH.

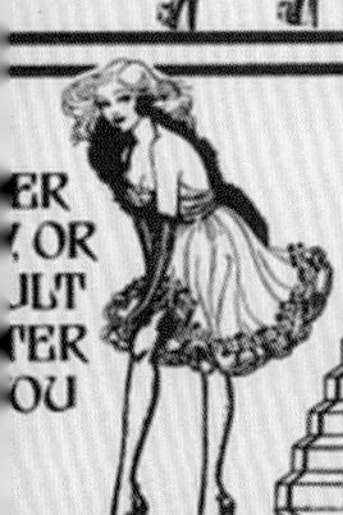

THANKS, PAL

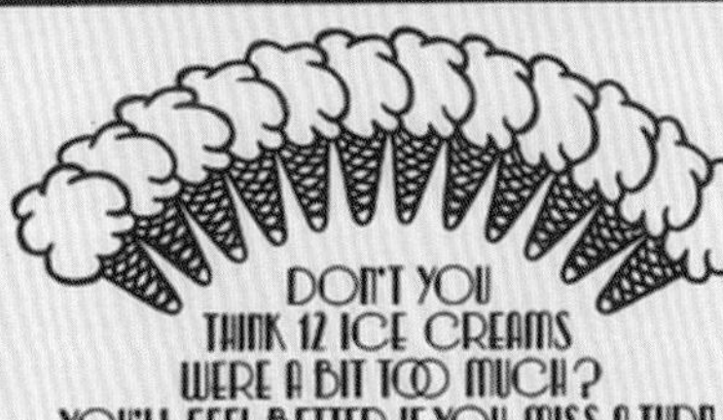

DON'T YOU THINK 12 ICE CREAMS WERE A BIT TOO MUCH? YOU'LL FEEL BETTER IF YOU MISS A TURN.

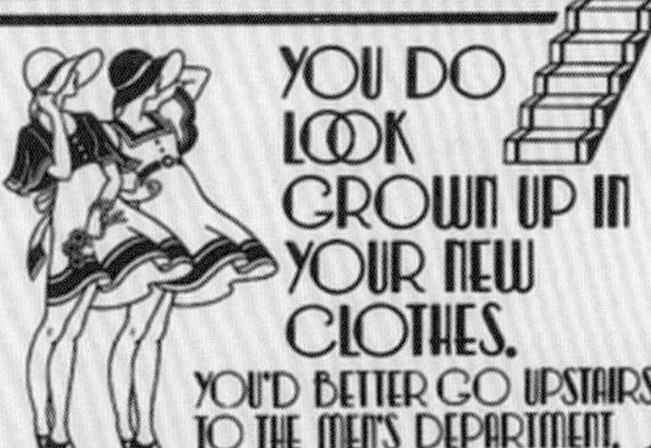

YOU DO LOOK GROWN UP IN YOUR NEW CLOTHES.

YOU'D BETTER GO UPSTAIRS TO THE MEN'S DEPARTMENT.

...ER
..., OR
...ULT
...TER
...OU

THE WEIGHT WATCHERS ARE WATCHING YOU. DO THOSE TROUSERS FEEL TIGHT? POP DOWN TO THE HEALTH FOOD COUNTER AND

THINK THIN

WELCOME TO THE GALLERY. DID YOU EVER SEE SUCH DELICIOUS UNDERWEAR BEFORE? OR NIGHTWEAR?

A FRIEND IN THE CHANGING ROOM 'BORROWS' YOUR LIPSTICK AND VANISHES. GO DOWN TO THE COSMETICS COUNTER AND BUY AN EVEN WEIRDER ONE

IT SERVES HER RIGHT.

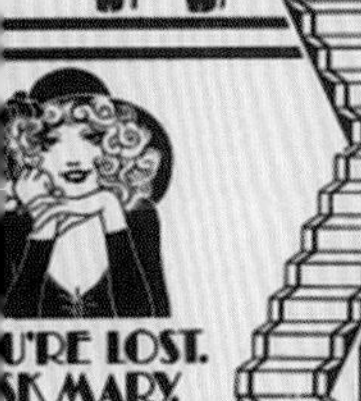

...U'RE LOST.
...SK MARY.
...RY SAYS YOU
...N HAVE AN
...RA THROW.

THE FLOWER SHOP SMELLS SO NICE. YOU MISS ONE TURN SNIFFING.

THE CASBAH: EXOTIC CLOTHES AND COSMETICS AND JEWELLERY AND RUGS AND GLASS... FROM TURKEY, TUNISIA, INDIA, MOROCCO, CHINA.

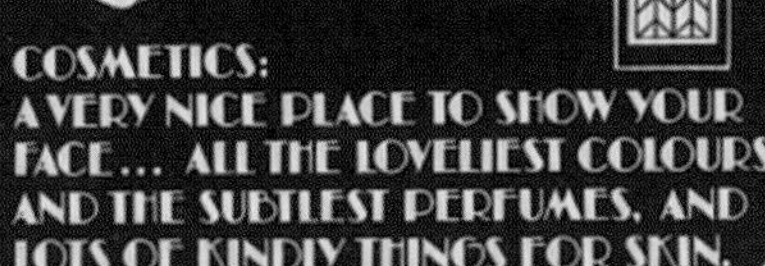

COSMETICS: A VERY NICE PLACE TO SHOW YOUR FACE... ALL THE LOVELIEST COLOURS AND THE SUBTLEST PERFUMES, AND LOTS OF KINDLY THINGS FOR SKIN.

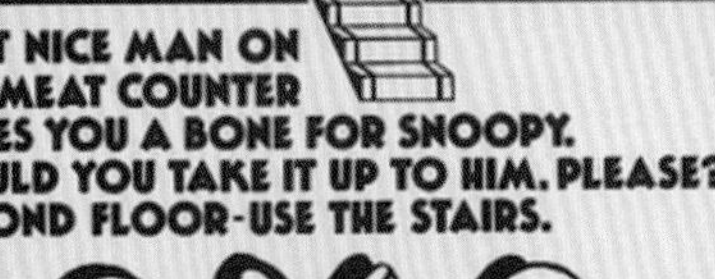

...T NICE MAN ON
... MEAT COUNTER
...ES YOU A BONE FOR SNOOPY.
...ULD YOU TAKE IT UP TO HIM, PLEASE?
...OND FLOOR-USE THE STAIRS.

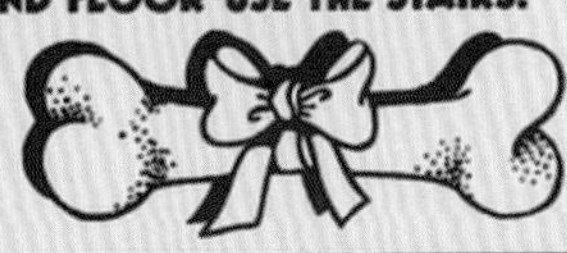

NICE THIN FOOD

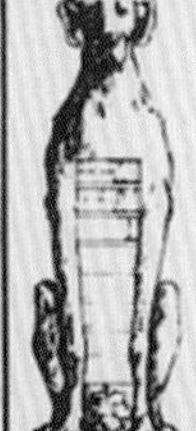

OTHELLO LIKES YOU. THROW THE DICE AGAIN.

YOU'VE GOT ALL THE FOOD FOR YOUR PARTY.

BUT SOME INCENSE WOULD BE FUN. COME WITH ME TO THE CASBAH...

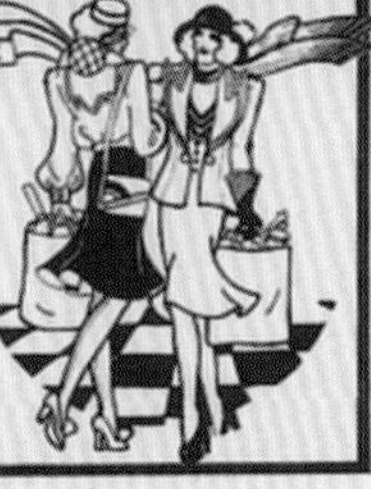

BIBA SECOND FLOOR FOR BABIES, CHILDREN, LOLITAS AND PREGNANT LADIES.

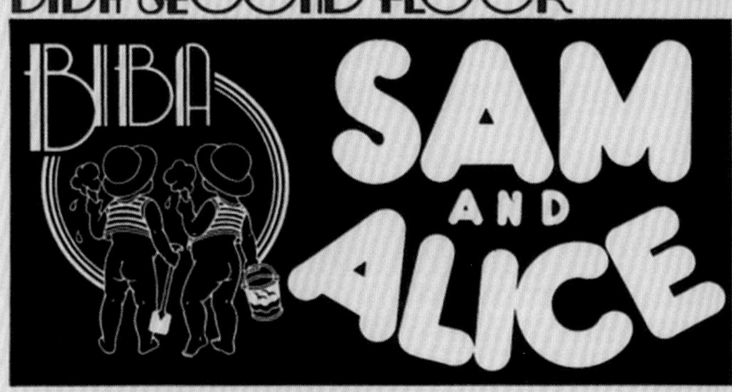

ONCE UPON A TIME, SAM AND ALICE WENT TO BIBA TO BUY SOME NEW CLOTHES, ON THE SECOND FLOOR THEY FOUND LOTS OF SPECIAL HOUSES. EVERYONE WAS DRESSING UP AND -LIKE MAGIC-LOOKING MUCH, MUCH HAPPIER

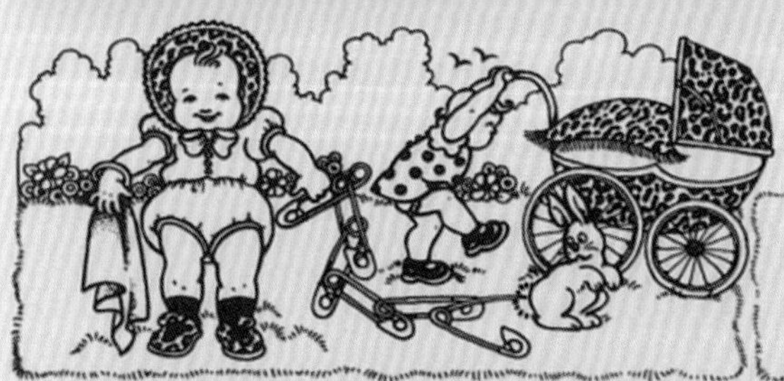

BABIES WERE CHOOSING NEW NAPPIES AND COTS AND SAFETY-PINS.

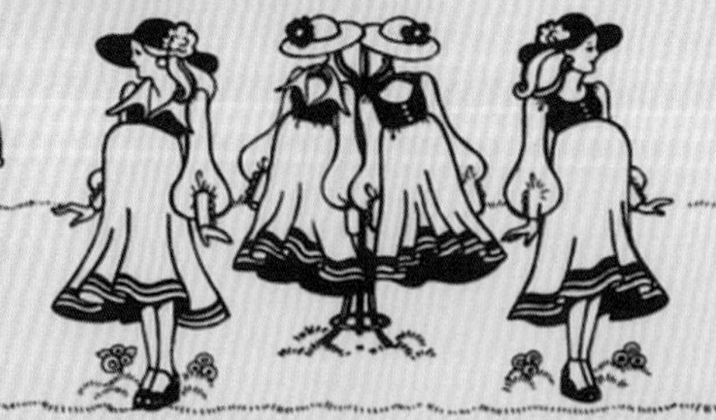

AND LADIES WHO ARE GOING TO HAVE BABIES WERE TRYING ON SMOCKS.

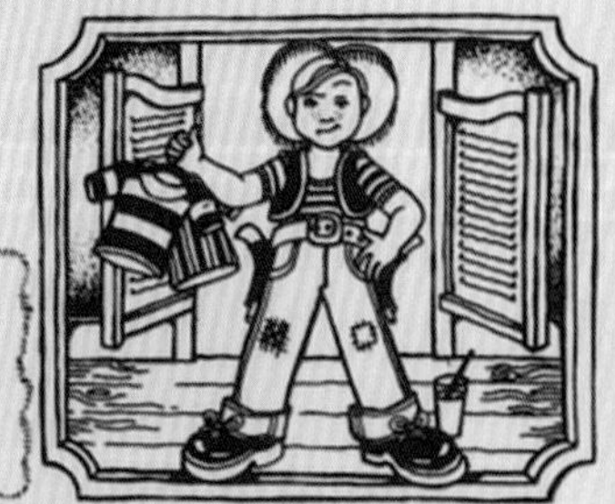

SOME BOYS WERE CHOOSING SHINY NEW SHOES IN THE SALOON.

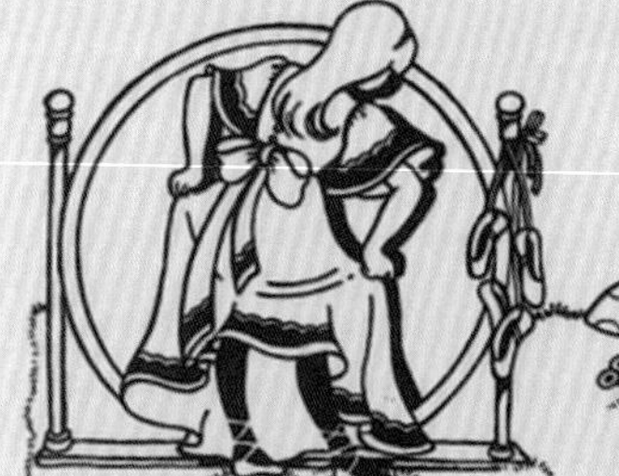

LITTLE GIRLS WERE PICKING BALLET SHOES FOR THEIR NEXT PARTY...

...AND EVERYBODY WAS EATING ICE CREAM.

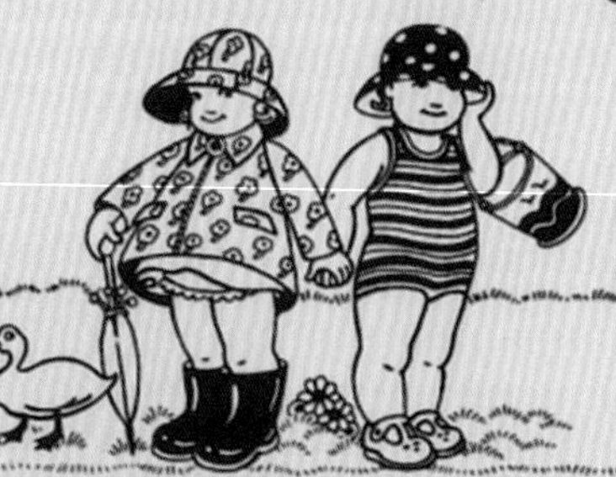

THERE WERE MACS AND WELLIES FOR WET DAYS, AND SWIMSUITS FOR DRY DAYS....

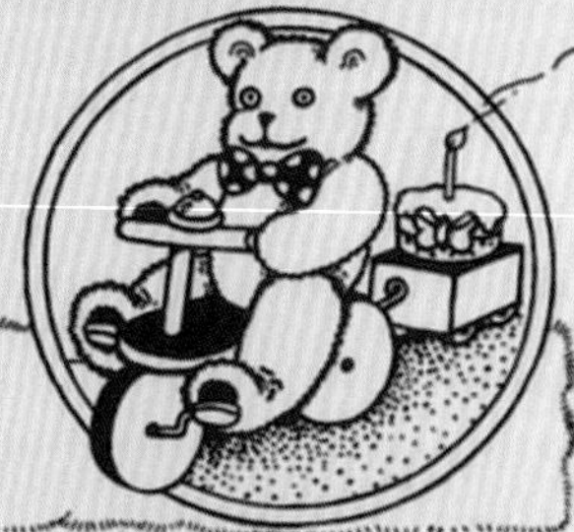

...AND TOYS FOR BIRTHDAYS.

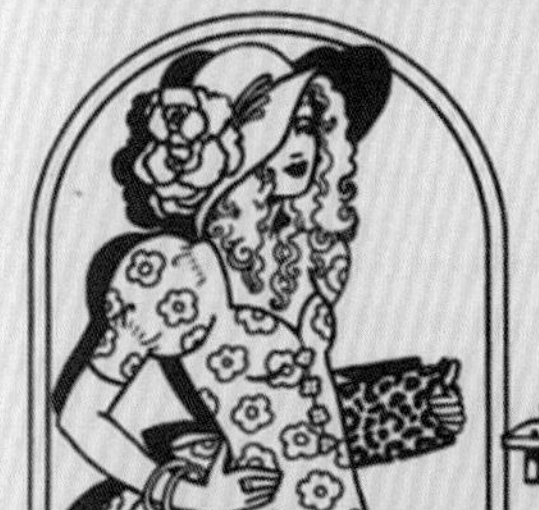

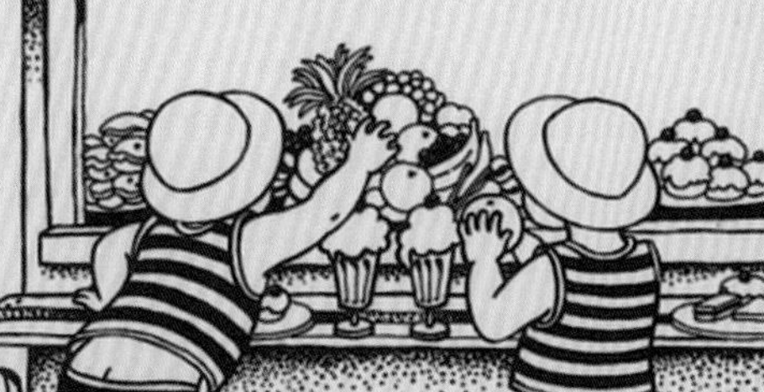

THEY SAW AN OLDER GIRL COME IN LOOKING PRETTY, AND GO OUT LOOKING BEAUTIFUL! SAM AND ALICE FELT HUNGRY, SO THEY HAD QUITE A LOT TO EAT.

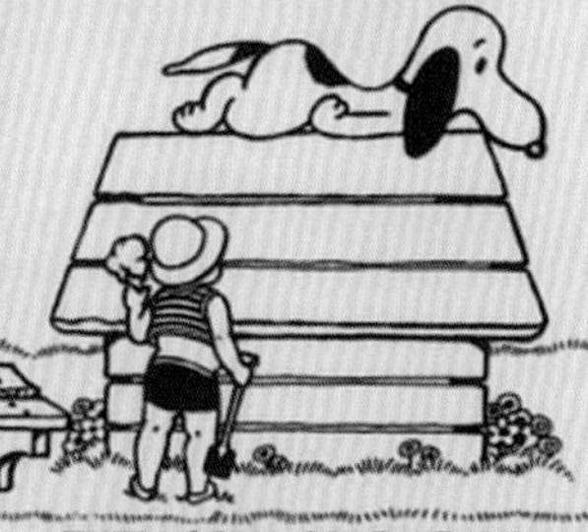

THEY SAW SNOOPY ON HIS KENNEL...

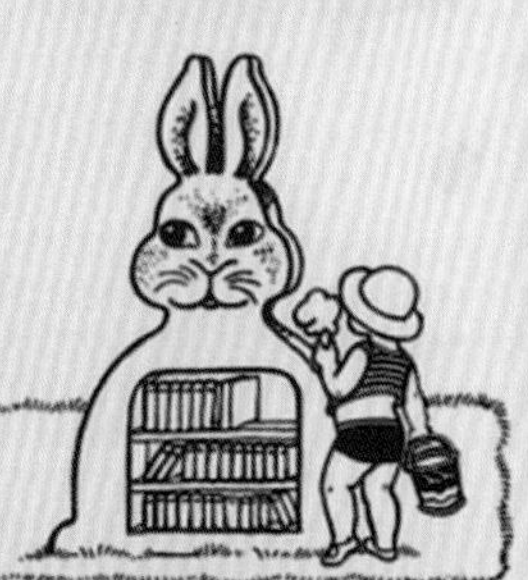

AND PETER RABBIT NEAR THE ROUNDABOUT

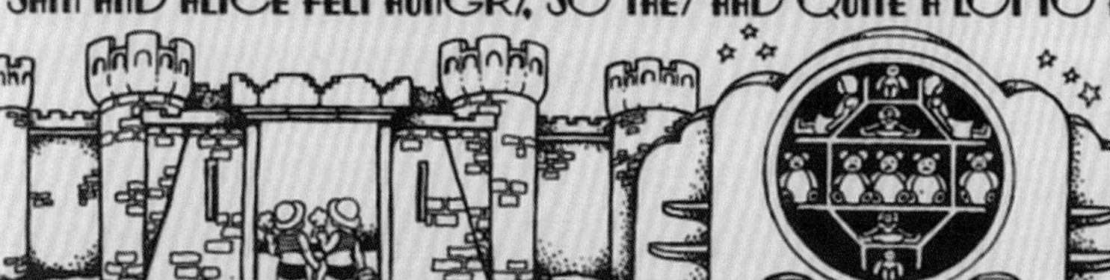

THEY LOOKED AT SOME BOOKS IN THE CASTLE......................

AND LISTENED TO THE BIGGEST RADIO IN LONDON.

UNTIL THEY WERE SO TIRED, THEY WENT HOME TO BED.

AND EVERYONE LIVED HAPPILY EVER AFTER.

YOU CAN COLOUR THIS PAGE WITH YOUR CRAYONS WHEN YOU GET HOME, DO IT CAREFULLY, AND BRING IT ALONG WITH YOU NEXT TIME YOU COME TO BIBA'S SECOND FLOOR-WE WOULD LIKE TO SEE IT!

MEN ONLY

THIRD FLOOR

Biba's third floor is for men of any age, from 10 to 100. So fathers can bring their sons, or sons their fathers. Just think of it as a very large walk-in wardrobe and dressing-room, with a small games-room at the side. Jeeves would approve.

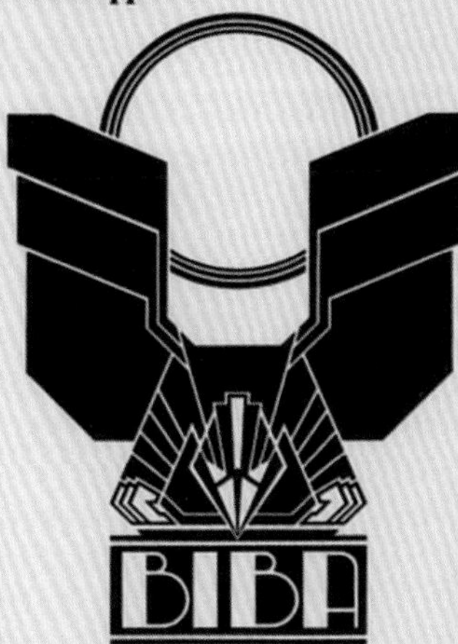

In addition to the clothes, there is an active sports section, which could be useful if you're an active sport. Feel free to drop in at any time for a game of bowls, or a desperate trial of skill at darts.

If you have reached the age of content, venture into the Mistress Room. Life, after all, is for loving.

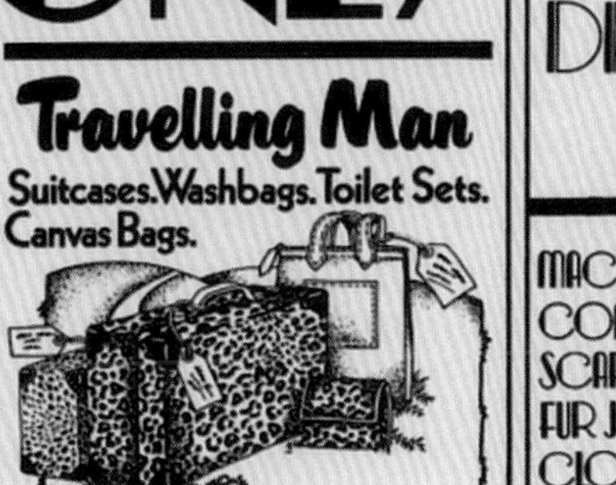

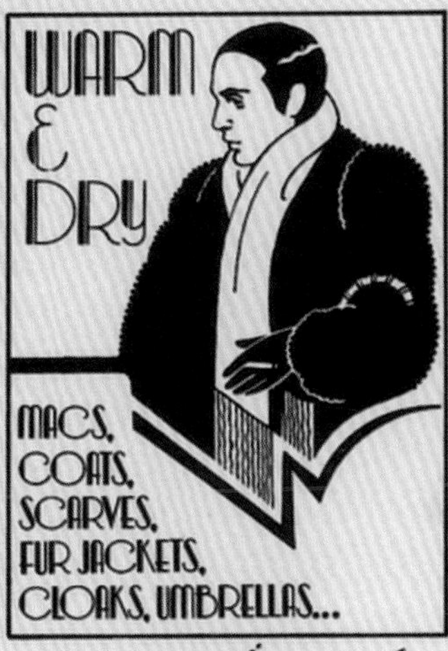

Dressing to KILL

Shirts, Waistcoats, Jackets, Suits, Trousers, Canes, Ties...

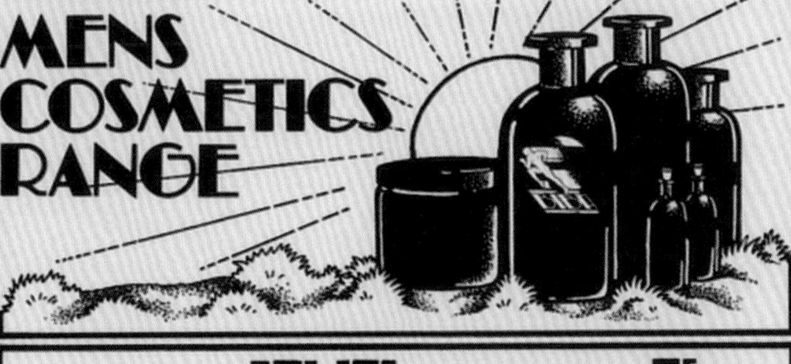
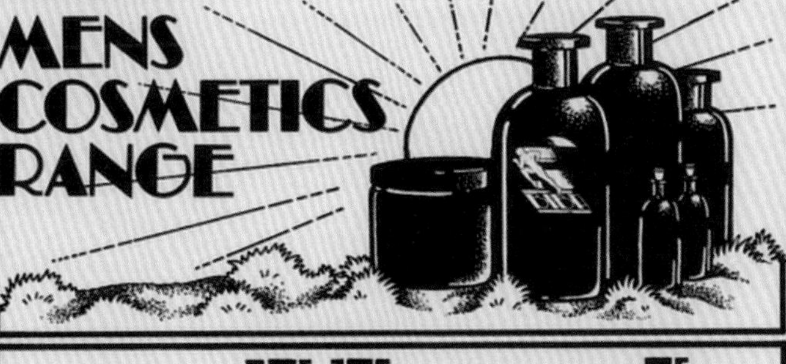

THE INNER MAN

VESTS, Y-FRONTS, SOCKS, BELTS, BRACES.

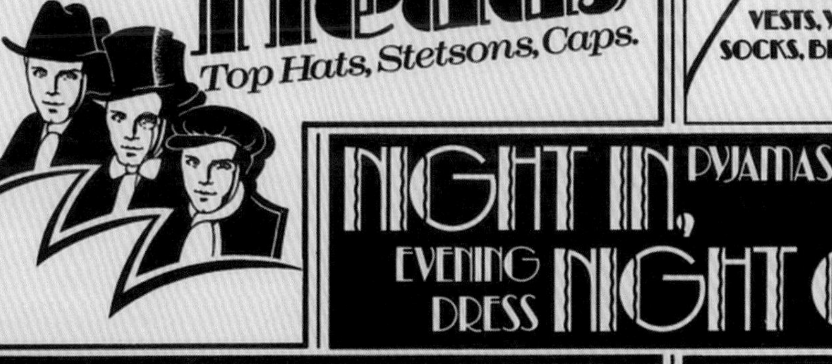

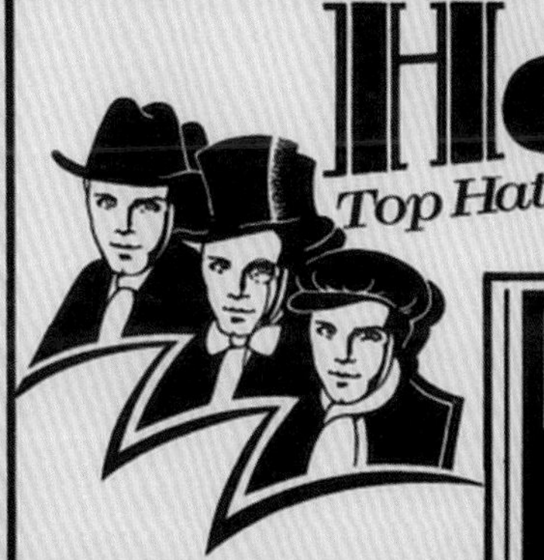

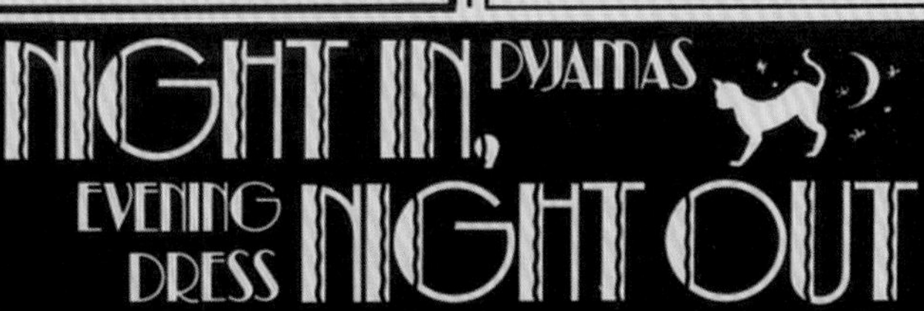

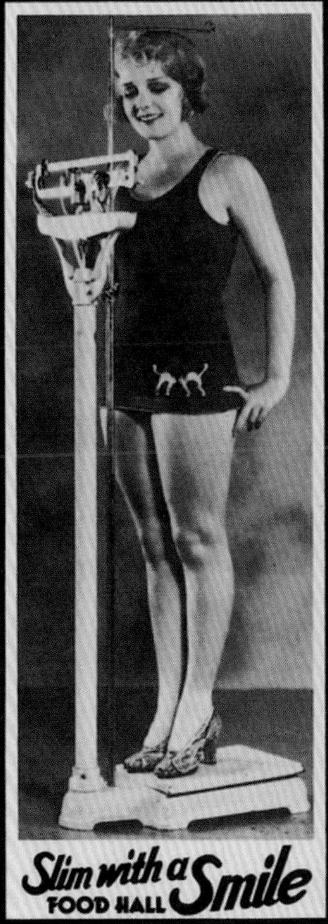

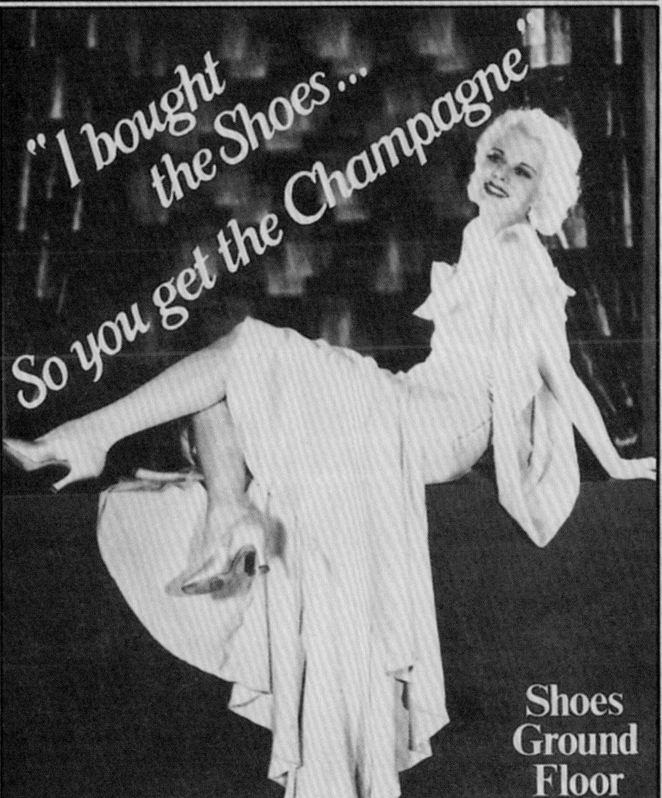

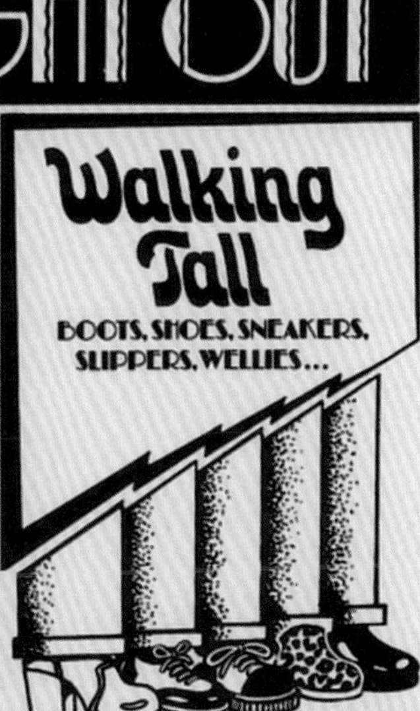

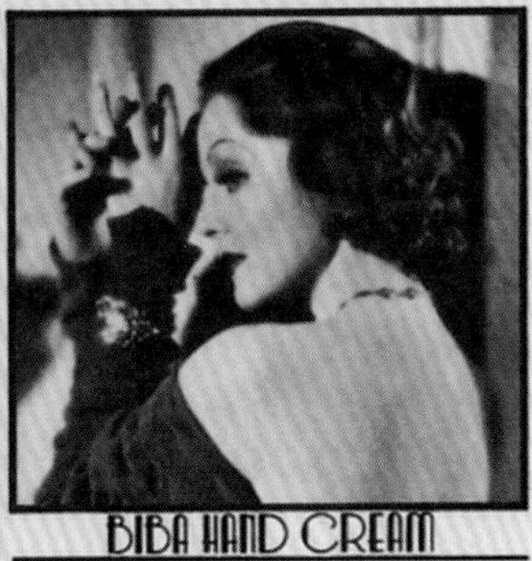

BIBA HAND CREAM

BIBA FOR BOYS

Boys *under* 10 will find everything to keep them happy on the second floor. But from 10 to 15 or so, they can kit themselves out for any occasion in their own section on the third floor – and after 15, they graduate to the men's department proper.

Biba boys' clothes are tough and practical, but they also have a distinct touch of the dandy about them, which the girls seem to like.

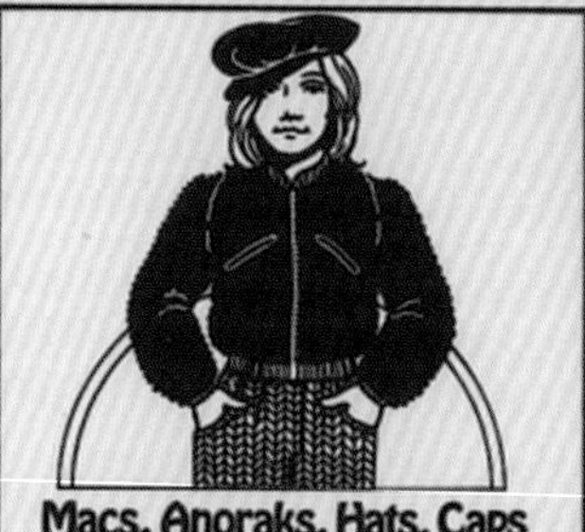

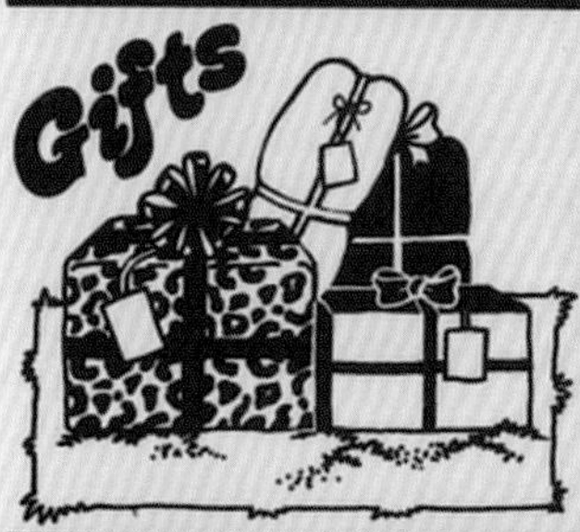

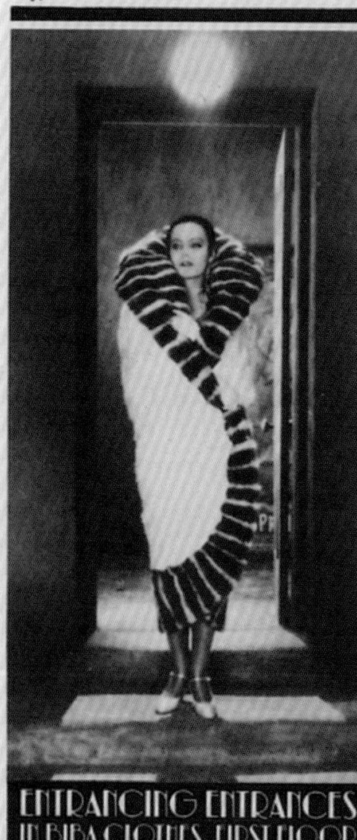

BIBA SPORTS

Even if you only play fast, competitive ball-games like roulette, there is something for you in Biba's sports section. The kind of kit that guarantees you'll be picked for the team – sweaters, T-shirts, ski-suits.

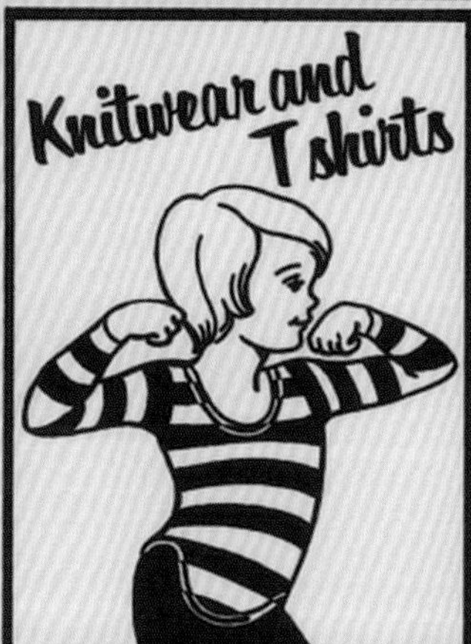

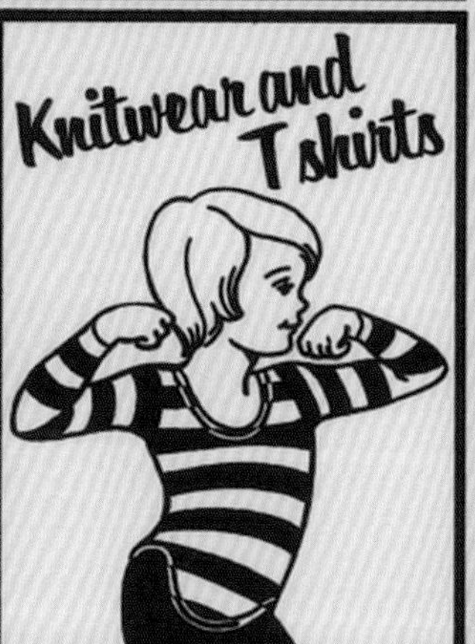

Underwear and Pyjamas

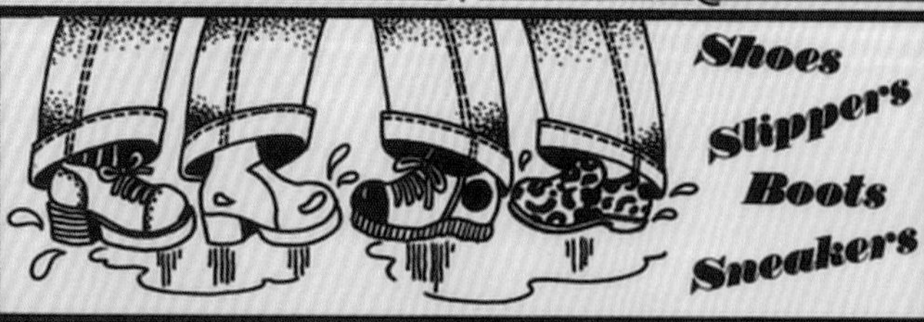

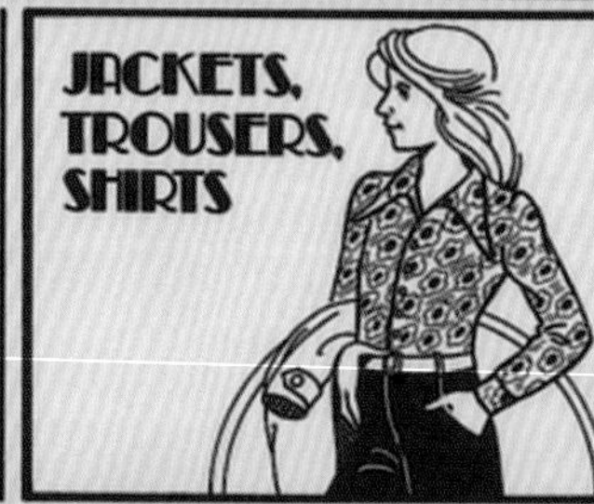

COME UP AND SEE THE MISTRESS SHOP SOME TIME...

Darling – the garters! The G-strings! The utter wickedness of the underwear! All too naughty. They have a whole safe-full of sparkling jewels. Dark, sinful chocolates. Subtle lotions and potions for the bath. Leopardskin cushions and slinky satin sheets. All most aphrodisiac. "Beulah – peel me a grape."

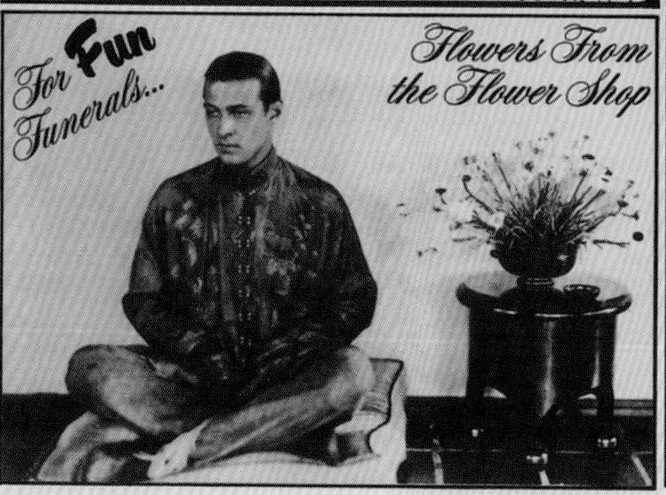

You can also kit yourself out with enough professionally approved sports gear to scare off the opposition long before the referee appears . . . football boots, boxing gloves, cricket bats.

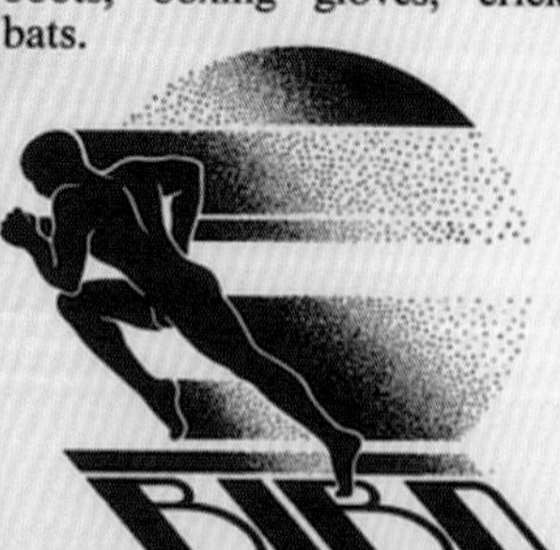

Biba also stock some exercising devices that help the thin muscular man who's fighting to get out of every fatso.

ONE EYED JACKS

Biba sells monocles. Instructions for use: fit monocle into left eye (fig. 'A') or right eye (fig. 'B'). Now say "By Jove, dash it all, don't you know." There – a monocle suits you, doesn't it?

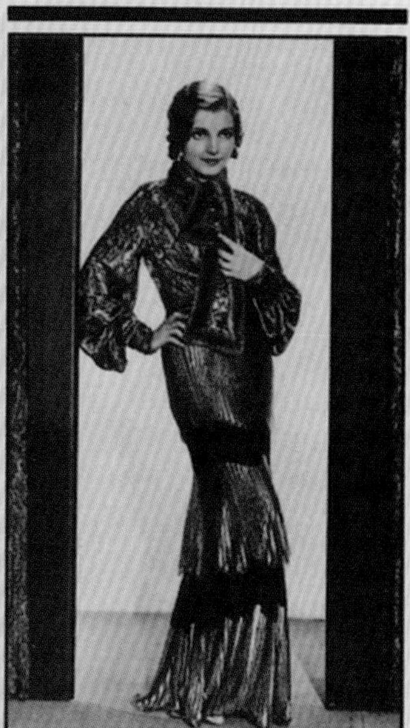

Curtain Call

Household Fourth Floor

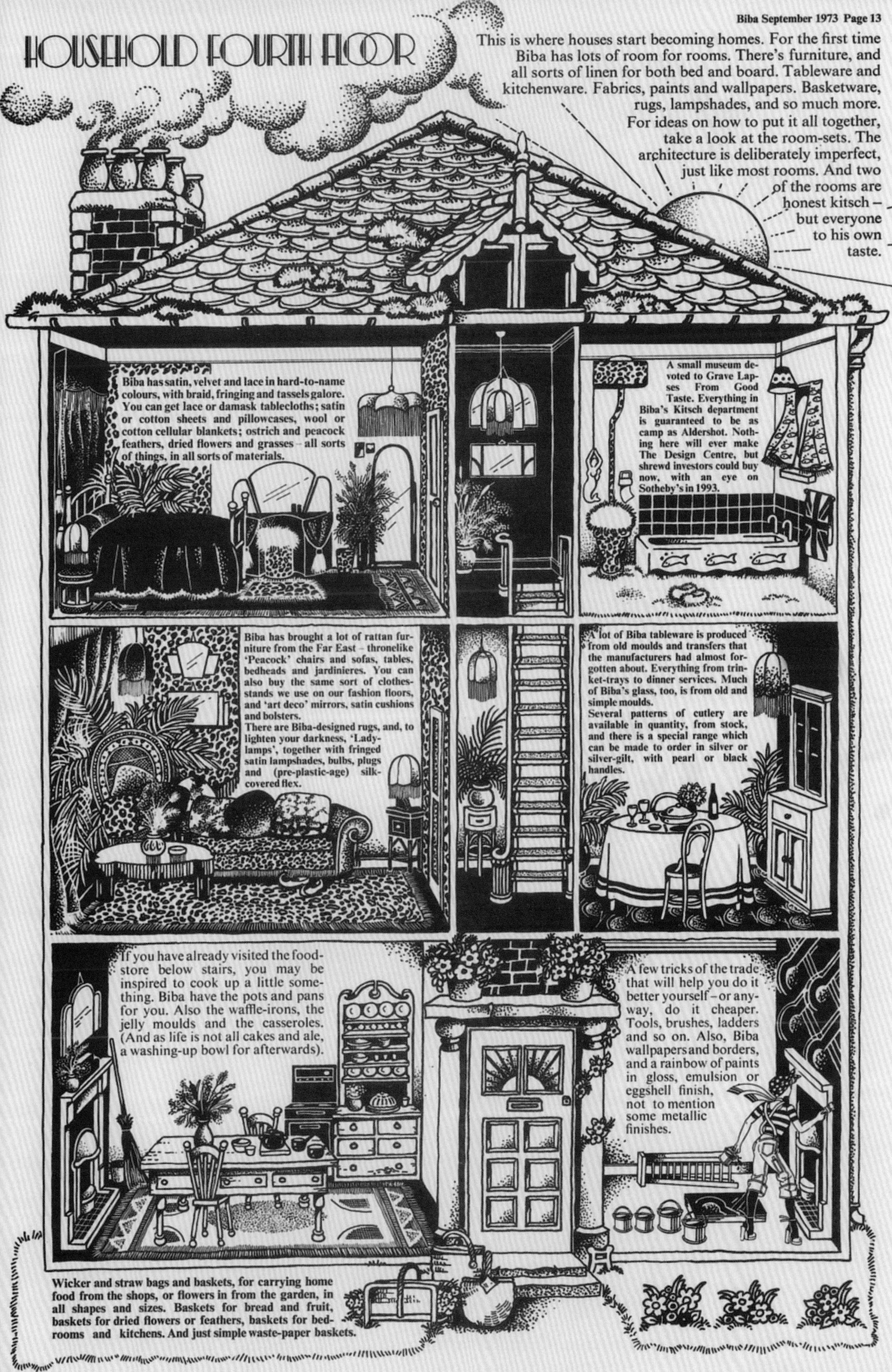

HOUSEHOLD FOURTH FLOOR

This is where houses start becoming homes. For the first time Biba has lots of room for rooms. There's furniture, and all sorts of linen for both bed and board. Tableware and kitchenware. Fabrics, paints and wallpapers. Basketware, rugs, lampshades, and so much more. For ideas on how to put it all together, take a look at the room-sets. The architecture is deliberately imperfect, just like most rooms. And two of the rooms are honest kitsch – but everyone to his own taste.

Biba has satin, velvet and lace in hard-to-name colours, with braid, fringing and tassels galore. You can get lace or damask tablecloths; satin or cotton sheets and pillowcases, wool or cotton cellular blankets; ostrich and peacock feathers, dried flowers and grasses – all sorts of things, in all sorts of materials.

A small museum devoted to Grave Lapses From Good Taste. Everything in Biba's Kitsch department is guaranteed to be as camp as Aldershot. Nothing here will ever make The Design Centre, but shrewd investors could buy now, with an eye on Sotheby's in 1993.

Biba has brought a lot of rattan furniture from the Far East – thronelike 'Peacock' chairs and sofas, tables, bedheads and jardinieres. You can also buy the same sort of clothes-stands we use on our fashion floors, and 'art deco' mirrors, satin cushions and bolsters.
There are Biba-designed rugs, and, to lighten your darkness, 'Lady-lamps', together with fringed satin lampshades, bulbs, plugs and (pre-plastic-age) silk-covered flex.

A lot of Biba tableware is produced from old moulds and transfers that the manufacturers had almost forgotten about. Everything from trinket-trays to dinner services. Much of Biba's glass, too, is from old and simple moulds.
Several patterns of cutlery are available in quantity, from stock, and there is a special range which can be made to order in silver or silver-gilt, with pearl or black handles.

If you have already visited the food-store below stairs, you may be inspired to cook up a little something. Biba have the pots and pans for you. Also the waffle-irons, the jelly moulds and the casseroles. (And as life is not all cakes and ale, a washing-up bowl for afterwards).

A few tricks of the trade that will help you do it better yourself – or anyway, do it cheaper. Tools, brushes, ladders and so on. Also, Biba wallpapers and borders, and a rainbow of paints in gloss, emulsion or eggshell finish, not to mention some metallic finishes.

Wicker and straw bags and baskets, for carrying home food from the shops, or flowers in from the garden, in all shapes and sizes. Baskets for bread and fruit, baskets for dried flowers or feathers, baskets for bedrooms and kitchens. And just simple waste-paper baskets.

THE RAINBOW RESTAURANT

FIFTH FLOOR

You can eat and run, in the Rainbow Restaurant, or take your time over a more relaxed lunch or dinner. It's open from 9.30 until 2.30 in the morning from Monday to Saturday, and from 10 am to Midnight on Sundays.

Outside the store's opening hours, use the entrance in Derry Street, and the direct lift service to the 5th floor. At night, there is parking space in the loading-bay off Derry Street; please don't park in Kensington Square.

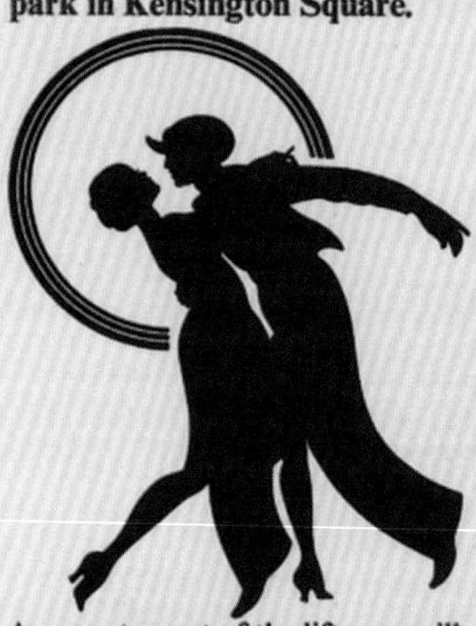

As you step out of the lift, you will see some serving counters on the left. Here you can choose soups, hot and cold dishes, and salads, as well as health-food or vegetarian dishes. Just make your choice, and take them on a tray to your table. There is a special counter serving children's food. (All of these counters close at 8pm; after, there is table-service only.)

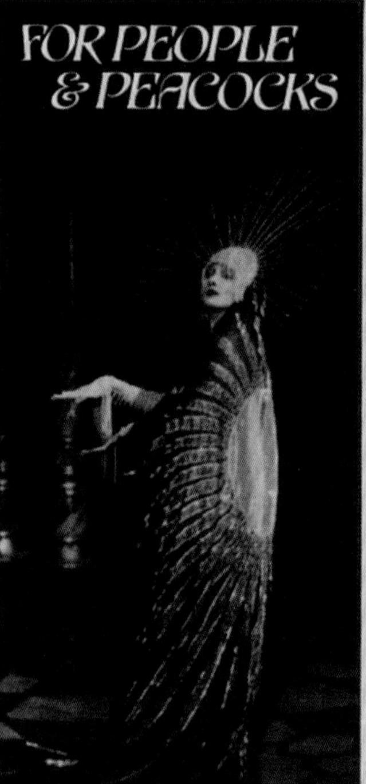

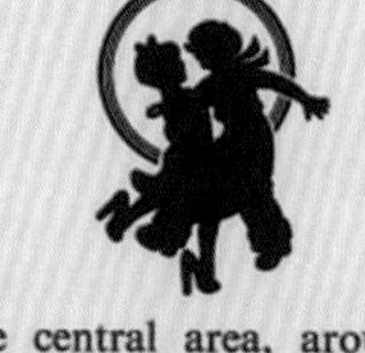

In the central area, around the banquettes under the Rainbow Ceiling, there are tables served by waiters or waitresses. The menu is unusual, not the sort of food you find everywhere. And the prices are sensible – most main courses cost under £1, and that includes potatoes and two vegetables.

On the right, you will find a cocktail bar, and some comfortable club chairs where you can wait for friends before your meal.

THE CLUB ARMCHAIRS

Restful. Soothing, if you're waiting for someone with a slow watch. Comfortable place to chat with friends. Good to loiter in, over coffee and a nice sticky liqueur.

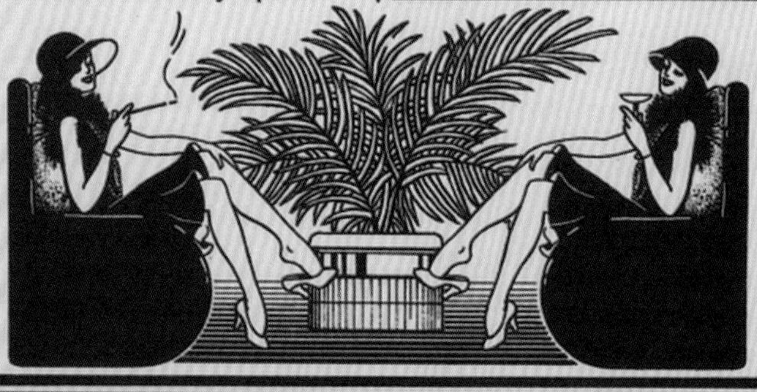

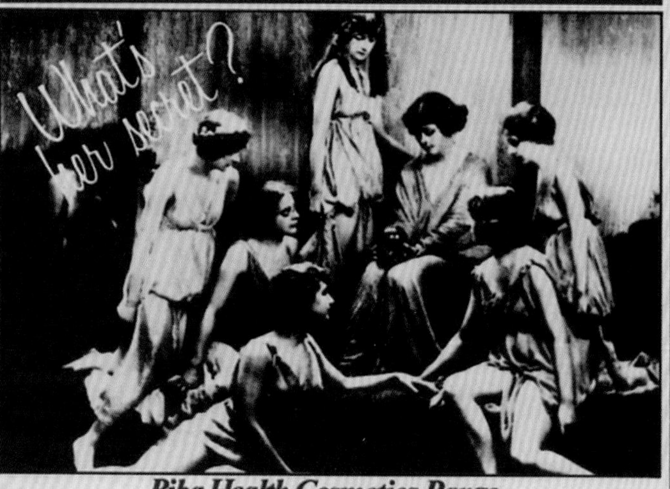

Biba Health Cosmetics Range

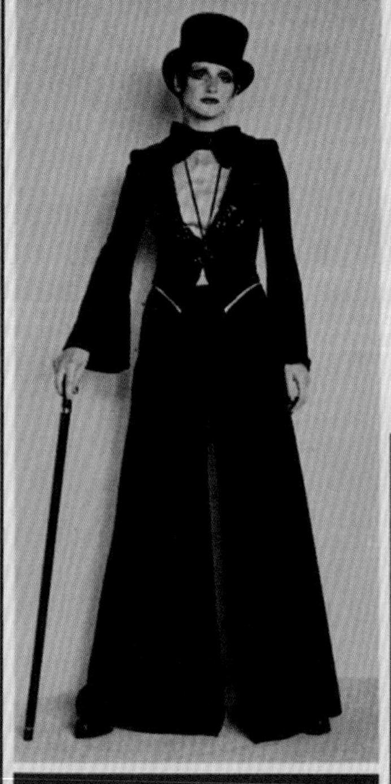

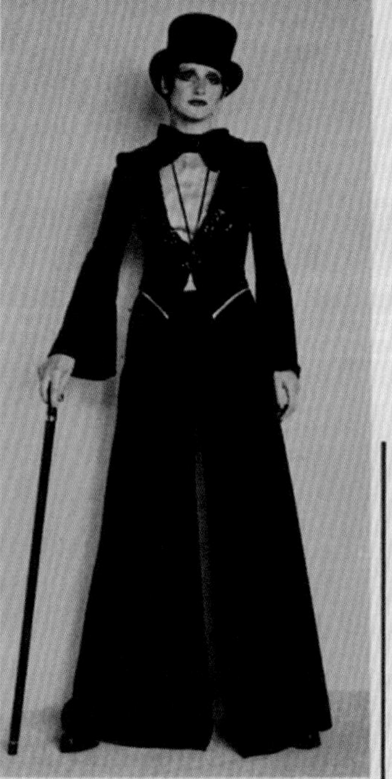

THE RAINBOW BAR

All the usual straight drinks and mixes, but also some less usual ones. We found them in an old copy of The Savoy Cocktail Book and they seemed well worth all that measuring and shaking. Rainbow Cocktail, anyone? There are also some long Italian drinks, made with fresh fruits or vegetables.

RAINBOW RULES

There are two tiresome phrases you will *not* hear in the Rainbow Restaurant. One is "The bill doesn't include service." No tipping is required, or expected. The second is "I'm sorry, Modom, but we don't serve unaccompanied ladies." We do – a girl alone is every bit as welcome as a man alone.

We must keep our licence if everyone is to enjoy themselves, so NO alcoholic drinks can be served without meals, and NO alcoholic drinks for those under 18.(In the Bar area, in the restaurant the normal rules apply.) Sorry, but that's the law.

HEALTH FOOD AND VEGETARIAN COUNTER

There is more to healthy eating than a limp lettuce leaf, some tinned fruit salad, and stale dandelion coffee.

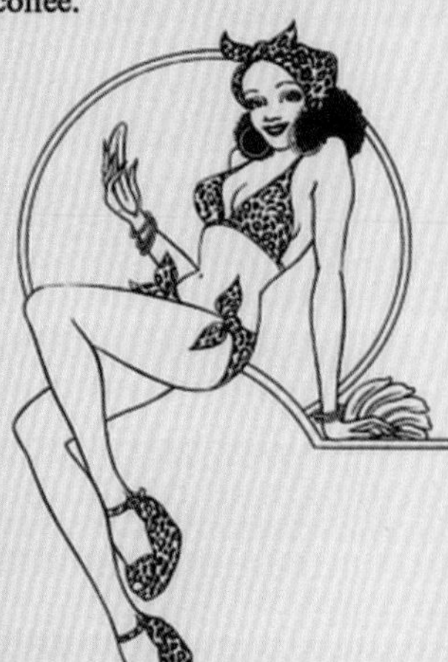

You'll find a good wholesome spread of hot and cold dishes, to suit all fancies. Freshly blended or juiced fruits and vegetables. Macrobiotic food. Organically-grown food.

CABARET TIME

As often as possible there will be live music in the Rainbow Restaurant. A gypsy violinist, or a tinkling cocktail-hour pianist. On occasion, we shall be aiming higher

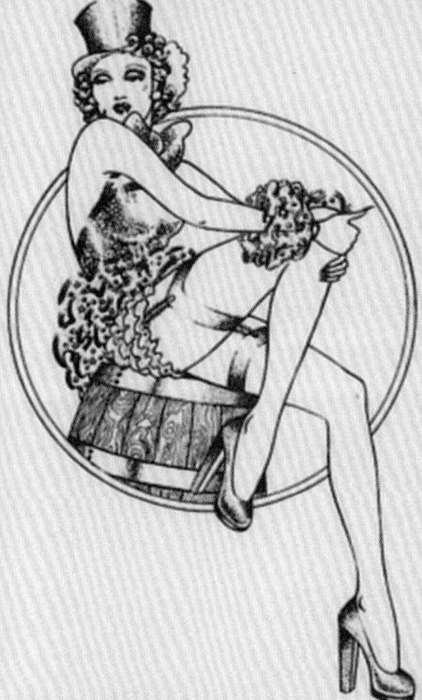

for some really big names. (The dressing-rooms behind stage are star quality.) Then it will be Cabaret Time at the Rainbow Restaurant but the price will *not* go up.

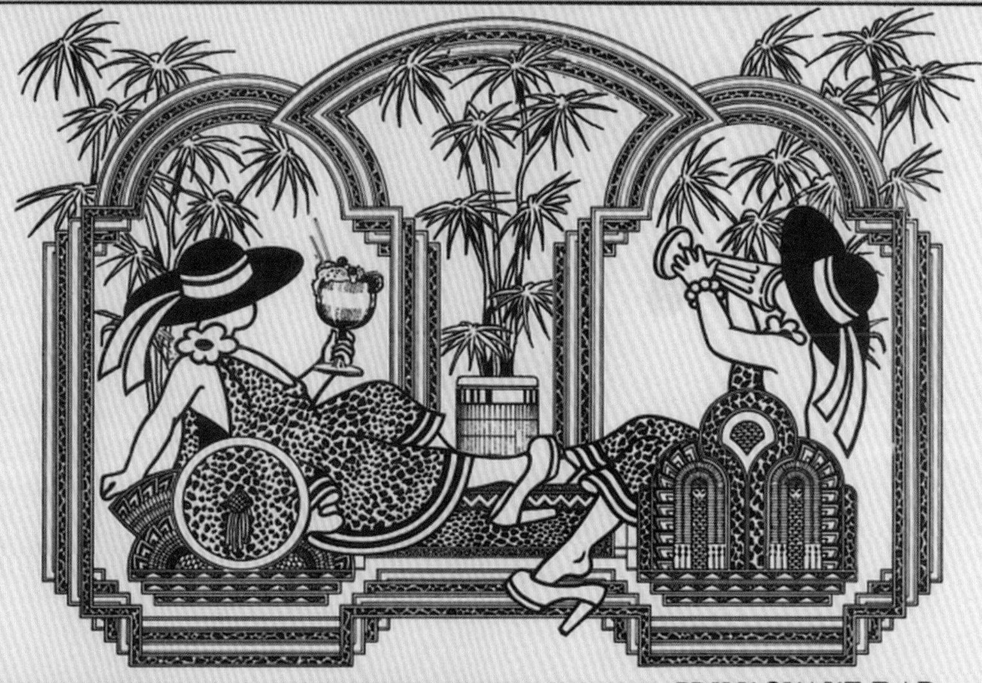

ROOF GARDEN

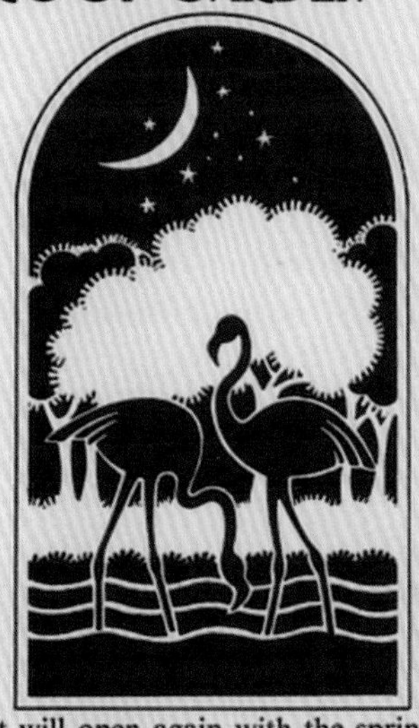

It will open again with the spring flowers of 1974, we promise. Then you will be able to watch the flamingos and ducks, and listen to the birds.

MENU

RAINBOW ROOM

MENU

STARTERS

Fish Sausage
Fish Tart
Mackerel Pate
Crudite and dressing
Smothered Ham
Herb Frittata
Briani with Yoghourt
Fish Soup
Chinese Noodles

MAIN COURSES

Boiled Beef and Carrots
Roast Beef
Roast Lamb
Roast Pork and Crackling
Turkey and Walnut Pie
Saudekraut and Kassleribben
Ham and Pease pudding
Chicken and Cherries
Fishsnacks
Fish stew with Saffron Rice

PUDDINGS

Biba Rainbow Cake
Pouffs Pudding
Ginger syllabub
Hindi dessert
Strawberry Mousse
Yoghourt, nuts and raisins
Spotted Dick
Sorbets

A shortened example of the menu, which will alter seasonally. Main courses include potatoes and two vegetables, and remember – no tipping.

WINE LIST

RAINBOW ROOM

WINE LIST

BIBA CARAFE WINES

Biba White
Biba Rainbow Pink
Biba Red
(75p per half litre)

BIBA ESTATE BOTTLED

Blanc de Blancs (£1.50)
Rose Premiere Goutte (£1.50)
Rouge Nature (£1.50)

CHAMPAGNE

SPARKLING WINES

Cold Duck (£2.50)

Red and White Bordeux
English Wines
Red Burgundy
White Burgundy
Mead
Alsace
Rhine and Moselle
Loire
Rhone
Spanish Bottled
Italian Bottled

Our actual wine-list is much longer. Sorry, but no alcoholic drinks can be taken without a meal. By the way, Biba's own house wines are on sale downstairs in the food hall.

MILK SHAKE BAR

For hungry children of almost any age – Tizer, and milk shakes, and the sort of food they never seem to leave on their plates: crisps, bangers, baked beans, that sort of thing. As seen on television.

THE POWDER ROOM

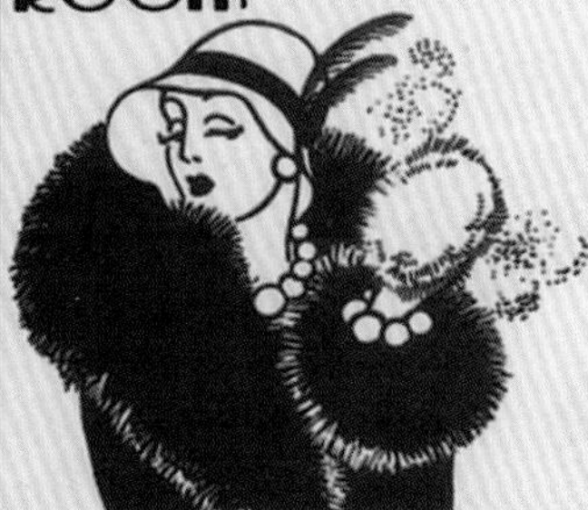

There is a particularly chic ladies' powder-room off the Rainbow Restaurant – worthy of a 1930 Cunarder. The gentlemen's loo is not quite so spectacular, but that's life.

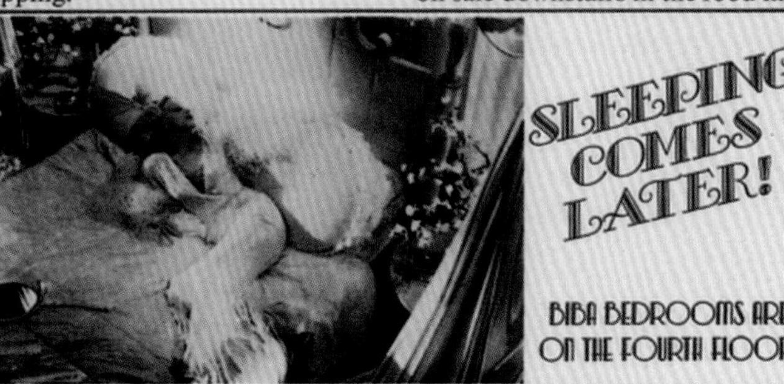

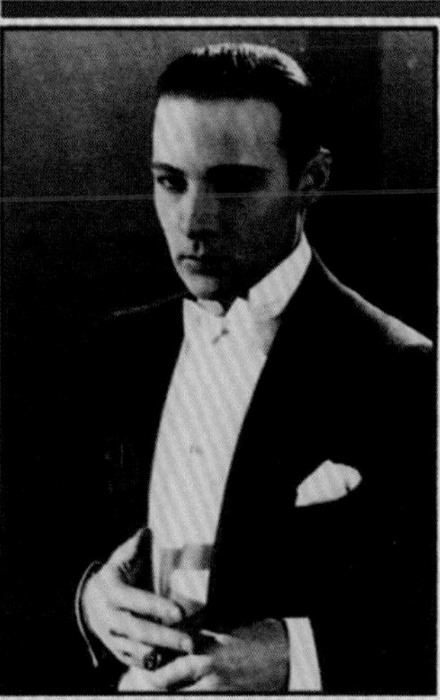

BARMEN WANTED
Strong silent type prefered
Must be willing to please
Rainbow Restaurant
Fifth floor

BELOW STAIRS

FOOD HALL

Biba food is good food. That means it's fresh, and clean, and tastes of itself and nothing else.
Feast your eyes first, on a dairy, a quayside for fresh-landed fish, a wine-cellar, and as many market-stalls as you'd find in many French towns.
Behind the scenes there are spotless kitchens and cold-rooms, and, far away, foraging-parties buying up the best that Smithfield, Billingsgate and Covent Garden have to offer.
Most of the counters are self-service – just take a wicker basket and help yourself; you pay at the cash-tills. But there are assistants to blend your coffee, or slice your bacon, or help you choose your meat or fish. The best of both worlds.

THE DAIRY

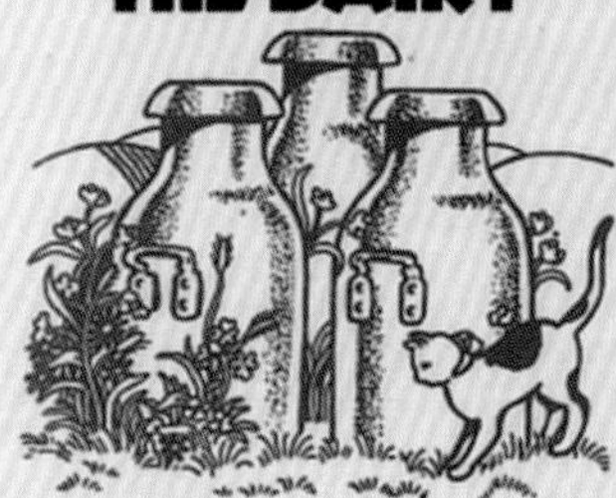

Guernsey and Jersey, gold top and silver top, milk and cream, double and single, fresh or soured. Very versatile animals, cows.
Butter, too, salted or unsalted, from the world's greenest pastures. And, close by, a very big cheeseboard. France, they say, produces 365 cheeses – and to be honest, we don't stock *all* of them. But try the Biba camembert, made for us in Normandy. There are all the noble British cheeses too – Stilton and Caerphilly, Wensleydale, good honest Cheddar, and the rest.

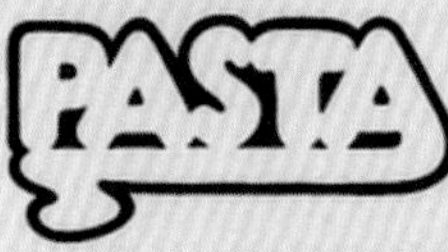

If the French can offer a different cheese every day of the year, the Italians have a different form of pasta for every week – lasagne, tagliatelle, fettucine, macaroni, ravioli, ragatoni, spaghetti, and so on. Biba also stocks rice for curries, paellas, risottos or simple rice puddings.

BISCUITS & CAKES

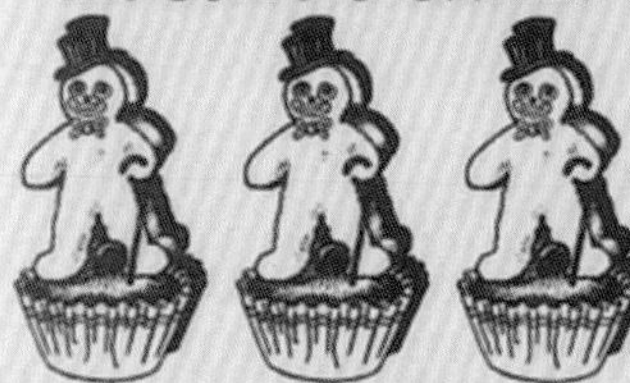

Nice, Digestive, Marie, Tin Captains, Bath Olivers, Sweet Tea, Thin Wine, Garibaldi . . . Britain has a biscuit for every taste, sweet or savoury, and so does Biba.
Nice cakes, too – homely everyday ones, as well as more decorative offerings for special occasions.

KITCHEN EQUIPMENT

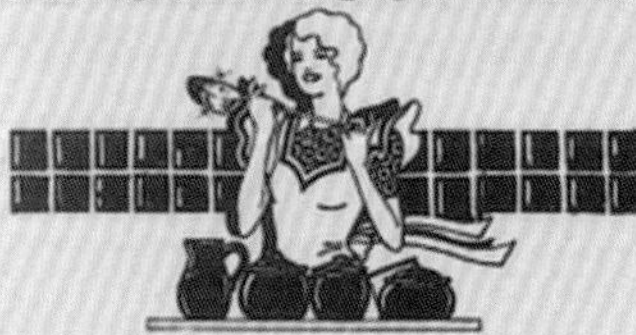

You will find Biba kitchen equipment, china, glass, cutlery and table linen on the 4th floor in the Household department, together with the pick of French kitchen practicalities.

On almost every counter you'll find some new products bearing the Biba label . . . soups and cheeses and wines, and a whole range of flans, and much more besides. (The wines are the same 'house' wines we serve in the Rainbow Restaurant.) All are specially prepared for Biba, and are the result of two years of tasting, testing and choosing.

MEAT

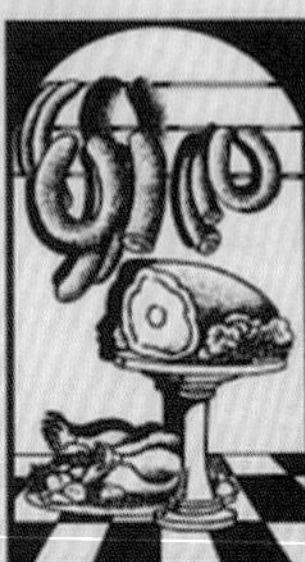

Biba has an early-rising friend at Smithfield, so the meat counter is stocked with properly-hung, neatly cut meat – the best from Ayrshire or Canterbury or Wiltshire. You'll find poultry, too, and game in season, and frozen meat out of season. Everything, in short, from a baron of beef for twenty, to a lamb cutlet for one.

BREAD

'Tell me where is fancy bread' as Shakespeare almost wrote. The answer is, at Biba, in our big bread bin. Not just fancy bread either, but bread wholesome and wholemeal, brown or white, sliced or in the loaf. Buns, rolls and pastries, too.

COOKBOOKS

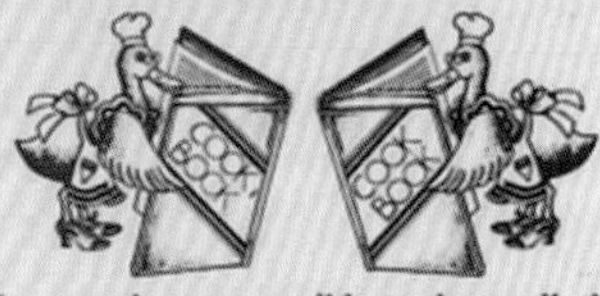

It seemed more sensible to keep all the recipe books near the food, rather than one floor up in the bookshop.
Publishers appear to issue about ten new ones every month, and Biba will try to keep up, even if it means more shelves. Meanwhile, more power to Elizabeth David's elbow.

ICE CREAM

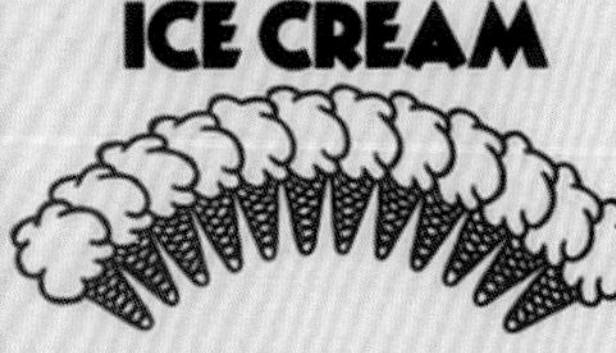

You'll find it on the sort of barrow you see in Venice, where they take ice cream equally seriously. Velvety smooth ice creams and cooling water ices – so stop us and try one.

TAKE HOME MEALS

Biba offers a very wide range of take-home meals, inspired by some of London's more interesting foreign restaurants – Chinese, American, Indian, Armenian, Greek and Russian.
You will also find salads and cold dishes prepared on the premises by our own chefs. (It's worth remembering that 10% VAT would be levied on this food in a restaurant, but take-home meals are exempt.)

WINES

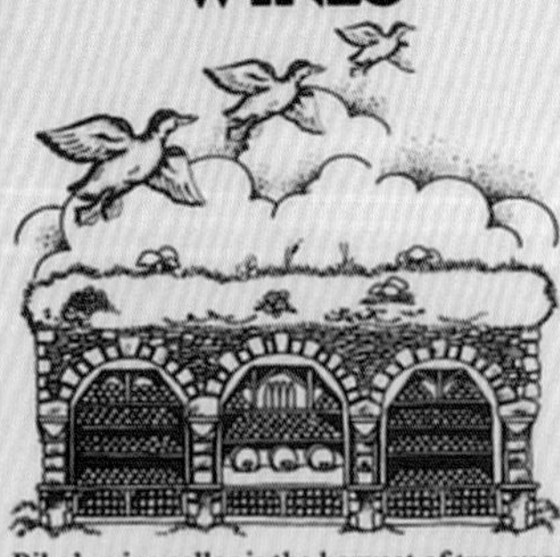

Biba's wine cellar is the harvest of two years of travel through the vineyards of Europe. If you enjoyed our house wines in the Rainbow Restaurant, you can buy them here to drink at home for a very modest sum – red, white or the attractively tawny rose.
From these daily table wines to the hugely expensive Chateau bottled premiers crus, Biba aims to run the whole gamut of vinous pleasure. Not to mention liqueurs, spirits, aperitifs, minerals, cyders, British and French spa waters, and even meads.

HEALTH FOODS

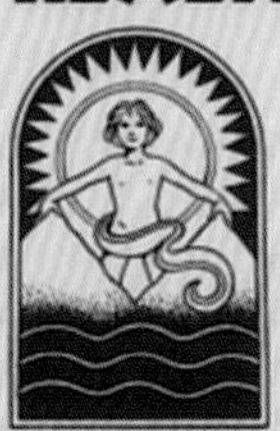

Eating to stay fit is not just a matter of how much, but what. You are what you eat, aren't you? So at Biba you can be everything from Macrobiotic rice to pure lemon juice. And don't forget that you can eat in an amazingly healthy way upstairs in the Rainbow Restaurant. (If you want to stay slim, run up the stairs.)

TEA & COFFEE

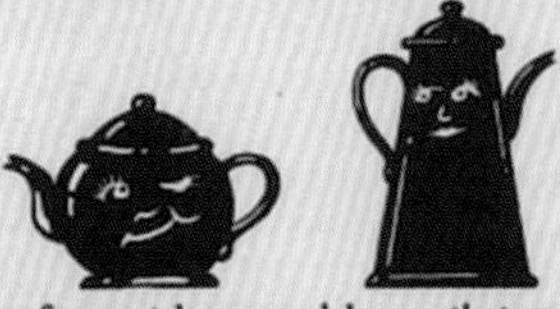

The fragrant beans and leaves that make work so nice to take a break from. Coffee, ground for your pot, or in beans, roasted just so and blended to your taste. Tea in bags or tins or loose, from China to India. Altogether a very soothing, stimulating display.

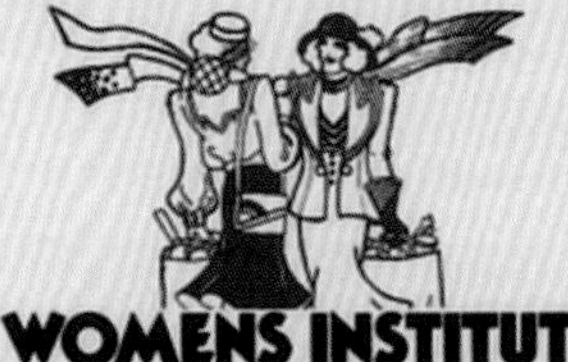

WOMENS INSTITUTE

Home-made cakes, biscuits and sweets, made with loving care from old family or country recipes. Come try, come buy.

PET FOODS

Meat for the Inner Dog, and fish for the Inner Cat, stacked up inside a slightly larger than life Great Dane.

VEGETABLE FRUIT & SALAD

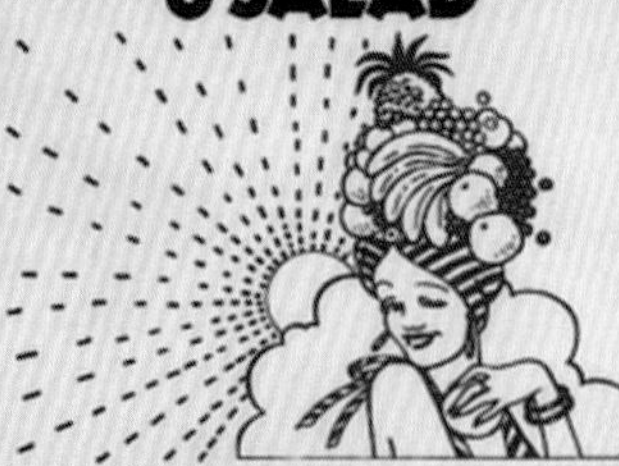

Covent Garden may be moving to Nine Elms, but the Biba buyer will still be up before the birds. On the fruit and vegetable stalls you'll find all the good things that grow out of the earth – in or out of season, home-grown or imported from the four continents.
And apart from fresh salad vegetables, you'll be able to take away ready-made salads to eat at home. These are freshly prepared in Biba's kitchens, under a very beady eye indeed.

FISH

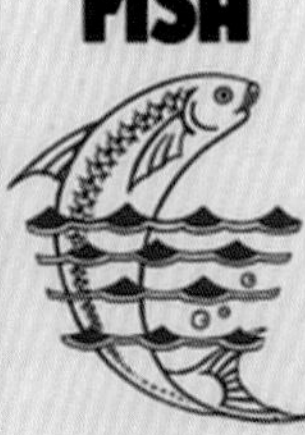

Step over to the fish-quay and imagine this silvery catch being unloaded. Every size of fish, from a shrimp to a lobster, and every shape from cockles to cod. Shoals of soles, creels of eels, grabs of dabs . . . fresh, salted or smoked, from rivers, seas and oceans.

Food Food Food

The big sardine, Heinz, and Old Oak Ham tins sell just what you would expect – those products. You'll also find bottles and jars. In fact, if you can't buy it fresh, Biba almost certainly have it put up in a tin, or in glass. And very good too.

HERBS & SPICES

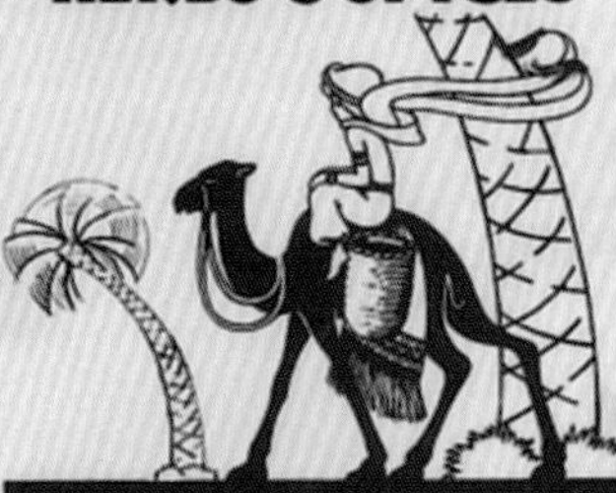

They come from all over the world to your kitchen. Food would taste very dull without them, so stock up with a jar or two.

SUDS

Biba now has its own detergent powder, side by side with all the heroes of television soap opera. You won't see ours on the box, but try it all the same – it washes quite white. On this counter you'll find all the other products that get things all washed up, and sparkling clean.

THE PHARMACY

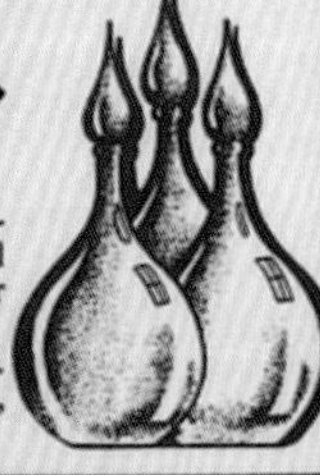

Not for serious hypochondriacs – you'll only see some rather nostalgic soap brands, and candles. We do have Aspirin, though.

STORE DESIGN: WHITMORE-THOMAS ASSOCS.
GRAPHIC DESIGN: Whitmore-Thomas Assocs.
ILLUSTRATION: Kasia Charko
TEXT: David Smith
PHOTOGRAPHY: Rolph Gobits
PRINT: C.P.A.

BIBA SECOND FLOOR

AABCDEEFFGGHHIJKLMNNOOOPQRRSTUVWXYYZ& (.,:""-!?

$£1234567890"%/

BIBA 2ND FLOOR BOLD

AABCDEEFFGGHHIJKLMNNOOOPQRRSTUVWXYYZ& (.,:""-!?

$£1234567890"%/

BIBA RAINBOW

AABCDEFGHHIJKKLMMNNOOOPQRSTUVVWXYZ & (.,:?!"

1234567890∞ ¼ ½ ¾ £/%-=+×*

BIBA RAINBOW SOLID

AABCDEFGHHIJKKLMMNNOOOPQRSTUVVWXYZ & (.,:?!"

1234567890o∞ ¼½¾ £/%-=+×*

BIBA FITZ FACE

AABCDEFGHIJKLMMNNOOOPQRSSTUVWXYZ& (.,:;!?--)

£12334567890⅓/%

BIBA GROUND FLOOR BOLD

AAABCDEFFFGHIJKKLMN

OOOPQRRSSSSTTTTHUVWXYZ& (.,:?!-"")

1234567890o∞$£/%

BIBA BASEMENT

AAABBCDDEEEFFGHHIJKLLMMNNOOOPPQR

SSSTTTTHUVVVWXYZCCFILbLTROZPT&.,:;-""!?(

£1234567890∞/%